Catholics
and
Canadian
Socialism

GREGORY BAUM

Catholics and Canadian Socialism

Political Thought in the Thirties and Forties

James Lorimer & Company, Publishers
Toronto, 1980

This book is published with the assistance of the Ecumenical Forum of Canada as part of its continuing programme on the Christian church in modern society.

ISBN 0-88862-295-3 cloth
       0-88862-294-5 paper

Design: Don Fernley

6 5 4 3 2 1   80 81 82 83 84 85 86

Canadian Cataloguing in Publication Data

Baum, Gregory, 1923-
    Catholics and Canadian socialism

Includes index.

ISBN 0-88862-295-3 bd.   ISBN 0-88862-294-5 pa.

1. Socialism and Catholic Church — Canada.
I. Title.

BX1396.3.B38   261.7'0971   C80-094111-X

James Lorimer & Company, Publishers
Egerton Ryerson Memorial Building
35 Britain Street,
Toronto M5A 1R7, Ontario

Printed and bound in Canada

Contents

To Father Eugene Cullinane

Foreword

In the Seventies the Catholic church's official teaching in regard to socialism underwent a significant change. The total condemnation of socialism, democratic and revolutionary, pronounced by Pius XI in 1931 and upheld by Church authority in the subsequent decades, was replaced by the open attitude taken by Paul VI in 1971, permitting Catholics to belong to socialist parties as long as these are not identified with a materialistic ideology. During the Seventies Catholic social teaching also refined its critique of contemporary capitalism. This shift to the Left, paralleled by similar developments among Protestant church leaders, raises the interesting question of where the Canadian churches and Canadian Catholics were during the Depression of the Thirties, when capitalism underwent an extraordinary crisis. While the impact of the Protestant Social Gospel on Canadian socialism and the formation of the Cooperative Commonwealth Federation (CCF) have been studied by historians and political scientists, the relation of Catholics to this Canadian movement has never been analyzed. It is the topic of this book.

The outline of this history is well known. The CCF was condemned by the Catholic bishops of Quebec, while in English-speaking Canada the Catholic bishops only warned Catholics of the new party without formally forbidding them to vote for it or take an active part in it. But no one until now has examined in detail how the bishops perceived the CCF, how they understood the Church's social teaching and what arguments they put forth against Canadian socialism. The negative approach of the Church to the CCF, as we shall see, was based on a particular reading of the papal teaching, one that differed from the way other Catholics understood it. Catholic bishops in England, for

7

instance, believed that the papal condemnation of socialism was in no sense aimed at the Labour party. It is this conflict of ideas and interpretations that is of interest to me in this study.

While the Catholic church recommended social reform, in actual fact it put its weight behind the defenders of the existing economic system. Until now, little attention has been given to the Catholics who disagreed with the bishops, who refused to endorse the existing order, and who either supported the CCF or engaged in some other form of critical political action. The great contribution of non-conformist Protestants to critical thought and social action in Canada has been studied in detail. Non-conformist Catholics were fewer in number, and they were on the whole unprepared to adopt many of the more radical stances taken by representatives of the Social Gospel. Still, the contribution of Catholics who swam against the stream deserves attention. They demonstrated the diversity within the Catholic church even in a period when great stress was put on conformity. Some of these non-conformist Catholics embraced positions that were later to become more widely held in the Church and eventually achieved recognition in the Church's official teaching.

The subject matter demands that this book be divided into two parts. Part I deals with the Catholic church's official reaction to Canadian socialism. Chapter 1 examines the political philosophy of the CCF in the Thirties, chapter 2 presents an analysis of papal teaching on socialism during the Depression and chapter 3 records the reactions of the Canadian Catholic hierarchy to the CCF. Part II deals with the Catholics who swam against the stream. Chapter 4 offers a brief account of the voices crying in the wilderness and points to the areas where historical research still has to be done. No one, for instance, has studied the relation of Catholics to the labour movement in Ontario. The subsequent chapters tell three stories of Catholic protest against the social misery of the Depression years. Chapter 5 deals with Catholics who supported the CCF in Saskatchewan, chapter 6 with Catholics in Quebec who responded to the CCF by creating a social movement of their own and chapter 7 with the innovative social projects of the Catholics in eastern Nova Scotia.

The reader may ask why I refer to the social thought of the

CCF as Canadian socialism. The reason for this is that the other form of socialism found in Canada in the Thirties, the Communist party, regarded the Russian model of revolution as normative for all working-class parties, understood the struggle for socialism in Canada as linked to the world political purposes of the Communist party and hence repudiated not only the CCF but the very idea of a Canadian socialism, that is, a Canadian way to a socialist society.

I must inform the reader that I am not a historian. My special field of interest is the interaction between theological and political ideas and their relationship to social change. In this study I have relied on historical research available in published books and articles as well as in dissertations written at Canadian universities. I have, moreover, interviewed a considerable number of people in Ontario, Quebec, Saskatchewan and eastern Nova Scotia in regard to their memories of the Thirties and Forties. These people included former social activists, politicians, labour leaders, social organizers, teachers, priests and ministers, among them Catholics who participated in the CCF in the early years. These people have contributed enormously to my understanding of the Catholic reaction to the Depression, both the official response and the action of the non-conformists. The list of the men and women who were willing to give me their time and reply to my questions is long indeed. I am grateful to all of them.

The book is dedicated to Father Eugene Cullinane, a priest who joined the CCF in the Forties and whose activity in the party was curtailed in 1948 by ecclesiastical authority. Father Cullinane's story has never been told, nor have the papers on the CCF he wrote during this time ever been examined. I am grateful to him for giving me permission to make them known in this study. The manuscript of this book has been read by several friends of mine, professors of history, political science and religious studies: Irving Abella, Paul Cronican, Gad Horowitz, Roger Hutchinson and Norman Penner. They have recommended changes and at the same time greatly encouraged me in my work. To them I express my sincere thanks.

— G.B.

Part I
The Catholic Church's Reaction

1
Canadian Socialism

While in European countries, from the turn of the twentieth century on, nationwide socialist movements have challenged capitalist society and in many instances produced parties that played a major role in the political evolution of these countries, this has not been true in North America. The significant exception was the Canadian socialist movement of the Cooperative Commonwealth Federation (CCF), founded in Calgary in 1932, which grew rather gradually in the Thirties and became a major party in the early Forties. At that time it appeared to follow the European pattern of becoming the principal alternative to the traditional parties. In 1944 the CCF won the provincial election in the province of Saskatchewan and formed the official op-position in three provinces, British Columbia, Manitoba and Ontario. Yet in 1945 the forward movement of the CCF was stopped. It remained the government of Saskatchewan and gave that province a special political style, but it was unable to make its own brand of socialism the great alternative for the Canadian people.

The CCF survived as a significant minor party in Canada. It continued to propose new social legislation in Parliament and pushed the government to accept at least some of its proposals; and it continued to be a mainstream national movement in which Canadians critical of capitalism could clarify their ideas and work out their positions. In 1961 the CCF reconstituted itself in alliance with the Canadian Congress of Labour as a new political party, the New Democratic Party (NDP).

Because of its peculiar position in North America, Canadian socialism has attracted the attention of historians and social

13

scientists. No political party in Canada has been as carefully studied as the CCF.[1] These studies have been written from a variety of viewpoints. Since in this book we are interested in the Catholic reactions to Canadian socialism, it is necessary that in this first chapter we examine the CCF in the light of questions important in Catholic social thought. We shall introduce the CCF through its founding conventions at Calgary and Regina, examine the various groups and movements that cooperated in its creation and then outline the special features of Canadian socialism.

The Founding Conventions

The CCF was founded in 1932. In July of that year the western labour political parties, which had been meeting yearly since 1929, held a conference at Calgary that was also attended by various radical farmers' organizations and a small group of members of Parliament from Ottawa. Present was J.S. Woodsworth, MP, a socialist, for years elected on a labour ticket in Winnipeg North Centre. Since the Calgary convention manifested sufficient unity among the workers' and farmers' organizations, the participants decided to launch a new national party called the Cooperative Commonwealth Federation, which was to replace the competitive, profit-oriented Canadian system by a cooperative economy oriented toward use. The early Thirties, we recall, were the darkest years of the Great Depression. The convention elected Woodsworth as the party's first president. It was decided to hold a meeting in the following year, the summer of 1933, at Regina, a meeting to which were also to be invited workers' and farmers' organizations from eastern Canada. The Regina convention was to work out the plan and programme of the CCF and publish it as a manifesto addressed to the Canadian people.

How could this cooperative commonwealth be achieved? The Calgary programme advocated "a planned system of social economy for the production, distribution and exchange of all goods and services."[2] It advocated "social ownership" of the banking, credit and financial systems — a point of importance to the radical farmers — and the "social ownership" of utilities and natural resources. The programme did not specify what was meant by "social ownership." It demanded "security of tenure for the farmer on his use-land and for the worker in his home." From the reference to "use-land," it sounded as if the new party favoured the social ownership of all land and wanted the farmer to use but not to own his homestead. The question of private property became a controverted issue in the CCF over the years. In the Calgary programme of 1932, the word "use-land" simply referred to land used for productive purposes. Only working farmers were to be protected, not land speculators.

The programme encouraged the development of cooperative enterprises, which were regarded as "steps to the attainment of the cooperative commonwealth." Again, as we shall see, this identification with the cooperative movement was a significant aspect of Canadian socialism. Finally, the programme asked for more advanced welfare legislation, the extension of insurance plans dealing with crop failure, illness, accident and old age, the socialization of health services — and for unemployment insurance "during the transition to a socialist state." Here again a characteristic of Canadian socialism emerged at the beginning: the association of radicalism with social reform.

The news of the new party spread rapidly through Canadian society. Several labour and farmers' organizations decided to come to Regina in the following year to affiliate with the CCF. A group of intellectuals, mainly in Toronto and Montreal — who in 1932 had created the League for Social Reconstruction, the Canadian equivalent of the British Fabian Society — looked to the CCF as the social movement that corresponded to their own social ideals. In the same year, a Protestant church organization in Toronto adopted a socialist position and in due time endorsed the CCF programme.[3]

On 1 February 1933, J.S. Woodsworth initiated a famous debate in Parliament on the reconstruction of Canadian society. He proposed the resolution: "That the government should immediately take measures looking to the setting up of a cooperative commonwealth in which all natural resources and the socially necessary machinery of production will be used in the interest of the people and not for the benefit of the few."[4] The members of the traditional parties were appalled. The government claimed the proposal was communist. Support came from Henri Bourassa, the well-known MP from Quebec, who thought the new movement had much in its favour.[5] On the basis of Catholic principles he agreed with the attack the CCF made on contemporary capitalism, thought it absurd to denounce the new socialism as communist and claimed that he, for one, was not afraid of the label "socialist." The main thing that worried him was whether this socialist commonwealth was to be based on the cooperation between public institutions and classes — in keeping with Catholic principles — or on the victory of one class over another. The parliamentary debate gave the CCF great visibility in the country.

Almost immediately after the debate in the Commons, a group of Catholic priests in Quebec felt the need to work out a public stance toward the new party. On 9 March 1933 a meeting of Catholic ecclesiastics — thirteen altogether — was held in Montreal, under the auspices of the Ecole sociale populaire, to examine the programme of the CCF and formulate a response from the Quebec Catholic perspective.[6] The speaker who had been asked to explain and evaluate the CCF position listed the groups and organizations associated with the new party, reported the positive response the party had elicited in various parts of Canada, praised the intelligence and education of the leaders, especially Woodsworth, and concluded that the new movement was not a passing phenomenon but a new and important force in Canada that deserved to be taken seriously.

In July 1933 the first national convention of the CCF was held at Regina. J.S. Woodsworth, in his introductory remarks, expressed the hope that the new party would create a distinctively Canadian socialism. "Perhaps it is because I am a Canadian of several generations, and have inherited the individualism common to all born on the American continent; yet with political and social ideals profoundly influenced by British traditions and so-called Christian idealism; further with a rather wide and intimate knowledge of the various sections of the Canadian people — in any case, I am convinced that we may develop in Canada a distinctive type of socialism. I refuse to follow slavishly the British model or the American model or the Russian model. We in Canada will solve our problems along our own lines."[7]

The convention was then presented with the draft of a manifesto that had been worked out by Frank Underhill, one of the founders of the League for Social Reconstruction.[8] The draft was discussed, amended and eventually approved and promulgated. The socialist orientation of the Regina Manifesto was strongly expressed in its opening paragraph and final sentence.[9] "We aim to replace the present capitalist system, with its inherent injustice and inhumanity, by a social order from which the domination and exploitation of one class by another will be eliminated, in which economic planning will supersede unregulated private enterprise and competition, and in which genuine democratic self-government based upon economic equality is possible." And at the end: "No CCF government will rest content until it has eradicated capitalism and put into operation the full programme of socialized planning which will lead to the establishment in Canada of the cooperative commonwealth."

The manifesto elaborated why capitalism is the source of injustice and exploitation. Capitalism produces inequality of wealth, chaotic waste and instability, reduces vast sections of the population to poverty, concentrates power in the hands of the few and produces an inevitable oscillation of the economy between feverish prosperity, from which profiteers and speculators reap the highest benefits, and catastrophic depressions. These ills can be resolved only, we are told, by a planned and socialized economy in which our natural resources and the principal means of production and distribution are owned, controlled and operated by the people."[10]

While the opening paragraph of the Regina Manifesto was clearly socialist, bent on replacing the present economic system by another, the careful reader will notice that it was not a Marxist document. The language of "replacing the capitalist system" was Fabian. What this Fabian spirit was, precisely, we shall see further on. No mention was made in the manifesto of the proletariat and its mission. Since the CCF was a coalition of workers and farmers, it was impossible to invoke the Marxist terminology that singled out the workers as the revolutionary class. The sentence that mentions the exploitation of one class by another does not specify what sections of society were being referred to. While in Marxist sociology farmers, as owners of their land and tools — their "means of production" — are often regarded as petit-bourgeois, Canadian socialism considered the working farmers of the West primary producers, as dependent on the capitalist system as industrial workers. Farmers engaged in single-crop farming were dependent on prices, freight rates, costs of fertilizer and farm machinery, credit and loans — that is, on the large industrial and financial corporations including the government, as were the miners, primary producers who did not own their means of production. From this point of view at least, the farmers had the same interests as the workers.

We also note that the Regina Manifesto, after considerable debate on the point by the convention, sought to overcome the present economic chaos by social ownership of natural resources and the principal means of production and distribution. Saying "principal" instead of "all" means of production, the manifesto revealed the pragmatic, non-doctrinaire origin of its socialism. It is not surprising, therefore, that in the subsequent paragraphs the manifesto committed the CCF to British constitutionalism. "This social and economic transformation can be brought about by political action, through the election of a government inspired by the ideal of a cooperative commonwealth and supported by the majority of the people. We do not believe in change by violence. We consider that both the old parties in Canada are the instruments of capitalistic interests and cannot serve as agents of social reconstruction, and whatever the superficial differences between them, they are bound to carry on government in accordance with the dictates of the big interests who finance them. The CCF aims at political power in order to put an end to this capitalistic domination of our political life. It is a democratic movement, a federation of farmers, labour and socialist organizations, financed by its own members and seeking to achieve its end solely by constitutional methods."[11]

The manifesto here bypassed the Marxist understanding of the state, according to which the very instruments of democracy represent and hence inevitably favour the ruling class. While the manifesto admitted that the traditional parties stood for the interests of the capitalist class, the democratic institution itself was an instrument of power that could be used by the majority to reconstruct the social order. Socialism was here regarded as the extension of democracy to the economic realm.

After the introductory paragraphs, the manifesto put forth fourteen points, the first thirteen of which dealt with the projected cooperative commonwealth, while the last one offered an emergency programme of immediate reform. Again, we see the refusal to create an opposition between radical change and social reform. The first emergency recommendation was the creation of a national planning commission, made up of a small body of economists, engineers and statisticians, whose task it would be to plan production, distribution and exchange of all goods and services necessary for the efficient functioning of society. The Fabian spirit of this recommendation is apparent. The influential planners of society shall be not the workers — the proletariat, the oppressed class — but a new group of dedicated experts and specialists, described as "public servants acting in the public interest and responsible to the people as a whole" (section 1).

The Regina Manifesto expanded upon the recommendations made a year earlier in the Calgary programme. The first goals were the socialization of the financial machinery, then social ownership of transportation, communication, electric power and "all other industries and services essential to social planning." The manifesto indicated that social ownership had several distinct forms: national, provincial and municipal. While the CCF envisaged an overall planning of the essentials of the economy, it was opposed to a highly centralized bureaucracy. "The CCF does not advocate a bureaucratic state socialism," Woodsworth said in the parliamentary debate.[12] Whether this was realistic or not, the CCF never equated social ownership with state ownership: instead the party hoped that the public ownership of the means of production could be decentralized and distributed over the whole of Canadian society.

How should this socialization take place? The manifesto recognized "the need for compensation in the case of individuals and institutions which must receive adequate maintenance during the transitional period." But since governments in the past have often been obliged to socialize companies that were no longer making money, the manifesto added that "a CCF government will not play the role of rescuing bankrupt private concerns for the benefit of promoters and stock and bond-holders" (section 3). The whole issue of socialization, as we shall see, remained open to debate.

The manifesto included an extensive farm programme. It promised "security of tenure for the farmer on his farm" (section 4). Since western farmers were often unable to meet their mortgage payments in periods of low world prices for wheat, they were constantly threatened with eviction from their home-steads. The first recommendation of the CCF was, therefore, the assurance of tenure. We note in passing that the reference to land-use found in the Calgary programme was dropped at Regina. The CCF came out unambiguously for the ownership of land by the working farmer. The manifesto recommended other measures of benefit for the farmers, the control of wheat prices, the removal of tariffs and especially the promotion, by adequate legislation, of cooperative enterprises for purchasing farm equipment and marketing farm products. Since in the prairie provinces, especially in Saskatchewan, the cooperative movement, the Wheat Pool in particular, had been a school of joint political and economic action for the farmers, it was an integral part of CCF socialism. The manifesto promised "the encouragement by public authority of both producers' and consumers' cooperative institutions" (section 6). The ideal of Canadian socialism, so strongly influenced by the cooperative philosophy, always included participation of the people in the institutions that serve them.

The same cooperative emphasis was found in the Regina proposals regarding labour. A "national labour code" was de-manded "to secure for the worker maximum income and leisure, insurance covering illness, accident, old age and unemployment, freedom of association and effective participation in the manage-ment of his industry and profession" (section 7). The proposals envisaged not only adequate working rules for industries but also, through "work councils," a share in the control of industry.

The same emphasis on participation and responsibility was found in the proposals demanding freedom of speech and freedom of assembly for all. This section of the manifesto spoke of an alarming fascist trend among Canadian government authorities. Freedom of expression and assembly had been denied workers and other citizens whose social views did not meet with the approval of those in power. Immigrants had been harassed and deported. The manifesto declared, "We stand for full economic, political and religious liberty for all" (section 12).

Concern over the inhumanity of modern society was also expressed in the proposals on "social justice" (section 13). Here the manifesto deplored the fact that in matters pertaining to crime and punishment, the administration of the law was usually inspired by fear and vengeance. It demanded that a committee, made up of psychiatrists, psychologists, social-minded jurists and social workers, devise a system of prevention and correction consistent with the other features of the new social order. This point as well as the previous ones on cooperatives, participation and freedom are of special interest to us, since some of the later ecclesiastical documents condemning the CCF accused the new party of being exclusively concerned with economic matters to the neglect of the moral dimension. We shall return to this topic farther on.

The manifesto recommended, finally, the reform of the British North America Act. It demanded the "amendment of the Canadian constitution, without infringement upon racial and religious minority rights or upon legitimate provincial claims to autonomy, so as to give to the Dominion government adequate powers to deal effectively with the urgent economic problems which are essentially national in scope" (section 9). The manifesto also urged abolition of the Canadian senate, which we are told was "one of the most reactionary assemblies of the civilized world." The section on the B.N.A. Act revealed that the CCF recommended the centralization of power in the Dominion government only with reluctance. The farmers and workers of western Canada had resentments of long standing against the federal government in Ottawa; they understood that a vast country such as Canada, made up of regions disparate in character and embodying different cultural traditions, could not be ruled effectively by a highly centralized government. They asked therefore for increased centralization not on principle, but only for the control of those aspects of economic life that affected the entire dominion. This cautious principle of centralization corresponded, as we shall see, to a principle in

44758

traditional Catholic social thought, the principle of subsidiarity.

The same section of the Regina Manifesto revealed an enormous weakness of the CCF programme, namely, the absence of any recognition of the binational character of Canadian society. The only reference in the entire manifesto to French Canadians, to Quebec, to the other founding people of this country, was the brief allusion to "racial and religious minorities." Needless to say, French Canada has never understood itself as a racial and religious minority. For Quebec, Canada was a country made up of "two majorities." The people of French Canada considered themselves a nation conquered and colonized by Britain. In 1867 they had joined the unequal union of Confederation with some trepidation, in the hope of achieving equality of partnership. While Woodsworth and his colleagues were opposed to British imperialism[13] and wanted to liberate the people from the impact of colonialism, they were caught in the perspective of western Canada, where French Canadians appeared as one minority among others, and hence never learned to appreciate the French/English duality that forms the central, defining axis of the Canadian reality.

The manifesto ended with proposal 14, a series of urgent recommendations for immediate reforms, dealing with unemployment, housing and the promotion of public well-being. The last sentence, already quoted above, reaffirmed the socialist aim of all reform. "No CCF government will ever be content until it has eradicated capitalism and put into operation a full programme of socialized planning."

We hasten to add that the Regina Manifesto did not express a unified political philosophy to which the affiliated organizations were unhesitatingly committed. It represented a political platform from which to build a party and promote a movement. The document left room for a great variety of emphases. The moderates were not happy with the radical socialist language at the beginning and the end of the document and the radicals, especially the representatives from British Columbia, were not satisfied with the reformist tone of CCF policy. But since a federation of parties and groups such as the CCF was the only way in which these organizations could achieve a national presence and political influence, they were quite willing to give up something of their own aims, agree upon a wide common denominator and cooperate in a joint political movement. It was this pragmatic spirit, rarely found in the Left, that characterized Canadian socialism. To get a better understanding of this indigenous socialism, let us now take a closer look at the various groups and organizations that joined in the federation and influenced the new movement.

The Antecedents of the CCF

We shall turn first to the radical farmers' movement in the prairies, especially in Saskatchewan, that united with western urban labour organizations who followed British socialist ideas. Both of these groups deserve our attention: they constituted the centre of the CCF. This was true above all in Saskatchewan, where they involved the entire province in a new style of political action and eventually, in 1944, saw the first socialist provincial government elected in Canada. In addition we must look at the workers' groups of British Columbia with their Marxist orientation; the League for Social Reconstruction, founded in Toronto and Montreal, which became the think tank for the CCF; and finally the Social Gospel movement.

1.

Agrarian radicalism in the United States and Canada was a phenomenon that has been carefully studied, even if scholars have come to different conclusions regarding it.[14] Contrary to common expectations, single-crop farmers, especially the wheat farmers, in the northern states of the American Midwest and in western Canada produced an opposition movement to big business and monopoly capitalism that eventually came to advocate policies that, in a North American context, sounded radical if not socialist. The wheat farmers were dependent for their survival on factors that immediately involved government policy as well as the major institutions of the nation. They depended on the price of wheat, which was determined in part by government policy and in part by the large corporations; they depended on fertilizer and farm machinery, the prices of which were determined by large industrial firms that in many instances held monopolies; they depended for the marketing of their products on the freight rates set by the railways or governments. In addition to these handicaps, farmers were vulnerable to crop failure through storms and bad weather, so that to assure their survival they needed either government subsidies or special crop insurance. While farmers owned their means of production, they were as dependent on the corporations and on government as were many of the industrial workers. In fact, farmers were more exposed to the complex system that controlled their income than workers. While workers received their pay envelopes and never encountered the agencies that determined the amount they received, farmers found themselves constantly at odds with industrial companies in regard to the prices they charged, with the government in regard to tariffs and transportation costs, with insurance companies and banks at times of loss, and so forth. Hence it was the very mode of production of single-crop farmers that affected their consciousness and prepared them to become radicals when times were bad — and businessmen when times were good.

In the Eighties and Nineties of the last century, agrarian radicalism was strong in the United States. It was a form of populist reaction against the hegemony of the eastern states. In the wheat-growing regions, the so-called wheat belt, the populist movement produced a radical critique of monopoly capitalism and of the kind of government that protected the large corporations. The radical farmers sought allies among the workers in order to form a political party. In the 1890s, the American Federation of Labor, which at that time was under strong socialist influence, refused to ally itself with the farmers because some of these were employers of labourers. It was only the non-socialist labour organizations, such as the Northern Alliance, that were willing to join the farmers in the creation of independent farmer/labour parties in the northern states of the American Midwest. According to Seymour Martin Lipset, in these agricultural states even the workers voted for socialist parties in greater strength than the workers in the eastern states, even though the latter were more highly industrialized and the workers wielded much greater power there.[15] Yet in the United States, the farmer/worker parties never assumed nationwide proportions. After the First World War their influence declined altogether. Lipset writes, "The destruction of the socialist party during and after the first world war by a combination of government persecution and Communist splits prevented the development of an American agrarian socialism."[16] During the Depression years we find a revival of radical organizations such as the Non-Partisan League or the Minnesota Farm-Labour Party, but they were unable to create a national movement based on the unity of workers and farmers. Then came the New Deal. When the Roosevelt government, through the new legislation, offered substantial help to the farmers by setting a minimum price for their products and providing crop insurance and extensive aid projects, it gave the farmers what they had striven for and laid to rest their incipient radicalism. In 1935 in Chicago, an attempt to create a new national party that would unite farmers and workers in a common struggle was unsuccessful.[17]

Agrarian radicalism in western Canada was produced by similar economic conditions. The farmers, as we have seen, were wholly dependent for their survival on economic forces outside their control. In addition to the dependencies described above, Canadian farmers were prevented by special government tariffs from dealing with companies in the United States that were often closer to them geographically and offered them better prices. It was the policy of the Dominion government, for nationalist and economic reasons, to keep the prairie provinces linked to the industrial development of eastern Canada. In the Twenties, the western farmers became vocal critics of the Dominion government, which ruled the country to the benefit of eastern economic interests, of the banking institutions that allowed credit agencies to foreclose their mortgages, of monopoly capitalism that was able to manipulate the wheat price and the prices of fertilizer and machinery, and of the railway company that controlled their marketing through transportation costs.

The radical farmers were also at odds with the townspeople of the West. The towns in the prairie provinces were made up largely of small businessmen, who acted as middlemen between the large producers and the farmers and were therefore often regarded as symbols of the exploitation of the farmers. To eliminate the middlemen, the prairie farmers created their own cooperative institutions for buying equipment and consumer goods and eventually for selling their wheat, the so-called Wheat Pool. It was the cooperative struggle to create and operate the Wheat Pool that produced among western farmers a collective self-understanding and a political style without which the formation of a new political party in the Thirties would have been impossible.

One of the curious political phenomena in Canadian history, one that has been frequently examined, was the divergent development of agrarian radicalism in Alberta and Saskatchewan.[18] Already in the Twenties, Alberta sent a considerable number of Progressives to Ottawa and in fact elected a United Farmers of Alberta (UFA) government in their own province. The UFA were conservatives, willing to listen to populist demands and put pressure on the federal government to pay more attention to the needs of the farmers. Toward the end of the Twenties, especially after the collapse of the economy, when even the Wheat Pool broke down, the farmers became more desperate and more radical. The United Farmers of Canada (UFC), under the leadership of George Williams, adopted policies that sounded socialistic: they asked for the social ownership of industries, natural resources and transportation — and in some groups even the nationalization of land so that the working farmer could remain on his homestead and continue to operate the farm in times of financial loss. The radical farmers' organizations began to negotiate with the labour groups and socialist movements in western Canada and eventually decided to send representatives to the meeting of the western labour political parties held at Calgary in 1932 and cooperate in the creation of a national party, the CCF.

In Saskatchewan the farmers stood behind the new party. They had already, prior to the Calgary meeting, joined with the Independent Labour party of Saskatchewan in a common political struggle. Now they enthusiastically endorsed the nationwide farmer/labour party. The cooperative networks they had created all over the province now served as the organizational basis for the new party. In Alberta, on the other hand, the radical farmers who supported the CCF at the Calgary meeting were unable to secure wide popular support for the new party. Alberta had already tried one radical government, the UFA government of the Twenties, so that the popular response after the Depression was to leave radicalism alone.

In 1935, however, a new populist movement was created in Alberta, promoted by an evangelical preacher, William Aberhart, who blamed the banks and financial institutions for the poverty of the country and advocated a new financial policy to give more purchasing power to the people. Aberhart regarded the banks as independent agencies and did not analyze how they were tied into the system of production and distribution. He advocated the revitalization of capitalism through a government strong enough to interfere with the banks and stimulate the flow of money in the country, Aberhart founded Social Credit, a new party that corresponded to the populist aspirations of the Albertan farmers in the Thirties. While Saskatchewan moved in the direction of agrarian socialism, Alberta moved in a strongly anti-socialist direction. Canadian social thinkers have tried to explain the divergent development in the two provinces. Among the significant factors they mention is the disappointment of Albertans with the radical government of the Twenties and the cultural difference between the two prairie provinces: Albertans were largely American in origin, while in Saskatchewan the British settlers predominated.[19]

Radicalism among farmers is an unusual phenomenon. Subsistence farmers (such as we find in Ontario) who rely on mixed farming are basically conservative. Though the United Farmers of Ontario, at the low point of the Depression, sent delegates to the Regina convention and joined the CCF, they soon decided to sever their relation with the party. But the single-crop farmers of the West, whose position and survival were threatened by a combination of forces that involved the whole of modern capitalist society and whose joint action in the cooperative movement produced a network of organizational links among them, entered upon a new collective awareness. This awareness had several features. The common ownership of the cooperative enterprises summoned forth in people a new sense of belonging together, of having some power to deal with economic matters beyond the boundaries set by the system of privately owned industry and business. The struggle for the establishment of the Wheat Pool made the partici-

pants aware of the difference between the dominant cultural outlook, defending free enterprise, and their own more collectivist
ideals, advocating an economic system beyond individualism and
competition.

According to Max Weber, we have class formation in the strict
sense when groups whose life chances are determined by the same
economic forces, under the conditions of the commodity or labour
market, become conscious of precisely what these forces are.[20]
When the contrast between the economic conditions of groups in
society becomes clearly visible, then class consciousness emerges,
Weber tells us, in proportion as the connection between the causes
and their consequences become more transparent. Continued
protest and representation, accompanied by the cooperative
movement and its organizational network, made the reasons for
their insecurity and poverty transparent to the prairie farmers.
They acquired class consciousness.

Still, while the farmers recognized the oppression produced
among them by monopoly capitalism, by the government that
protected industrial interests and by the intermediary businesses
in their own communities, they wanted to protect the ownership
of their own homesteads and use cooperative organizations to
promote the development of their own property. The farmers
wanted to be entrepreneurs and make the most of their agricultural operations, and it was in the defence of these things that they
were driven to a radical critique of modern capitalist society. This
has been called the paradox of agrarian radicalism.[21] An entrepreneurial approach to their own farming operations was coupled
with a radical stance toward the capitalist system. Their class consciousness was not without a certain contradiction. While the
forces of oppression had become transparent to them, they did not
question the implications of their own economic struggle.

In his important study on agrarian socialism, Seymour Lipset
defends the idea that the Depression moved the radical farmers
toward socialism. When the Wheat Pool failed and the farmers
advocated a compulsory wheat pool, they moved beyond the
entrepreneurial outlook that had characterized their struggle
until then and acquired a collectivist vision of economic life. Other
writers think that Lipset exaggerates here.[22] It is true that under
the leadership of George Williams, the United Farmers of Canada

in 1930 advocated a compulsory marketing pool set up by law, the abolition of the competitive system, the substitution of a cooperative of manufacturing, transportation and distribution, and the nationalization of natural resources, including the land, public utilities and means of transportation. In the midst of the Depression, this platform was a cry of protest against a society that was destroying the farmers. Subsequent sociological research has brought out, however, that despite the radical platform of the UFC, the majority of farmers were not socialists in any theoretical sense. They opposed monopoly capitalism and its protection by the government, and they wished to create social and economic conditions in which hard-working farmers could make a decent living and enjoy happiness with their families. They were against the evils and the abuse of capitalism, not against the economic thrust that created it in the first place. Yet to call this spirit "petit-bourgeois" seems unjust to me: these farmers did not resemble the owners of small shops and businesses, who kept away from physical labour, were removed from production, and enjoyed a certain independence and security. Lipset may have exaggerated the extent to which the farmers had become socialistic, but his critics have often underestimated the change of consciousness that did take place in them through their common struggle. If the notion of class is used in its Weberian sense, as indicated above, then it makes good sense to say that the radical farmers constituted a distinct class. They had acquired a new consciousness, and they were aware of how their perception of the social reality differed from that commonly accepted by the dominant culture.

Thanks to the farmers of Saskatchewan, the CCF was from the beginning associated with a grass-roots organization, with experience in popular participation and a system of communication between centre and periphery. In a sense this association laid the foundation for the remarkable development of the CCF in Saskatchewan. It was this popular participation that not only gave the CCF a special character in Saskatchewan and led to its victory in 1944, but also affected the entire province and produced a social awareness and political culture that had no parallel in any other Canadian province. The effects of this remarkable development are still very visible in Saskatchewan at this time. It is not surprising that the American S.M. Lipset, when engaged in his extensive study of agrarian radicalism at the end of the Forties, fell in love with Saskatchewan. He regarded it as a miracle on the North American continent, a successful social movement against the cultural mainstream.

2.

We must now turn to the urban workers of the prairie provinces, who had developed a socialism of their own. They were organized in independent labour parties, mainly in Winnipeg and Regina, and cooperated with the farmers in the creation of the CCF. In this context we recall that the majority of Canadian workers, especially in the East, were organized under American auspices and had to conform to the philosophy of the American Federation of Labour, which, since the turn of the century at least, had repudiated the alliance of labour and politics. This was the philosophy of Samuel Gompers, the successful American labour leader, who defended the view that labour in North America should remain non-partisan and avoid linking itself to a political party. Labour should consider itself simply as a pressure group in society, vote for the friends of labour, whatever their party affiliation, and refrain from systematic criticism of the economic system. The urban workers of western Canada objected to Gomperism; they followed the British way, according to which labour holds a philosophy critical of established society, expresses itself in a political party and seeks to change society through industrial struggle as well as political action. The western workers formed local labour parties and were able to elect labour representatives to the federal parliament.

The leaders of these workers were men who had played an important part in the history of western radicalism and were now, in the Thirties, active in the creation of the CCF. J.S. Woodsworth, since 1921 the leader of the Independent Labour party (ILP) of Winnipeg, and M.J. Coldwell, the leader of the corresponding party (ILP) at Regina, were the principal architects of the national farmer/labour movement. They were both socialists in the British tradition, acquainted with the politics of the British Labour party and the philosophy of the Fabian society. They were conscious that in Canada, at that time still predominantly rural, a labour party could be successful only if linked to the farmers' organizations, and they understood the need to rethink the theoretical foundations of socialism to suit this special situation. They advocated a Canadian form of socialism, a viewpoint clearly expressed by Woodsworth in his opening address at the Regina convention.

Woodsworth is the most important single figure of the Canadian socialist movement. A former Methodist minister, he was deeply committed to the biblical ideal of justice and the brotherhood and sisterhood of man — so much so that at one point, in 1916, he resigned from his church because he thought it was too much identified with imperialism and the interests of the ruling classes. He left his church in Winnipeg and went to British Columbia, where he worked as a longshoreman and helped form the Federated Labour party; he returned in 1919 to Winnipeg, where he took an active part in the General Strike and later created the Independent Labour party. He was soon elected as an independent labour representative to the House of Commons. Woodsworth was a moralist, a spiritual man, a gifted organizer and a charismatic figure. We are fortunate to have excellent biographies of this remarkable Canadian.[23]

Canadian socialism, in contrast with European and British socialism, did not produce major works of social theory. Canadian society was still engaged in the basic struggle for economic development: its culture had not yet entered the theoretical, self-reflective stage. Since Canadian universities on the whole did not encourage exploration and in many instances even censured nonconformist professors, very few intellectuals in Canada had elaborated a systematic critique of capitalist society. Woodsworth himself was not a theoretician; he was an educated man, a thinker in his own way, but he communicated his ideas to workers, not to university audiences. He published his understanding of Canadian socialism in a set of articles that appeared in the *Western Labour News* during the years 1918 to 1920.

What were Woodsworth's ideas?[24] Already at that time, the labour leader discerned a movement arising in Canada, made up of many groups and organizations, including workers and farmers, who differed among themselves but shared a common passion for justice and reached out toward a new ideal of brotherhood. Relying on this incipient movement, Woodsworth foresaw a new political party in Canada, a party that could not simply represent labour as in Great Britain but would include workers, farmers, returned soldiers and other disadvantaged groups, as well as progressive men and women from every walk of life. He wanted to unite in a single movement all who were oppressed by the dominant system. For this reason Woodsworth refused to speak of the proletariat and its special mission. "We fight not against abstract capitalism," he wrote, "but against capitalism in league with militarism, with imperialism, with protection, with authoritarianism in religion and education, with a subsidized press and soporifics and palliatives in the form of amusements and 'welfare provisions.'"[25] Could the oppressed in Canada be united in a common struggle? Woodsworth realized that in Canada the regional differences and national and ethnic loyalties tended to work against nationwide solidarity, yet he saw the creation of such a solidarity precisely as the task of the new party.

Woodsworth recognized that the class structure of Canada was quite different from that of the European countries. Canada had never known an aristocracy, and hence the bourgeoisie had never experienced itself as a revolutionary class, bent on overthrowing the social system. The Canadian middle class was not a true bourgeoisie at all. Neither did Canada have the equivalent of the European peasant. Canadian farmers were not traditional peasants who defined themselves against the landed gentry that held vast property, nor were they themselves landlords with large holdings. Woodsworth wrote, "Our scientific friends" (he meant his Marxist colleagues in British Columbia) "claim that the farmers are not class-conscious and should be considered as part of the bourgeoisie."[26] Woodsworth disagreed with this. He recognized that farmers were not wage-earners, and that they owned their own tools of production, but this did not give them independence: the mortgage company owned their lands, and the banks, railroads and manufacturers had them at their mercy. The cost of production and prices for their goods were fixed by forces over which they had no control. Under such conditions, Woodsworth argued, the old individualism was breaking down and farmers were becoming organized industrially and politically.

Canadian socialism never looked upon farmers (or fishermen) as petit-bourgeois. They were producers who laboured; they were not estranged from manual labour as were the petty bourgeoisie. Since they ran their own farms, they were knowledgeable about agriculture, acquired the technical skills to look after and repair their machinery and were acquainted with the methods of business. And since they were exploited by the same economic forces that exploited labourers — this was especially true in the prairies — the mode of production that introduced them to many skills also demanded that they organize in their struggle for greater justice. This is not to deny that in more prosperous times successful farmers who expanded their land holdings and ran their farms mainly with hired help easily entered a new class situation akin to that of entrepreneurs.

In most parts of Canada, Woodsworth argued, the lot of the farmers was so insecure that there was an exodus from the land to the city. Farmers often preferred to sell their labour power to industry rather than continuing to live in constant insecurity in the country. Even the more secure farmers sent their children away to get an education so that they would be able to leave the land and create a better life for themselves in the city.

Woodsworth realized that in his day the Canadian working class was far too small to create a mass movement. What he advocated therefore was the creation of a joint farmer/worker movement, supported by all groups suffering oppression from capitalism. This would include all employees, all wage-earners and, he thought, even many small businessmen, who were almost as exploited as the workers since their survival depended on policies made by the large corporations.[27]

In British Columbia, Woodsworth argued against the Socialist party, which followed a doctrinaire Marxist approach and had no use for the farmers. In 1917 he founded his own political organization, the Federated Labour party (FLP), in which he developed the views and positions that he later proposed as Canadian socialism. This is how he characterized the programme of the party. "The creed of the Federated Labour Party is remarkable not only for what it says but also for what it does not say. There is no mention of 'surplus value,' of 'the materialistic interpretation of history,' 'class-conscious wage slave,' and the other well-worn phrases so familiar to us all."[28] The FLP was leaving "scientific orthodox groups and the revisionist groups to fight out their theories but takes the great underlying principle stressed by Marx, viz. the collective ownership and democratic control of the means of wealth production."[29] Woodsworth avoided terms such as proletariat and wage slave, which suggested workers and farmers were in wholly different class situations and hence easily widened the rift between them.

Canadian socialism also avoided talk of "surplus value." According to Marx, wealth is produced by labour. The labourers produce the wealth of the nation, yet they are deprived of it by the owners of industry. By "surplus value" Marx designated the wealth produced by the workers, after the amount of money they need for their own and their families' sustenance has been subtracted. What happens to this surplus value? In capitalist society, it is appropriated by the owning class. Marx declared that the surplus value of industry is rightfully owned by the workers who produced it and should be used by them for the well-being of the entire community. Marx took his model for talking about surplus value from the early form of capitalist production. The capitalist supplied the tools of production and the raw materials, and the workers then produced the goods. Here the workers alone produced wealth: they did "productive" work, while the work of the owners and distributors of the goods was "unproductive." In this system the owners and those dependent on their wealth lived off the exploitation of the workers.

But in modern industry, the production of goods is done in an industrial setting that demands many services. What about the men who repair the machines? What about the cleaning staff that works at night? What about the people employed in services and transportation? What about the secretaries in the office? What about engineers, planners, technical specialists? What about those who manage the industries? Is their work "non-productive"? Are they parasites living off the wealth produced by the workers? Canadian socialism refused to divide people into productive and non-productive workers: it tried to show that all employees, whether industrial or white-collar workers, workers employed in services or workers who use only their brains, have a common interest and must struggle against a common enemy. This, I think, is the reason — or one of the reasons — why Canadian socialism did not speak of "surplus value."

There is, however, a wider and more acceptable understanding of surplus value. It is true that industrial enterprises produce wealth. They do this in a process involving a multitude of employees, within the enterprises and even beyond. After the workers in the industries, the offices and the service sector have been paid, and after the taxes necessary to support the public utilities used by the enterprises (roads, post office, railways and so forth) have been subtracted, the remaining money made by the enterprise is "surplus value." The Fabian socialists called this "rent." They spoke of the outrageous "rent" that the workers who produced the wealth had to pay to the owners of industry for use of the productive tools. Socialists held that this "rent" should be publicly owned and spent on behalf of the entire community. Canadian socialism did not differ in this from Marxism, as Woodsworth said clearly in the above quotation. But since their class analysis did not single out the industrial workers among other workers and farmers, Canadian socialists sought a vocabulary that would strengthen the solidarity among these groups in Canada.

According to Marx, in the final stage of the classless society surplus value will disappear altogether. In that society it will no longer be necessary to work so hard, to produce so many goods, to increase the wealth of the nation. In the end, the wealth created by the workers will equal the amount needed for them and their families, leaving no surplus. At that time the very nature of work will change and become a higher form of human creativity. We note that Canadian socialism did not follow the Marxist theory of history.

Canadian socialism refrained from speaking of "the materialistic interpretation of history." Following the pragmatic nature of British socialism, Woodsworth and Coldwell were unwilling to commit themselves to a particular view of history. This does not mean that they failed to discern a forward movement in history, leading toward a socialist society. They were in fact convinced, and expressed this conviction with great fervour, that the present widespread misery produced by capitalism was destined to be overcome through a movement organized by the exploited in society: the workers, the farmers, the underprivileged.

Some historians have stressed the messianic element in the

CCF campaigns and compared it to the preaching of a new gospel. I suppose any radical movement, struggling against power structures and the cultural mainstream, must be carried by the conviction that its success is written into the flow of history. Marxists think that the inner logic operative in history can be calculated because the contradictions present in society constitute the motor that moves history forward. Many Christians hold that the forward movement of history is assured by the divine promise made and ratified in the great biblical events. While there was a certain evangelical tone, derived from the Social Gospel, in the proclamation of Canadian socialism, the new society to be created was never regarded — as in Marx — as the final stage of history and the passage from the realm of necessity to the realm of freedom.

Woodsworth's programme of the early Twenties anticipated the CCF programme of the Regina Manifesto. It was divided into an outline of the future social order and a set of demands for social welfare now. Woodsworth envisaged a new society, defined by the socialization of the natural resources, transportation, communication and the financial institutions. He also foresaw a gradual socialization of the major industries and the expropriation of unused land — if possible, with compensation for the present owners. The socialized industries would be controlled by the workers. This description of the new society was accompanied by welfare recommendations to be introduced immediately by law: free medical service, free compulsory education, the equality of women and insurance for unemployment, accident and old age. Woodsworth thought the state should pay mothers and housewives for their labour.

What was typical in this programme was that the outline of the radical goal was accompanied by welfare demands. This refusal to split radical politics and reformist plans became a characteristic of Canadian socialism. In Parliament, Woodsworth, the other labour leaders elected in the Twenties and the CCF in the Thirties supported all legislation that sought to improve conditions for the working class. Woodsworth never accepted the view that reform is the enemy of radical change: he never wanted to magnify the contradiction of capitalism at the expense of the workers to hasten the coming of the great revolution. He said in

Parliament, "As long as workers are content to sell their life's energies in the market, they must accept the conditions which the fluctuations of that market entail. We shall accept reforms to strengthen our position, but our ultimate objective is the socialist state."[30]

Woodsworth's programme of the early Twenties reflected his position after his experience of the British Columbia labour movement and the Winnipeg strike. When we compare it with the programme of the Socialist party of Canada (later of British Columbia), we note that the latter calls only for a radical reconstruction of society without making demands for immediate changes. In the mid-Twenties, Woodsworth, then leader of the Independent Labour party in Winnipeg, worked out another programme, which proved to be more moderate than his first. The Winnipeg programme did not speak of socialism at all but only of the cooperative commonwealth. It demanded "a complete change in our present economic and social system" but did not offer a description of the new society; instead it provided a fourteen-point programme of immediate reform.

The British-style socialism of Woodsworth and Coldwell, adapted to the Canadian situation, was firmly committed to the parliamentary system. The labour leaders believed that the class struggle in Canada had to be carried on in a democratic manner. The principal weapon in this battle was the ballot. They hoped that a farmer/labour party could gain the support of the vast majority of Canadians and eventually constitute the government; and they counted on a general strike to wrest the power from the old elite if they should refuse to surrender it to the legitimately elected government. Canadian socialism envisaged a strategy that combined the political struggle with industrial pressure. In 1919 Woodsworth wrote, "Whether the radical changes may be brought about peacefully largely depends on the good sense of the Canadian businessmen who now largely control both industry and government in this country."[31] If the rulers of the country would not accept the newly elected socialist government, then those in power would have to use the appropriate means to impose the will of the majority on the recalcitrant elite. Woodsworth's remark of 1919 was often quoted against him. Yet he himself repeated and defended it in Parliament.[32] This reference to emergency measures in no way weakened his or his party's commitment to the parliamentary system.

In the Twenties J.S. Woodsworth and William Irvine, another prairie radical elected to the Commons, were able to unite the independent labour representatives and several Progressive members in a so-called ginger group, which defended the underdog in the Canadian West. Members of this group attended the Calgary conference; hence when the new party was founded, it was immediately represented by a small but significant caucus in the House of Commons.

3.

We must now take a look at the socialist organizations of British Columbia, which participated in the making of the CCF and represented its radical wing. The labour movement in British Columbia had been class-conscious from the beginning.[33] The reason for this was the crass visibility of the class line between the owners and managers of very large enterprises — mainly mining companies but also lumber yards and large-scale farming — and the great majority, who were in fact workers. At the turn of the century there was almost no secondary industry in British Columbia that might have produced a broad middle class to disguise the gap between rich and poor. Nor were there many farmers taking care of their own homesteads. Under these conditions the labour movement in British Columbia was much more radical than in eastern Canada — with the exception of Cape Breton, Nova Scotia, where the economy was as dominated by the extractive industries as in British Columbia.

Socialism was alive and well in British Columbia during the first decade of this century. In the 1916 provincial election, the Socialist party of Canada almost became the official opposition in the province, but internal strife weakened the workers' movement and undermined the party's success. The British Columbia socialists were Marxists. Though the labour leaders were almost exclusively British, that is to say immigrants from Great Britain, they did not advocate British labourite socialism: they endorsed the class struggle in more divisive fashion. They saw themselves as revolutionaries, readily used Marxist concepts and regarded the proletariat as the key class of social transformation. It has been pointed out that the British Columbia socialists had among them no intellectuals; their Marxist rhetoric was highly stereotyped, not based on careful research into the conditions of Canadian society.[34] In her study of Ernest Winch, perhaps the most important British Columbia socialist leader, Dorothy Steeves has shown that the vehement Marxist rhetoric used in the Socialist party had a ritual purpose: it enabled the frustrated workers to express their indignation over the economic system that made their lives so miserable.[35] Though the workers were not joined by any intellectuals, they were quite able to create organizations that exerted considerable influence on the politics of the province.

Woodsworth, though a personal friend of Ernest Winch, did not side with the Socialist party. Woodsworth held that a workers' party that showed no interest in the farmers and engaged in stereotyped Marxist rhetoric could never build a nationwide socialist party in Canada. For this reason, as already mentioned, he started his own political party in British Columbia, the Federated Labour party. In the late Twenties, however, the Socialist party sought association with other independent labour parties in western Canada, sent representatives to the 1932 Calgary meeting and eventually cooperated in the founding of the CCF.

The British Columbia socialists were regarded as the radicals in the CCF. At the Regina convention they challenged the moderate approach of the manifesto. They did not want this public document to say that the CCF excluded altogether social change by violent means, nor did they want to limit the activity of the party to solely constitutional means. They were not satisfied with a programme demanding that only the principal means of production be socialized, or with the promise of compensation made to the owners of the industries, and finally they defended the socialization of land against the position adopted in the manifesto. On all these issues, the British Columbia delegation was outvoted. But since they were firmly committed to the creation of a nationwide movement and party, "farmer, worker, socialist," they were quite willing to tone down their own political views. Dorothy Steeves tells us that on the whole, the British Columbia delegation was pleased with the Regina Manifesto, more especially of course with the last sentence.[36]

The labour leaders of British Columbia knew their constituency: they used the radical language the people expected of them and for the sake of which they had been elected to the provincial legislature. To many Canadians east of British Columbia, Ernest Winch appeared a terrible revolutionary. He was known mainly through the outrageous statements he made from time to time and for which in later years he was occasionally reprimanded by the national office of the CCF in Ottawa. The opponents of the CCF used Winch's statements to argue that the CCF was a revolutionary party and thus went against the cultural tradition of Canada. It was only in British Columbia that Winch was understood as a rhetoretician of revolution who was in fact deeply committed to reformism in the legislature. He used his political influence to help people in trouble. He was always, under all circumstances, on the side of the underdog. While he sometimes repudiated reformist policies in his speeches, he spent most of his time working on reform legislation in the provincial house. His son, Harold Winch, became a political leader in the CCF and often imitated his father's radical rhetoric.[37]

Canadians often believed that the Marxist socialists of British Columbia were in fact communists. This was not the case. On the contrary, the Russian Revolution and the creation in 1919 of the Third International, the first communist International, produced turmoil and division among the socialist parties of Europe and America. While socialists everywhere looked with admiration at the revolution taking place in Russia, they were greatly divided in their response to the Third International, established as it was on Leninist principles. A new, authoritarian, centralized socialism was being created. The Moscow Executive Committee of the Third International demanded complete control over the communist parties in different parts of the world.[38] This new socialism ridiculed parliamentary democracy, recommended participation in it only as a way of destroying it and hoped to replace it by the dictatorship of the proletariat, exercised by the communist party. In 1921, the Moscow Executive Committee worked out "conditions of affiliation" for the Communist International that removed from the affiliated parties all independent action and reflection. This new communism split the socialist parties down the middle: some members became communists and created communist parties in compliance with the statutes of affiliation, while others remained socialists and retained the freedom to determine their own policies. In 1921 the Canadian Communist party was founded. The Socialist party in British Columbia did not join it. These socialists remained true to their own tradition, for which they were vehemently attacked in communist publications.

While the socialist parties in Europe and America did not permit themselves to be pulled apart by the conflict between revolutionaries and gradualists prior to the Russian Revolution, socialism after 1917 was torn asunder over this difference. The social-democratic parties of Europe were now obliged to clarify their own positions. In the manifesto *Labour and the New Social Order*, the British Labour party defined its own policy on the socialist reconstruction of society, "revolutionary in its goals and constitutional in its methods."[39] This also was to define the direction of Canadian socialism. When Woodsworth was asked how the CCF differed from the communists, he gave a reply that scandalized many of his listeners: he said that the CCF had the same goal as the communists but the methods chosen to reach this goal were quite different. Many Canadians did not realize that this was a direct reference to the manifesto of the British Labour party.

While the CCF was often classified by its opponents, and particularly by Catholics, as part of the threatening communist wave, in reality the Communist party of Canada (CPC) and the CCF were antagonists.[40] Already in the Twenties, just after its foundation, the CPC opposed the socialist parties in Canada, including the independent labour parties in the prairie provinces. According to the directives of Lenin, the reformist socialist parties were the principal social bulwark of the bourgeoisie and for this reason had to be opposed in a relentless, systematic and, in many instances, open struggle. This was Lenin's emphasis at the first three congresses of the International, held in Moscow. The second of these congresses, in 1920, adopted the conditions of affiliation. Lenin insisted on that occasion that reformism was the principal enemy and that the delegates must not leave the assembly without the firm determination to carry on the struggle to the very end. One supposes that what Lenin had in mind was the German situation, where the socialist party, the largest in the world, had firmly opted against revolution. The fight against democratic socialism was stepped up by Stalin. At the 1928 congress of the International, Stalin denounced the dangerous role being played everywhere by the principal enemy, the social democrats, whose ideology had "many points of contact with the ideology of fascism."[41]

The CPC accepted this doctrine fully. At the 1929 convention, the party committed itself to struggle against labour parties and reformism in all its forms. In a report given at this convention, Woodsworth was called "one of the most dangerous men in the working class,"[42] because he wanted to lead a working-class movement without commitment to revolution. After the founding of the CCF, the CPC came out very quickly with its condemnation. An extensive article appeared in *The Worker*, 24 July 1933, and it was followed in February 1934 by a full-length book, *Socialism and the CCF*, written by an author who called himself G. Pierce but who seems to have been the communist organizer Stewart Smith.[43] The book represented a vicious attack on social democracy and in particular on the CCF. Canadian socialism was called simply liberal labourism plus farm reformism: it played the role of "social fascism" in Canada, similar to fascism in Germany. In the death struggle against the CCF, said Pierce, it was important to concentrate on the "left wing" in the party, who considered themselves Marxists, and in particular on the socialists of British Columbia.

Stalin's decision in 1928 to make social democracy the principal enemy of the progressive movement prevented the communist and socialist parties of Germany from working together against the rise of fascism. As we shall see, Pope Pius XI's decision in 1931 to forbid Catholics to support the social-democratic parties of Europe splintered the opposition to fascism even more. Perceptive observers of political developments in the early Thirties, for instance Trotsky and Simone Weil, recognized the utter folly of the Stalinist position. It was only two years after Hitler's rise to power, in 1935, that Stalin switched policy and advocated a common front in the struggle against fascism. The CPC, following the official switch, then offered its cooperation to all progressive elements in Canada, including the CCF. Woodsworth opposed this cooperation; other party members favoured it. The new tactics produced strife in the CCF and often confused its members as well as the Canadian public. Norman Penner points out that the CPC never repudiated Pierce's *Socialism and the CCF*. The continuing struggle between CPC and CCF was most pronounced in the labour movement over the leadership control of the industrial unions. The tactical switches of the CPC, following the directives of Moscow, continued to pit the party against the CCF. From 1939 to 1941, the CPC opposed the war against Hitler, and in 1945 it supported the Liberal party under Mackenzie King.

Despite the changing tactics of the CPC, the courage, dedication and human compassion of many party organizers and members of the rank-and-file created an idealistic movement in the Thirties that belongs to the great moments of Canadian history. The party initiated people into a new consciousness that released extraordinary powers of sacrifice and self-surrender. Moreover, since the party organizers represented many ethnic groups in Canada and hence had facility in many languages, they were often more successful in organizing workers and setting up unions than were CCF organizers, who tended to be confined to the English language.[44]

4.

Agrarian radicals, urban socialists, British Columbia Marxists — what other groups were influential in the formation of the CCF? We must take a brief look at the League for Social Reconstruction (LSR), a society of intellectuals dedicated to the cause of socialism, founded in January 1932 by Frank Underhill and Frank Scott, professors at the University of Toronto and McGill University respectively.[45] The league understood itself quite consciously as the Canadian equivalent of the British Fabian society, which had existed since 1883 as an intellectual powerhouse for the creation of a socialist Britain. This remarkable society, made famous by members such as George Bernard Shaw, Sidney Webb and his wife, Beatrice Webb, eventually exerted a good deal of influence on the British Labour party and produced the research and economic analyses necessary for policymaking and socialist planning. This is what the LSR wanted to do for Canada. The members of the league asked J.S. Woodsworth to be their honorary president, and they were in solidarity with the new party that was being created at Calgary in July 1932. It was in fact the LSR, especially Frank Underhill himself, who composed the draft for the Regina Manifesto. In this document Underhill tried to bring together the political aspirations of the various groups constituting the CCF; and since the draft was accepted with minor modifications, one must conclude that he did his work admirably well. At the same time, as we noted above, the Regina Manifesto revealed the Fabian socialism of its original drafter.

The LSR remained the brain trust of the CCF. The members of the LSR were called upon by members of Parliament to do research and prepare briefs on the topics of special concern for the CCF. In 1935 the league published a large collection of papers and articles entitled *Social Planning for Canada* and a condensed version of it, *Democracy Needs Socialism*. These works put into the hands of the CCF a scholarly analysis of the social and economic reality in Canada.

It is important for our purpose to have an idea of what is meant by "Fabian socialism." It was a peculiarly British school of thought, combining scientific rationalism and utilitarian ethics in the promotion of a socialist economic system.[46] The Fabians believed that rational analysis could demonstrate the superiority of socialism over the capitalist economy. "No reasonable person who knows the facts can fail to become a socialist — or at least be converted to the socialist policy on any topic presently under discussion."[47] To make these empirical findings known, the Fabian society produced pamphlets, called *Facts for Socialists*, to educate the Englishmen of their day. The Fabians believed in rational persuasion. Their economic views were socialist: they advocated nationalization of the major industries and held that the "rent" — the equivalent of Marx's "surplus value" — should be returned to the workers and used collectively for the good of the community. They tended to equivocate on whether previous owners should receive compensation. At the same time, the Fabians were gradualists. They trusted in the power of Parliament and were convinced that democracy and socialism belonged together and that neither one could preserve its full integrity without the other. If the greatest happiness of the greatest number was the rational norm for social action, they believed it possible to persuade the public that socialism was the most suitable means for promoting this happiness; and then the public opinion of the vast majority could be forced upon the owners of the means of production by the parliamentary system. In the Fabian perspective, the state was not — as for Marx — the paid jailer of the owning class who kept the prison of the workers tightly locked; the state was rather the supreme court executive of the people's votes. The Fabians were socialists and liberals at once. When work councils are introduced in England, Bernard Shaw once said, they would be called "her Majesty's soviets."

How did Fabianism differ from Marxism? The Fabians did not provide a profound critique of capitalist society nor analyze the cultural impact of the present economic system, and so did not look upon socialism as the coming of a qualitatively new society, in the building of which people would experience deep personal transformation. The Fabians were not yearning, as Marx was, for the overcoming of egotistic man: they were in fact quite pleased with the rational personality, motivated by usefulness and economic advantage, that capitalism had produced. Socialism for them was simply a more rational economic system leading to greater happiness for all. They trusted that liberty, personal initiative and, within limits, free enterprise would remain. They did not favour revolution, but spoke of the *reconstruction* of society — a word, incidentally, that became central in the CCF vocabulary. According to the Fabians, the aim of the class struggle was not the conquest of one class by another, but rather the cooperation of the classes in a system that provided the maximum of happiness for all.

Nor did the Fabians accept Marx's philosophy of history. They did not recognize in society the emergence of contradictions that moved history forward, through a series of major upheavals, toward the classless society. They were idealists in the Marxist sense of the word: that is to say, they trusted that the ideas, demonstrable truths regarding economic policy, could be inserted into the course of history by the power of persuasive arguments and the democratic system. Marx's important insight had been that the orientation of history was produced by the struggles of oppressed people, and consequently that ideas have power only if they are linked to social groups that are actually struggling to achieve emancipation. For Marx, ideas had power only when their time had come. Yet the Fabians did see a movement in history: they believed, with many liberal thinkers of the nineteenth century, that operative in Western society was a movement toward equality that had produced political democracy over the centuries and was now leading society toward economic democracy, or socialism. What moved history ahead was not economic necessity but the ideal of equality.

Finally, the Fabians were not philosophers. They regarded the discussion of fundamental issues as a waste of time. They did not enjoy the examination of socialist theory and its implications for public and private life. They were strictly pragmatic. They worked out socialist policies for the various concrete problems that arose in the political life of the nation. The labour movement in the nineteenth century regarded the Fabians as upper-class theorists and unpractical snobs, but in the twentieth century, after the formation of the Labour party, labour and the Fabians became allies. While the labour movement was more geared toward class struggle than the Fabians and hence had a different style in its day-to-day politics, its leaders agreed with the Fabians that the state was not simply the agent of the ruling class but could become, through electoral victory, the protector of labour and the initiator of socialism.

To explain the phenomenon of Canadian socialism, it is important to emphasize that it was largely, if not exclusively, British in origin and style. It was the heir of the British labour movement, the cooperative philosophy and Fabian socialism. It is possible to exaggerate the contrast between the British style of socialism in Canada and the Central and Eastern European character of American socialism prior to the First World War. Before that war, Canada also had many socialist groups of ethnic origin. It is true, however, that the radicalism of the British immigrants (and this included Marxists) who came to Canada before and after the war could never be regarded as alien or foreign.[48] The British were at home in the Empire. After the decline of the socialist organizations in the years following the war, due to government persecution and communist strategy, almost the only socialist parties that survived in Canada were the British ones. European immigrants involved in socialist groups often feared, with good reason, discrimination and even deportation.[49] Among the leaders of the Winnipeg strike of 1919 there was a single non-WASP, A.A. Heaps, and he was a British-born Jew. When the immigrants were asked why they exercised so little political initiative and stayed away from radical movements, they explained that they were in too vulnerable a position and could be labelled as foreign agitators. The English and the Scots were not foreign. As we pointed out before, the CCF was a WASP phenomenon. In Ontario, for instance, the percentage of British Protestants in the CCF was higher than in the general population.[50] It was undoubtedly the British character of Canadian socialism, including the Fabian element, that helped it to become a Dominion-wide movement and constitute a major political party in the early Forties.

5.

The cultural recognition of Canadian socialism was also related to the fact that it drew upon the tradition of Christian socialism and that many of its leaders were originally Protestant ministers. The impact of the Social Gospel on the progressive movements in Canada and the formation of the CCF is usually recognized by historians, but they often pay little attention to it because they are under the impression that the social dedication of these Christians had lost its religious quality and become purely secular. However, as the Canadian Social Gospel is studied more carefully, it becomes apparent that the commitment to socialism on the part of significant groups of Protestant Christians was, properly speaking, religious and that the defence of the socialist position in terms of the Christian message gave credibility to the CCF in a culturally conservative country such as Canada.

Norman Penner argues that it was the Social Gospel as common heritage that enabled a group of radical Protestant ministers and ex-ministers connected with labour and socialist organizations to reach over and link up with radical farmers, and thus help bring about a single political movement in Canada.[51] These men could move back and forth between labour and farmer groups with relative ease.[52] That which is most specifically Canadian about the CCF and which distinguishes it from the British Labour party — namely, the union between workers and farmers in a single movement — is very largely due to the impact of the Social Gospel in western Canada.

What was the Social Gospel? The term usually refers to a Christian movement that heard in the Gospel a message of justice addressed to society. The Social Gospel heard in the preaching of Jesus and the prophets a judgment on the present social order and a summons to build a more just society, and it interpreted God's promise made through Jesus as an assurance that this transformation of society was part of man's divine destiny. In his study of the Social Gospel in Canada from 1914 to 1928, entitled *The Social Passion*, Richard Allen divides the Social Gospel movements into three categories, conservative, progressive and radical.[53] The conservatives understood the problems of society in traditional terms; they accused people of personal sinfulness and lack of virtue and called the country back to religious observance and greater fidelity. The progressives, who according to Allen constituted the mainstream, understood sin largely in social terms and hence saw the appropriate Christian response to sin mainly as active commitment to reform projects and progressive politics. The justice of God demanded the reform of the social order. The radicals, finally, held that sin had permeated the social order to such an extent that nothing short of a total reconstruction could make society more pleasing to God.

The radical Social Gospel reached a high point in Canada at the end of the First World War when a great number of Christians recognized the imperialistic designs of the war and discovered that, on top of this, the victory in no way improved the misery of ordinary people at home. The radicals at that time occupied important positions on church boards and were able to formulate the public policy of their denominations. The famous 1918 report of the Committee on Social Service and Evangelism of the Methodist church went farther than any other ecclesiastical document in projecting the ideal of a socialist society.[54] The report condemned all forms of special privilege in society, advocated the democratization of commercial organizations and demanded that all industrial enterprises call labour to a voice in management and a share in the profit. It then asked for the nationalization of the natural resources, such as mines, water power, fisheries and forests as well as all means of communication, transportation and public utilities, and condemned exorbitant profits and speculation on land and grain. The report also recommended legislative reform to assure the labourers fair wages and business a fair profit, then pass all profit in excess of these to the public. The other Christian denominations, especially the Presbyterians, followed the Methodists in the emphasis on the reconstruction of society, even if they did not adopt such a radical programme.

Richard Allen shows how the radical demands were usually made by a small ginger group in the denomination: they would get a hearing and be allowed to produce a provisional text, but then their demands would be reformulated in a more general way, made more acceptable to a wider public within the church and in the process purged of their socialist orientation, until the final position reached expressed a progressive or reformist spirit. In many instances even such positions were weakened until all that remained of the original movement was the church's recommendation of social justice in a general and abstract way. Again and again radical Christians found themselves obliged to leave the denominations of their origins.

Salem Bland, for a time a professor at Wesley College in Winnipeg, was a Christian radical who remained with the church and did not abandon theological reflection. His book *The New Christianity*, published in 1921, clarified the religious experience that stood behind the radical Social Gospel. Over against mainstream Christianity, which tended to look upon God as the heavenly father who guided and protected his creation from above and who, in the minds of the people, became the protector of the existing order, the radical Social Gospel saw God present in history as its forward movement, manifesting divine power in the struggle of the poor and oppressed for emancipation. God was here perceived as a transcendent agent, immanent in the historical process as call, as orientation, as power, as the final horizon of reconciliation. While the churches worshipped the God of order, the Social Gospel worshipped the God of justice, who was a principle not of stability but of social change.

Solidarity with the workers and the poor led these Christians to new religious experiences. Yet not all radical Christians expressed their convictions in theological form. Since the churches claimed a monopoly on religious language, many radicals, Woodsworth among them, produced a secular counter-language to express their basically religious convictions. For this reason it is not always easy to evaluate the religious position of the activists. The secular vocabulary adopted by them does not necessarily imply that the sense of urgency that moved them had lost its essentially religious quality.

After the decline of the Social Gospel in the late Twenties, a remarkable revival took place in the Thirties, this time in more sophisticated theological form, sponsored by Christian intellectuals who had become socialists during the Depression. The movement originated with a Toronto-based group of ministers of the United Church concerned with the state of society.[55] At a meeting in April 1931, they created the Movement for a Christian Social Order, later reconstituted as the Christian Socialist Movement. It was resolved that "the teaching of Jesus Christ, applied in an age of machine production and financial control, means Christian socialism."[56] The movement spread to Montreal and Ottawa, and in 1934 became the Fellowship for a Christian Social Order (FCSO), a Christian socialist organization that was dissolved only at the end of the Second World War. The fellowship was closely associated with the League for Social Reconstruction. In fact several founding members of the league were active in the new fellowship: Eugene Forsey, King Gordon, John Line, Gregory Vlastos and R.B.Y. Scott.

The new Social Gospel was based on a much more careful socio-economic analysis of the world's problems than the more popular Social Gospel of the Twenties. The theological foundation of the new movement was carefully worked out by the participants in critical dialogue with neo-orthodoxy, existentialism and the Marxist critique of society. The one major publication of the FCSO was a collection of articles entitled *Toward the Christian Revolution*,[57] which offered theological reflections in a socialist perspective that actually anticipated the "political theology" and "liberation theology" developed in the late Sixties by Protestants and Catholics on the Left.

The contributors to *Toward the Christian Revolution* improved the inadequate theological reasoning of the traditional Social Gospel and argued against liberal theologians who fought the politicization of the Christian message. In particular, they argued against Reinhold Niebuhr, the great American theologian, who by that time had repudiated the Social Gospel.[58] Niebuhr had reasoned that the Christian message addresses man in his human situation, which is the same everywhere, independent of social location and the problems of society. By relying on existentialist philosophy, Niebuhr described the human situation as anxiety-producing. Torn between the finitude of his natural endowment and the infinitude of his aspirations, man is deeply troubled by an anxiety that is the source of his sins and the wound from which he is healed by the Christian message alone. The FCSO regarded this as an ideological use of human anguish. If people are in fact anxious, if they are inwardly torn, theologians must first analyze the contradictions in the social system that generate conflicts in individual persons (and for this a careful sociological analysis is necessary) and then turn to a political movement that promises to change the anxiety-producing social institutions. Niebuhr's speedy turn to metaphysical anxiety allowed him to look away from the oppressive structures in society.

Niebuhr, moreover, in line with Christian neo-orthodoxy, accused the Social Gospel of expecting the coming of God's kingdom into history. He held that this was historically naive, did not recognize the dimension of sin operative in earthly existence and gave a false interpretation of God's promises. God was totally other and thus not identified with any historical movement. The FCSO argued that the theological foundation of their political involvement was not the expectation of God's kingdom on earth, even though the promised kingdom affected the course of human history. But when confronted by a conflict between the rich and poor, the "haves" and the "have-nots," as Christians in the Thirties were, they would find that the Christian message indicated clearly with which of these two sides they should identify. God's identification with the poor as revealed in the scriptures was the theological foundation of socialist involvement. The FCSO represented a new theological movement.

The spirit of the Social Gospel as well as its organizational connections had a considerable impact on Canadian socialism, especially in western Canada. We mentioned that the number of
Protestant ministers and ex-ministers in CCF leadership positions was considerable. The CCF made a special point of presenting its social doctrine as in keeping with the social teaching
of the churches. The party produced a series of pamphlets that
displayed quotations from ecclesiastical documents, including
papal encyclicals, as well as more personal statements made by
ecclesiastical leaders to demonstrate that the ideals of the party
were in fact endorsed, at least in principle, by the Christian
churches. When the CCF was attacked by churchmen, especially
by Catholic bishops and priests, the party made it a policy never
to give an angry reply. The leaders sincerely believed that their
version of socialism was in keeping with Christianity, but that
they were a little ahead of the churches, who in due time would
also recognize the socialist implications of the Christian message.
For the time, some argued, there was a conflict between Christianity and "Churchianity." When CCF leaders did make angry
remarks critical of the churches, the Catholic church in particular
— this happened occasionally in British Columbia — they were
reprimanded by provincial or national leaders and their sentiments publicly disowned.[59]

It must be recognized that there was a good deal of hostility to
religion at the time among the rank-and-file activists of the labour
movement, especially in the industrialized parts of Canada, like
British Columbia and Ontario. The active socialists and union
organizers who had to struggle against the "respectable people" in
the towns and cities, among them the local churches with their
priests and ministers, sometimes adopted atheist rhetoric. The
churches appeared to them to be altogether on the side of the
exploiters. The Christian congregations in the towns were unaf-
fected by or, more likely, ignorant of the left wing in their own
denominations and the progressive declarations of their church
leaders. While the Toronto conference of the United Church had
repudiated capitalism — "it is our belief that the application of the
principles of Jesus Christ to economic conditions would mean the
end of capitalism"[60] — and Pope Pius XI had argued that capitalism
had become an evil system — "free enterprise has committed

suicide, economic dictatorship has taken its place"[61] — the local congregations tended to behave as if God were the protector of the present socio-economic system. Atheistic slogans uttered by a few empassioned activists only confirmed the Christian communities in the belief that they were defending God's cause in society. The Social Gospel represented a minority in the churches; its impact was felt strongly only in the prairie provinces.

The Character of Canadian Socialism

In this section I wish to examine the special features of Canadian socialism. After the foregoing it is by no means obvious why the policy and philosophy of the CCF should be called socialist at all. Some of the groups that constituted it, especially most of the prairie farmers, did not think of themselves as socialist. They hated monopoly capitalism, but they regarded it as an abuse of capitalism rather than its true nature. Still, it was in Saskatchewan that the party adopted the term "socialist" as the adjective that expressed its peculiar character. The CCF weekly, *The Commonwealth* (sometimes called *The New Era* in these years), not only used the term to designate the party and its policy but also tried to clarify the particular Canadian usage of the term. Under the rubric "What is Socialism?" the paper offered, issue after issue, new descriptions of socialism, drawn from the speeches of CCF members, that expressed a political vision of the CCF in terms acceptable to farmers and workers. Here is one of these definitions of socialism that represents the spirit and tone of them all: "The abolishment of unfair competition and the establishment of fruitful cooperation; the prevention of amassing of riches in individual hands, and the more equitable distribution of wealth; the institution of social and national endeavours for the common good in the place of private enterprise for the benefit of the few; the uniting of all the workers of the world for the establishment of international brotherhood by the elimination of the causes of jealousy and suspicion between the nations."[62] Canadian socialism wanted to replace an economic system based on competition and private profit by another defined in terms of cooperation and social planning; it sought to overcome the chaos of production and distribution characteristic of capitalism by introducing a planned economy for the essential industries.

These descriptive definitions of socialism left out many elements important to theoretically oriented comrades, yet they were useful for uniting diverse social movements in a single political party. The CCF, we recall, included groups that regarded themselves as socialists, either British or Marxist, and others that were simply opposing monopoly capitalism. It was also supported by liberals who regarded the party as a political agent for promoting extended welfare legislation. The definitions of socialism in *The Commonwealth*, reticent in regard to class struggle and public ownership of industry and banks but strong in regard to the cooperative nature of the new society and the planned economy, left ample room for the distinct emphases of the affiliated organizations. It can even be argued that CCF socialism was of considerable theoretical interest because it guaranteed that the new social and economic order would be based on cooperation and participation and hence excluded a "socialism from above,"[63] that is to say, the authoritarian imposition of socialist policies by a strong-arm government that comes to power representing only a small fraction of the population. Canadian socialism was to begin at the base. Despite the lack of theoretical consistency and the pragmatic nature of party unity, it is possible and, I think, necessary to speak of certain features characteristic of Canadian socialism. I wish to single out four of them: CCF socialism was democratic, libertarian, populist and, for want of a better term, moral.

1.

When I say that Canadian socialism was democratic, I am not referring simply to the fact that the CCF accepted the parliamentary system and promised to work within the confines of the Canadian constitution. The peculiar democratic nature of Canadian socialism was expressed in the manner in which the founding conventions perceived and organized the party. From the beginning the CCF was a federation of existing farmer, labour and socialist organizations, and there was no intention to remove from the affiliated groups their special styles and viewpoints.

Since Canada is divided into distinct regions, such a policy was imperative. The CCF wanted to preserve a pluralistic character — an aspect, incidentally, that was not highlighted when the party sought to establish itself in Quebec. Since the party gave Dominion-wide visibility and impact to disparate radical groups, it was taken for granted that each group affiliated with the federation would give up something of its own; yet the price for having a national party was never understood as perfect conformity to policies worked out at headquarters. Considerable diversity remained among the different CCF member organizations, a fact that sometimes confused the Canadian public.

Since individual citizens could not become members of the CCF during the Thirties, the party created new organizations, the so-called CCF clubs, that new members could join. These clubs brought CCF members together as comrades and friends; they became communities of action and education and laid the foundation for the kind of grass-roots party the CCF wanted to be.

In due time the need for greater centralization arose. The national convention of 1938 constituted the CCF as a national party with provincial sections, modelled after the Canadian federation and the federal structure of the traditional parties. As the party reached more people, became more influential on the national level and aspired to more power in Parliament, greater power was granted to the national office. At the same time the CCF struggled hard against the bureaucratic style of mass parties. Woodsworth was vehemently opposed to centralized bureaucracies. The organization of the party was of such importance to Canadian socialists because they believed that the style of a party contributes to the creation of political consciousness and hence determines the kind of society that would result from a movement.[64] In other words, they thought that political organization belongs to the infrastructure rather than the superstructure of society. An elitist vanguard political party with strict discipline that imposes its decisions on its supporters is bound to create, CCFers felt, an authoritarian society in which people are unable to contribute to the making of policy. They felt the Communist party, in particular, reflected an authoritarian ethos, at odds with the spirit of democracy, a political style possibly derived from the clandestine way in which socialist parties had to be organized in Czarist Russia.[65]

The CCF wanted to create a cooperative commonwealth in Canada. For this reason the party set itself up as a network of organizations where all groups, even the smaller groups at the base, were able to make an active contribution. There was to be easy communication between the local level and the central offices. The party had decided, moreover, that it should be financed simply by its members: it did not seek financial support from wealthy donors. In this it followed the basic cooperative principle laid down by the original Rochdale foundation. This practice was to give a greater sense of participation to the members and protect the party from the influence of business people. Election campaigns were run on very little money: they consisted mainly of public meetings and door-to-door canvassing by the members. By demanding the participation of every level and creating channels of exchange, the CCF tried to be at the same time a political party and a social movement.

In the correspondence of E.J. (Ted) Garland, an MP from Alberta through the Twenties and Thirties, we find a letter that articulated the ideal of the party.[66] He recognized, of course, the trend toward bureaucracy in the large parties and the pressure exerted on the party by the powerful in the community. Still he argued that the party system itself was not at fault; what was at fault, he wrote, was that the parties were unable to organize the people and did not know how to mobilize the people's collective intelligence. "Everything in the party system will remain the same after the first bloom is spent, unless there is an organization, permanent in character, involving the people who have voted and on whose participation the party must rely." Garland saw clearly that a party without grass-roots organization would need large sums of money for election campaigns, would turn to business groups and the wealthy, and then very soon — as he put it — "the old masters are in the saddle again."

This approach was particularly successful in Saskatchewan, where cooperative enterprises and the setting up of the Wheat Pool had brought the farmers together in grass-roots organizations. Since in those days, rural Saskatchewan was made up of a single class of farmers who did not differ much among themselves in terms of the land they owned and the income they made, the local groups were strongly united and thus gained considerable influence in making party policy. "The Saskatchewan CCF," Lipset writes, "has succeeded in involving more people in direct political activity than any other party in American and Canadian history, with the possible exception of certain similar [U.S.] farmers' parties."[67] The CCF asked for more from the people than their votes. People became dues-paying members of the party in large numbers, participated in their local organizations and took an active part in thinking through what socialism meant for their province. Participation in political discussions and active support of the party were so great that they produced in Saskatchewan a new political culture, a mass movement of informed, perceptive and principled people to which there was no parallel in North America. This was the cultural impact of Canadian socialism in the prairies. It was a "socialism from below":[68] it provided people with the possibility of becoming creators of their own society and, in doing so, modifying their own self-understanding.

The grass-roots party did not last forever. Party conventions remained assemblies where different groups in the party fought out their differences and where the policies of the party were discussed and decided by vote, but the forces of centralization and the multiplication of administrative procedures eventually reduced the influence of the local units, to some extent even of the conventions, and made the central offices, provincial and national, the actual decision-makers. Walter Young has analyzed this trend very carefully. He argues that "the law of oligarchy," formulated by Robert Michels, was operative to some extent at least in the history of the CCF.[69] According to this law, it is inevitable that a political party, whatever its ideology, will eventually be run in bureaucratic fashion by a small group of leaders, an oligarchy. Michels had focussed his research on the German Socialist party prior to the First World War and concluded that despite its radical principles the party, under the rule of the oligarchy, had become a bureaucracy without vision and imagination, insensitive to the aspirations of the members and the needs of the political situation. Walter Young has shown that the Canadian socialist party also came to be run by a small group of leaders who were accepted as the public spokesmen for the entire movement.

What is perhaps more remarkable is the persistence of the CCF in struggling against Michels' law, and thanks to this effort it remained a political organization quite different from the other Canadian parties. Young acknowledges this. "The CCF," he writes, "was an anomaly on the political landscape."[70] The CCF constantly carried on its debates and disagreements in the public eye, and while this had educational value for the members and gave them a sense of participating in the decision-making process, it allowed the opponents of the party to make use of the opinions uttered in these conflicts and castigate them as signs of irresponsible radicalism. The price the CCF had to pay for its democratic style was considerable. Still, the party did not slacken in its devotion to democracy. Father Eugene Cullinane's account of the CCF in the mid-Forties put great emphasis on "the passion for democracy" he found in the party, even and especially among the radicals, including the Marxists from British Columbia.[71]

2.

This takes us to a second characteristic of the CCF: the party's commitment to civil liberties. We recall that this commitment was clearly expressed in the Regina Manifesto. The party continued to defend freedom of expression and freedom of association throughout the subsequent decades, even when this was against its own interests. Civil liberties were a matter of principle for the CCF. Woodsworth and his party defended the civil liberties of communists, even though the Communist party of Canada was their declared enemy. Thus in 1934, when major demonstrations took place in Toronto after the sudden arrest of A.E. Smith, the prominent communist leader, and a new organization, the Canadian Labour Defense League (CLDF), was formed for the purpose of obtaining the release of Smith and other political prisoners, Woodsworth protested against the arrest in the Commons and defended the civil rights of communists.[72] At the same time, the CCF decided not to join the CLDF but to work for the liberation of political prisoners through their own organizations. This defence of civil liberties created problems for the CCF. Canadians opposed to social reform and left-wing movements, among them Catholic spokesmen, understood Woodsworth's plea on behalf of communists as a sign that he himself and his party were associated with communism. Yet the CCF did not weaken its position.

The place of civil liberties in Marxist socialism is ambiguous. Marx recognized of course that civil liberties were at one time the revolutionary demands of the rising bourgeoisie in its struggle against the feudal order. But when Marx dealt with the civil liberties proclaimed by the French Revolution and adopted, at least in principle, by the modern bourgeois state, he tended to look upon them as an ideological superstructure defending the freedom of the market and the interests of the owning class.

The civil liberties, he argued, apply only to the bourgeoisie: freedom is here defined in terms of political rights against traditional authority. The freedom for which the proletariat longs is the power to participate in the wealth of the nation. For the poor, freedom is first of all the freedom to eat, to work, to have access to the wealth they produce. For the successful middle class — industrialists and businessmen — freedom is principally the independence from the regulations and structures inherited from traditional society that limit them in their economic activity. In the name of freedom, they therefore oppose all traditions, both sacred and profane, that subordinate production and commerce to the needs of the community. The bourgeois demand for civil liberties after the demise of feudalism expresses the desire of the owning classes to free themselves from government interference and buy and sell as they please. Freedom here means freedom of the market.

For Marx, the rights of man are equally ambiguous. In the Marxist perspective, there is no "man as such" who could be the subject of rights. Any theory of human rights, he argued, disguises the uncomfortable fact that in every society there are masters and servants, and that man belongs to either one or the other of these two classes, with interests at odds with one another. Man as such is an abstraction that does not exist. The dominant class looks upon itself as representing the whole of society, and the rights it claims for itself are understood as the rights of man. The emphasis on human rights in bourgeois society is an ideology that blinds the proletariat in regard to its real freedom. The freedoms offered in capitalist society prevent the workers from discovering their bondage. The rights of man do not prevent the workers from being slaves in society, that is to say, from being obliged, for sheer survival, to sell their labour on the market. Marx says very little in favour of the human rights gained by the French Revolution: he does not clarify, except in occasional remarks, that the socialist negation of human rights is dialectical, that is, intent on preserving the positive content of these rights in the new society.

Marx's critical view of civil liberties is a useful paradigm for the sociologist who examines *to what extent* bourgeois legislation protects the successful classes. That Marx did not mean to discard human rights altogether is clear from his account of the classless society, in which all domination of man over man shall be overcome. Still, the ambiguous treatment of these rights in his political philosophy is at least partially responsible for the ease with which human rights are disregarded and violated in the Soviet bloc.

Marx's evaluation of human rights ties in with his view of the bourgeois state. The state is also an ideological superstructure: in the words of the Communist Manifesto, it is "the executive committee of the ruling class." The bourgeois state was created as the guardian of private property, and its legislation protects the owning classes against the property-less masses. In this situation even reform legislation ostensibly devised to help the workers and protect the interests of the poor in fact creates conditions that are of greater advantage to the owning class. Again, some scholars argue that this view of the state is not Marx's definitive verdict on modern democratic governments, but rather a paradigm or a hypothesis, to be used by social critics to study *to what extent* the state and its legislation actually favour the powerful in society. Associated with this view of the state is the most utopian of Marx's positions, namely, that after the revolution and the establishment of a socialist economy the state will eventually "wither away." There may be a brief period of domination during which the workers themselves will be the ruling class, when the revolutionary government will make decisions in favour of the working class just as the bourgeois state had legislated in favour of the owning class; but then, in due time, the state will slowly disappear altogether as the last principle of domination in society. This will be the end of the oppression of man by man. The state, then, in the perspective of Marx, is an instrument of domination.

British socialism never followed Marx on the question of the state and civil liberties. British socialists recognized the partiality of government toward the ruling class and saw clearly that the laws passed in Parliament were, on the whole, of greater benefit to the rich than the poor, but they refused to regard the state as nothing but the executive committee of the ruling class. They believed in parliamentary democracy. It should be possible, they held, to use parliamentary power to subdue the possessing class and establish a socialist society. Similarly, British socialists were sincerely committed to civil rights.

What were the reasons for this British approach? Some writers point to the special position of Britain in the nineteenth century, the successful expansion of the Empire and the wealth Britain derived from its imperialist connections, and then suggest that the workers in such an aggressive nation profited considerably from the existing system, especially if one compared their situation not with the ruling class of their own country but with the workers of other countries. Was the loyalty of British labour to democracy and civil rights simply due to its privileged position?

Such a theory, even if it were true of British socialism, does not explain the commitment of Canadian socialism to democracy and civil liberties. For Canada was a colony; its relationship to the Empire was a source of exploitation felt by workers and farmers alike. Woodsworth was a vehement opponent of imperialism. Following the British social thinker J.A. Hobson, Woodsworth believed that capitalist production, ever in need of expansion, pushed the industrialized nations toward imperialism, which in turn led to wars, small wars of colonial conquest and great wars among the competing powers for the extension and protection of the market.[73]

Woodsworth loved the British tradition, but believed that Canadians owed no allegiance whatever to the British Empire. Canada was an exploited colony: it supplied the mother country with raw materials and in turn bought from the mother country the finished products. Yet the Canadian socialists believed there was a British democratic tradition, of which they were proud and to which they were loyal. It is true, of course, that the democratic language used in Britain since the Magna Carta applied, strictly speaking, only to a small elite, first the nobility and then the owning classes; but the language itself, spilling over its first narrow application, generated an ever wider democratic expectation. The political struggle for the extension of the vote to the propertyless illustrated well the force of the democratic impulse beyond the intention of the original framers. As we shall see further on, the Canadian radical Salem Bland called this phenomenon "overspill."

The democratic character of British socialism, moreover, was related to the nature of Protestant Christianity. Associated with the bourgeois struggle for freedom and in some cases even preceding it, was the struggle of radical Christians against the hierarchical church. Religious liberty and freedom of association were the demands made by the Anabaptists of the sixteenth century, the left wing of the Reformation that repudiated traditional churches as well as secular authorities. For this they were mercilessly persecuted by Catholic and Protestant governments alike. The social foundation of this protest movement lay in the century-old struggle of the peasants against their feudal lords, successful at one time in Switzerland but brutally crushed in the sixteenth century, and related to this and derived from it, the tension between the country and the towns, events that antedate the rise of the bourgeoisie. The radical Christians' demands for separation of church and state and for freedom of association lie at the origin of civil liberties.

The Anabaptists were defeated. In the seventeenth century, Calvinist Christians in England opposed the established Church and the feudal order with which the Church was still identified and demanded religious freedom and the right of association. In defining themselves against papacy and prelacy, these Christian groups saw themselves as voluntary associations, freely called together, whose governing bodies were elected and empowered by their members. Democracy and liberty became essential elements of the Puritan heritage. While the class involved in these non-conformist churches was indeed that of the craftsmen and businessmen who strove for greater political power in society, it is impossible to understand their religious position purely and simply as a reflection of their class struggle. The Anabaptist spark was original. So was the Calvinist religious experience in Britain a century later.

James Luther Adam has pointed out that Max Weber only explored the economic ethic of Puritanism, while overlooking the political impact of Puritan religion on modern society.[74] The democratic and libertarian ideals particular to Anglo-Saxon Protestantism had great influence in establishing the constitutional governments in England and North America that protected the freedom of citizens to form associations for religious or secular purposes. The Puritans developed a strong sense of civic responsibility, which balanced the individualistic work ethic that has received so much attention. If this ethic had an affinity with the spirit of capitalism, it can also be argued that the social responsibility generated by Puritan religion had an affinity with the spirit of socialism, that is to say, with a personal life dedicated to the well-being of society.

In my opinion, the commitment of British (and Canadian) socialism to democracy and civil liberties was related to the Protestant tradition. This is one of the reasons, I think, why Marxism, with its anti-religious spirit and its cynical view of parliamentary democracy, was never accepted by the British labour movement, even though both Marx and Engels lived in England and were closely associated with English labour organizations. Since they practised democracy in their non-conformist churches, ordinary people believed that democracy was the appropriate ideal for their political organizations.

By way of contrast, let me recall that the Catholic tradition has had no such libertarian heritage. Sacramental worship and religious experience mediated through the authoritative Church produced among Catholics a strong identification with their religious community and made them accept as God-given the Church's hierarchical structure and the society that this Church had blessed. While there have been prophetic men and women in the Catholic church who have demanded freedom of expression, they have never been strong enough to modify the ecclesiastical system. It was only Vatican Council II that reconciled the Catholic church with liberal ideals. Still, in Catholic cultures democracy and civil rights are not seen as belonging to the essence of collective well-being. There exists a predilection for authoritarian rule. As late as the 1930s, Pius XI urged governments in pursuit of social reform to suppress socialist organizations in their countries.[75] The provincial government of Quebec revealed the same indifference to civil liberties up until the Fifties. Even the economic radicals of Quebec, about whom we shall have more to say in another chapter, did not feel compelled to object during the Depression to the curtailment of civil liberties by the provincial government. It has even been argued that whenever a Catholic population does turn to socialism, they are easily attracted to an authoritarian version of it.

3.

The next feature of Canadian socialism I wish to describe is its populism. The term "populist" has often been applied to popular movements in America and Russia, produced by the vehement reaction of farmers against the oppressive conditions inflicted on them by government and society. Populist movements organize farmers in a joint struggle for greater justice and, in many instances, give birth to political parties.

Populism is a highly ambiguous phenomenon. For if the populace does not analyze the cause of the common oppression correctly, it turns to unsound theories, slanders innocent groups, finds a scapegoat on whom to blame the common deprivation and becomes attracted to conspiracy theories of history. Thus populism can produce blind hatred of foreigners, immigrants or other races. But if the populist movement operates out of a correct analysis of the common ills, it becomes a power to be reckoned with and produces an important critique of the dominant institutions of society. It has been said that in the United States, the best truly native criticism of capitalist society during the second half of the nineteenth century was produced by populists. In the twentieth century, prairie populism produced the thrust of the CCF in Saskatchewan.

What concerns us in this context is the populist nature of the CCF. What we find in Canadian socialism is great trust in ordinary people. This spirit was again related, I think, to the nonconformist Protestant tradition. The confidence was shared that ordinary people, struggling to understand their situation, could easily come to see what was wrong with their world and find solutions for improving their lot. This was also the conviction of the cooperative movement, which was wedded to the CCF in western Canada. People could understand the cause of their economic plight, organize themselves around their economic needs and become masters of their own productivity. This trust in ordinary people was often associated with distrust of the major institutions, including the educational system and universities. Populism often reacted negatively to the expertise offered by the educated elite and their schools. This easily resulted in anti-intellectualism and, in religion, in a fundamentalist approach to the Bible. At other times, however, the mistrust of the educated strata of society was accompanied by the confidence that ordinary people were intelligent and able to learn what was important for their trade and for their lives and could become perceptive critics of the social order. The cooperative movement developed its own methods of populist education.

Populist education was the strength of the Antigonish movement, a cooperative movement in eastern Nova Scotia sparked by two Catholic priests, J.J. Tompkins and M.M. Coady, which had its beginning in the Twenties but became strongly organized only in the Thirties.[76] This movement formulated a clear educational policy. Already in 1921, Tompkins had expressed his views in a pamphlet entitled *Knowledge for the People*. He felt that the knowledge supplied by the university was quite useless. It made people more dependent on the elite and blind to the causes of their ills. But if one could get people to reflect on their plight, to study the causes of their exploitation and introduce them to methods of self-help, then they would discover a new self-confidence and find in themselves resources hitherto unexpected. As people organized in cooperatives and struggled jointly against the obstacles put in their way by the dominant system, they would begin to see more clearly how the injustices from which they suffered were woven into the whole of society. They would begin to see society in a new light and would opt for an alternative social order. Later popular educators have called this "the raising of consciousness." Education was here seen not as the extension of received and demonstrated wisdom to those who had been excluded from it until then; it was rather the entry into a new awareness that would enable people to understand the forces of oppression and would create in them a new sense of solidarity with others in a common struggle for justice.

That the CCF was committed to educational goals is generally admitted. From the beginning the CCF organized discussion and study clubs, published newsletters, papers and pamphlets, and sent speakers and teachers all over the country to introduce people to the new thinking. Even members of Parliament, although hard at work in their offices, were willing to travel long distances for the purpose of popular education. This great trust in education has been described by Walter Young as an expression of the liberalism and rationalism inherited from British Fabianism and mediated through the Canadian League for Social Reconstruction.[77]

It seems to me, however, that this refers only to one aspect, a minor one, of the educational policy of the CCF. The other aspect — the dominant one, I think — was the populist approach to education. It introduced people to a critique of the present order and offered them an alternative view of society; it was a process of consciousness-raising. Since the CCF was committed to the parliamentary system, it realized that socialism could come to the Canadian people only if they really wanted it and the vast majority involved itself in the political process, voted the CCF into power and were ready for a new kind of social responsibility. What the party tried to do — and I think that this goes beyond the liberal or Fabian model — was to create a grass-roots culture that would mediate a new consciousness to the people. An electoral victory alone could never introduce socialism, even if accompanied by a general strike and the use of force in setting up and protecting the democratically elected government, unless the political change had been prepared by a cultural socialism, that is, by a critical populist perception of reality, expressed in the people's style of life, forms of association, religion, art and entertainment. Canadian socialism exhibited a trust in the common man and woman that was untypical of liberalism and, for quite different reasons, of Marxism. The social philosophy of the CCF, following the British prototype, lacked a theory of alienation and thus inspired a populist trust in ordinary people, workers and farmers alike.

4.

Finally, I wish to mention a feature of Canadian socialism closely related to the preceding ones, namely its "moral" character. I mean "moral" socialism in contrast with a socialism that calls itself "scientific." Socialism is primarily scientific if it argues against the capitalist system in scientific terms, that is to say, if it analyzes the inner contradictions of capitalism and demonstrates that by its own inner logic the capitalist economy is bound to destroy itself. Scientific socialism, moreover, motivates the workers to join the organized struggles by demonstrating to them that the present system exploits them. The theory of surplus value purports to show that workers are deprived of the wealth they produce, even if they happen to be well paid, as long as they do not own the means of production. Scientific socialism appeals to the workers very largely in terms of their collective self-interest. It certainly expresses its outrage at present injustices, but since it tends to regard the whole of culture and religion as an ideological superstructure of the exploitative economic order, it does not appeal to traditional values. It does not condemn the present system in terms of the inherited morality.

Canadian socialism often presented scientific arguments against capitalism. CCFers argued that capitalism had produced the war, was responsible for the Great Depression and remained intrinsically incapable of planning production and distributing the goods to the people who needed them. Yet the main arguments employed by the CCF were moral: they showed that capitalism had led to poverty and insecurity and inflicted endless suffering on people. The capitalist system was immoral and sinful. Canadian socialism preached against the dominant system. In their political speeches the CCFers appealed to a traditional sense of justice, to the moral aspirations of the Canadian people and in particular to the biblical ideal of justice in order to persuade people to join the CCF and its socialist cause.

Scientific socialism tends to suppose that the "mores" are always on the side of the ruling class. For this reason, scientific socialists see themselves as being at odds with the inherited culture. In turn they are often looked upon by people as strangers, as persons who introduce foreign ideas unrelated to traditional wisdom. Canadian socialists, on the other hand, while repudiating the culture and religion of the dominant class, firmly embraced what they regarded as the highest values mediated by British political culture and the Christian moral tradition. CCFers often used the argument that Christians were increasingly unable to put up with capitalism because it offended the dignity of human persons and undermined the common brotherhood.

The Antigonish movement of Catholic origin even used Thomistic theology in a radical way.[78] The leaders would first describe the image of man and the truly human life according to the teaching of St. Thomas, and then compare these ideals with the grim social realities of the day, which inflicted indignities upon poor people and forced them to live under inhuman conditions. The present system was immoral, and the right thing for Catholics to do was to reject and repudiate it.

The most interesting theoretical analysis of the historical thrust toward socialism was made in Salem Bland's book, *The New Christianity.* He argued that in Western history two great interrelated ideals are at work — "brotherly love," derived from the biblical experience, and "democratic intent," drawn from the classical and European, especially British tradition — ideals that men have embedded in institutions and that then, by a phenomenon he called "overspill," stand in judgment over these very institutions as inadequate and make people work for their reconstruction.[79] Christian brotherhood created the church: but as soon as it was organized the same ideal of brotherhood stood in judgment over it and made people eager for structural changes. Similarly, the impulse toward democracy expressed itself in political institutions, but soon after their establishment the same impulse toward democracy made the excluded people recognize the elitist and oligarchical character of these institutions and reach for social revolution. The ideal always reaches beyond the institutions it brings forth; it achieves historical power through the section of the population inspired by this ideal that suffers from the contradictions of society and finds itself at the bottom. Societies that use the language of brotherhood and democracy generate, despite themselves, movements that unsettle them and try to revolutionize the social order. Love and justice are dangerous words: while they have been tamed by the institutions that mediate them, they produce a yearning for social revolution among the excluded people. This "overspill" constitutes the dynamics of Western history.

According to Bland, then, it was not class conflict defined in economic terms that moved history forward: it was rather the conflict between classes in a wider sense, between those who protected the inherited institutions as embodiments of justice and those who, enlightened by the same inexhaustible ideal of justice, recognized themselves as excluded from justice (brotherhood and democracy) and struggled to revolutionize the social order. Bland recognized the moral or, if one prefers, spiritual element in the movement toward socialism. He believed that the time had come when fellowship and democracy were to be introduced into the economic system. For this reason he advocated the dismantling of capitalism and the public ownership of resources and industries.

This theory expresses very well the spirit of Canadian socialism. The CCF appealed to the Christian message, even though it criticized the ecclesiastical institutions for being identified with capitalism. Similarly, CCFers found no difficulty in appealing to the British democratic tradition, even though they clearly recognized that in Canada democracy was in the hands of the ruling elite and was employed to oppress the nation. The CCF appealed to the moral sense of the Canadian people. It did not expect that this moral vision would be shared by all Canadians, by rulers and ruled alike; to entertain such an expectation would have made their socialism "utopian" in the sense defined by Engels.[80] What the CCF hoped was that the moral sense inherited from the best of the Canadian tradition would intensify the conflict between the bourgeoisie and the dependent classes and help the party, in the name of the dependent classes and in reliance on them, to gain power.

This moral socialism did not exclude the scientific element, nor did it seek to transcend the conflict between classes by proposing high ideals acceptable to all Canadians. Canadian socialism was not politics based on sentiment, a special pleading for the victims of society, a bleeding-heart approach to society. The CCF insisted that the dependent classes, farmers and workers in particular, were in fact the producers of wealth in the country and had the right and in fact the power to claim what was theirs; but it also believed that this claim was in keeping with the moral sense of the Canadian people, to which even the religious and political institutions gave witness, despite themselves.

2
Papal Teaching on Socialism

To understand the reaction of the Canadian Catholics to the socialism of the CCF, we must turn to the official position adopted by the papacy in the face of the Great Depression. In 1931 Pope Pius XI published the encyclical *Quadragesimo anno*, in which he summed up previous Catholic social teaching and extended it to meet the needs of the contemporary situation. In this document, which exerted a strong influence on Catholic bishops and, through them, on the Catholic population everywhere, Pius XI criticized the abuses of capitalism — he repudiated, in particular, monopoly capitalism — condemned socialism in its revolutionary and its moderate democratic forms, and advocated a third way, a middle road between capitalism and socialism, a Catholic policy for overcoming the present crisis.

Catholic Social Teaching

What is meant by Catholic social teaching? During the nineteenth century, the official Catholic church defined its socio-political stance in opposition to the liberal bourgeois state created by industrial capitalism and democratic or republican principles. The Church defended the feudal and aristocratic heritage of European civilization and paid next to no attention to the emergence of the new class of labourers and the oppressive conditions under which they lived. There were a few spirited Catholic reactions to the plight of the working class in various parts of Europe. These movements, often referred to as Social Catholicism,[1] advocated the protection of the workers by just laws: they criticized the bourgeois state — as did the official Church — but in addition accused capitalism of treating workers as commodities and demanded that governments encourage labour organizations.

Social Catholicism combined a pro-labour stance with opposition to socialism in any of its forms. The socialists criticized the new liberal society in the light of an imagined future, the classless society to be created in due time; while Social Catholicism worked out its critique of liberalism in the light of an idealized past, the organic society of the feudal age, when those who owned the land — then the ruling class — saw themselves as protectors of the people who lived and worked on their territories and as the promoters of the common good. Social Catholicism corresponded to what in the British tradition is sometimes referred to as radical Toryism. "Red Tories"[2] are critical of liberal society, resent the power of the bourgeoisie, deplore a society in which the imporant decisions are made under the pressure of commercial and industrial interests, and demand a government made up of responsible, disinterested, magnanimous men — an elite, as it were, high-minded enough to foster the common good of society and defend the urban and rural poor against exploitation by industry and business.

At the end of the nineteenth century, Pope Leo XIII wrote the first important social encyclical, *Rerum Novarum*, in which he adopted the stance of Social Catholicism as the Church's official position. This encyclical defined the direction of Catholic social teaching. Subsequent popes, bishops and theologians have expanded this teaching under the impact of changing social conditions. How have Catholics followed the Church's social doctrine? In a purely abstract way, all Catholics assented to the church's official teaching. It is only in recent years that socially concerned Catholics have examined papal teaching critically.

Before presenting the position of Pius XI's *Quadragesimo anno*, I wish to summarize under four headings the general orientation of Catholic social doctrine. There was first of all *the rejection of political and economic liberalism*. Catholic social teaching argued that modern liberal society had produced a new individualism, dissolved the inherited sense of community, detached people from traditional values and permitted the ambitious and economically successful to gain power in society, influence public policy and define the cultural ideals. Catholic teaching repudiated, in particular, laissez-faire capitalism. While economic competition within certain limits was morally acceptable and in fact socially useful, the unlimited competition that flowed from the free market was regarded as gravely harmful. Why? Because it created a new class of selfish entrepreneurs, subjected the working class to inhuman conditions, and produced in the bourgeoisie eagerness for high profits and growing insensitivity to spiritual values.

In the same breath, Catholic teaching also rejected liberal democracy. For a government that became democratic escaped the power of the traditional leaders of society, men with a sense of divine vocation and social responsibility, and fell instead into the hands of the newly arrived bourgeoisie, the propertied, who desired public authority to protect their own industrial and commercial interests. Democracy allowed pressure groups, especially the rich, to wield powerful influence in society and in particular to undermine the hold traditional values, religion among them, had on the people. Democracy led to the secularization of social institutions and made religion a purely personal and private affair. It undermined the organic unity of traditional society, with its hierarchies, secular and ecclesiastical, and promoted individualism and rationalism, thus producing the typically modern malaise.

What political and economic liberalism overlooked was that people were actually united by profound social bonds, religion among them, inherited from the past, which were the source of their vitality and creativity. To dissolve these bonds made people spiritually, emotionally and existentially empty. The only motivating forces that remained in such a situation were making money and improving the material standard of living. Political and economic liberalism also overlooked the fact that in their social interaction people were bound by objective norms of justice. There were just laws and just institutions and there was something like a just price and a just wage, norms that significantly limited the freedon of the owning classes. These standards of justice were called into question by capitalism, which settled prices and wages on the free market, and by liberal democracy, which made laws and created institutions in accordance with the interests of the bourgeoisie.

Secondly, Catholic teaching regarded *government as the promoter of the common good*. Against liberal social theory, which ascribed a minimal function to government — namely, the protection of law and order and the settlement of conflicts — and asked that the public authority refrain from interfering in the economic, cultural and religious life of the nation, Catholic social teaching, following the classical tradition, held governments responsible for the total well-being of society. In the Catholic view, society was not an aggregate of many individuals united by a legally constituted organization; it was rather a social body, that is, a people united in almost organic fashion through common values and institutions venerated by all. Catholic teaching defended the position that society had an objective common good that transcended the private goods of the individual members. The common good consisted of the values, structures and institutions that provided for the well-being of the people as a whole, including their economic, social, cultural and religious life. While it may have been difficult to give a concrete definition of the common good that satisfied all members of society, it was possible, in the Catholic view of things, to define the common good in general terms and be sufficiently concrete in certain areas of national life to formulate public policy.

In particular, government must protect justice in society, and this included a certain control over the economic life. Since the wealthy had enough power to look after their own interests, it was the special task of government to serve the well-being of the poor, to protect the workers from exploitation by commerce and industry, and to legislate in favour of the disadvantaged in society. The idea that government should not interfere in the economic and cultural affairs of the nation was wholly foreign to this tradition. What Catholic teaching presupposed was that public authority was superior to and independent from the particular interests of the various ranks of society: it expected government to act not as an agent of the owning class, as easily happens in liberal democracies, but as an arbiter in the midst of conflicting interest groups. Whether such presuppositions were justified is, of course, another matter. But at least according to Catholic social theory, those who govern were not appointed by a section of society and hence had no reason to rule in favour of those who elected them; they were rather understood to govern with an authority derived ultimately from God. They represented no section of society, but rather its totality, and hence they saw themselves as servants of the common good.

This aspect of Catholic social teaching has always been meaningless for Catholics living in North America — with the exception of those in Quebec. In the United States and English Canada, liberalism predominates. Society sees itself as made up of individuals, each seeking the abundance of life and free self-expression. The ideal of minimal government is taken for granted and government interference in economic affairs is grudgingly admitted as an exception to the rule — even though in fact the government has already acquired enormous regulatory power in economic life and the old liberalism has long been dead. There is an equal resistance to the presence of government in the cultural and religious life of the people. This liberal view of the state is part and parcel of the American way of life. Liberalism is so pervasive in the United States that to most Americans it no longer appears as a political option at all but as the true, objectively valid view of society. Any deviation from liberalism is looked upon as foreign, an import from another culture, in contradiction with common sense.

Since American Catholics in the Thirties were nourished by the myth of liberalism, they assimilated it into their world-view as had the rest of the population, and for this reason they found papal social teaching almost impossible to apply in their political action. At the time of Roosevelt's New Deal, however, social-minded Catholic leaders were able to use papal teaching to persuade the Catholic community, particularly the more cautious and anti-socialist among them, to give support to the new government policy.[3]

French Canada, as we shall see, had a Catholic tradition that enabled the people to make sense of papal teaching. Even English Canada, in contrast with the United States, possessed in addition to the dominant liberalism a certain authentic Tory tradition that had preserved an old-fashioned collectivist understanding of society, assigning to government the task of protecting the community and restricting the influence of commercial and industrial interests.[4] This Tory social philosophy survived in Canada largely because of the monarchy, Canada's colonial status and the influence of Empire Loyalists and their descendants. Tory social philosophy found expression in certain sections of the Conservative party, although it encountered strong opposition from the party's liberals, whose sympathies lay with the economic elite. Yet the Catholic population of English Canada — made up of later immigrants, mainly from Ireland at first and belonging to the lower classes — looked upon the Liberal party as their protector; hence they had no connection whatever with Canadian Toryism. For this reason papal social teaching on the role of government was as strange to English-speaking Canadian Catholics as it was to American Catholics.

Thirdly, Catholic social teaching recognized *the social dimension of private property*. Leo XIII and subsequent popes strongly defended private property, including land and the means of production, against nineteenth- and twentieth-century socialism. They connected private property with the natural law. A careful reading of the ecclesiastical documents makes it clear, however, that the papal view of private property was quite different from the liberal view that predominates in modern society. In modern society, private property means that people have the right to use, sell or destroy their possessions as they please. In the Catholic tradition, derived from the more organic society of feudalism, private property meant ownership associated with responsibility. In feudal times, private property consisted mainly of land; associated with it was the duty to protect and care for the land, and to distribute some of its produce to the people who laboured on it. The landowner was responsible for the well-being of serfs and tenants.

In line with this pre-industrial model of society, Catholic teaching claimed that private property had two dimensions, the first *private*, which defined ownership in the strict sense and affected such questions as inheritance; and the second *social*, which related the use of ownership to the promotion of the common good. The private side of personal property, even in small amounts, protected the freedom and integrity of persons in society (and hence demanded defence against its detractors), while the social side subordinated the use of this property to the alleviation of common needs and to the well-being of the community. This organic view of society significantly limited personal freedom. Here private property could not be defined as the right to use, sell or destroy, for the use of this property must serve the common good and hence was under the direction of public authority.

Catholic teaching on private property had little in common with the modern liberal view. It may not have been at odds with the modest and benevolent capitalism of small enterprises; that capitalism created a wealthy elite willing to look after its workers, spend its money to build up the community and decorate the land with works of art. But it was wholly opposed to the more developed, more consistent capitalism of large enterprises, whose workers remained strangers to their employers and derived no protection from them, and whose owners did not spend their money on the community but used it to expand their own operations and reinvest in other enterprises. A developed capitalism, even before it reached the monopoly stage, was at odds with Catholic social theory since the use of money, far from serving the common good, was systematically subordinated to the maximization of profit.

What this papal teaching meant in a modern liberal society was not clear. Church teaching insisted that the "social function" of property was actually advantageous to the owners. Why? Because wealth spent in support of the common good rendered the social order more stable and created conditions in which the further increase of wealth was possible. The neglect of this social service, on the other hand, would produce grave injustices in society, upset the social peace and prepare unrest and possible revolution. Catholic teaching favoured a planned economy. Since the model of society was the organic community, justice demanded that the production of goods satisfy the needs of the people and that these goods, when distributed, actually reached them. Yet in bourgeois society no government had this power. By advocating socialist ideas for a planned economy, at least in regard to the essentials of life, and by repudiating at the same time the socialist ideal of public ownership, the popes produced a teaching that was almost without application in modern society. Since it was impossible to go back to a pre-industrial, small-town-and country society, the Catholic demand for the submission of private wealth to the common good, and consequently for an economy guided by government to serve the well-being of all, created in some nations the longing for a strong man, a leader, who could affirm his power in comparative independence of landowners and the owners of industry and legislate or even dictate the just society from above.[5]

Fourthly, Catholic teaching demanded that *class conflict be overcome by class cooperation*, rendered possible through the submission of all to the identical principles of justice. The popes clearly recognized class conflict in industrial capitalism. We read this interesting sentence of Pius XI: "Toward the close of the nineteenth century, new economic methods and new developments of industry had in many nations led to a situation wherein the human community appeared more and more divided into two classes.... The first, small in numbers, enjoyed practically all the comforts so plentifully supplied by modern inventions. The second class, comprising the immense multitude of working men, was made up of those who, oppressed by dire poverty, struggled in vain to escape from the straits that encompassed them."[6] Pius XI recognized that "this state of things was quite satisfactory to the wealthy" while "the working class, victims of these harsh conditions, submitted to them with extreme reluctance and became more and more unwilling to bear the galling yoke."[7]

While papal teaching clearly recognized the existence of class conflict, Catholic social doctrine rejected the effort to overcome economic injustice by class warfare, that is to say, by the struggle of the proletariat to conquer the owning class and substitute itself as the governing class. It is true that Leo XIII already recommended the creation of workmen's associations or unions at the end of the nineteenth century, and hence approved of working-class solidarity and class action on behalf of greater justice. However, he asked that this struggle of the workers seek not conquest but an acceptable form of cooperation, in accordance with the objective norms of justice. Only in this restricted sense should class conflict become the lever that moves society ahead toward greater social and economic equality. The popes rejected the idea that class warfare was the necessary dynamic of history's forward movement.

Catholic teaching recognized the oppression of the working class in modern society, but defended the view that if workers were adequately paid — that is to say, if they received a "living wage" or a "family wage," a wage that enabled them and their families to live in modest comfort — their labour in the factory had dignity and was socially useful. Factory work, in a context of justice, was honourable and expressed the creative contribution of workers to the building of society. We find in Catholic social teaching nothing that corresponded to the Marxist theory of the alienation of labour, according to which wage labour, especially under the conditions of modern industry, estranges the workers from their human substance. Nor did Catholic teaching follow the Marxist position that the wealth produced by industry belongs entirely to the workers and that therefore the profit the owner derives from the industry is actually stolen from them. In contrast to this, Leo XIII taught that labour and capital need one another; one cannot operate without the other.[8] The ideal toward which industrial society must strive was cooperation between the classes, each respecting the rights of the other and obeying the norms of justice.

Were there institutions that promoted industrial cooperation? While industrial capitalism itself produced conflicting classes, Catholic doctrine recommended, following the model of the medieval guilds, that men organize themselves in vocational or professional groups, associations made up of owners, managers and workers involved in the same branch of production or the same branch of industry. The many different forms of primary and secondary production could give rise to groupings that represented not the interests of one class but the concerns of an entire trade, which would have been heard by government as voices beyond the class conflict. If the workers were paid a just wage, determined in part by their families' needs and in part by their contribution to the total production, then the new professional and trade associations linking owner, manager and workers would be able to work out government policies capable of overcoming the gap between the classes. This ideal is sometimes called "corporatism."[9]

This brief characterization of Catholic social teaching has shown that modern industrial society was here criticized in the light of an ideal derived largely from the past. The social ills could only be remedied if the Christian people returned to the faith they had inherited, recognized the demands of justice on society and restructured the social order in accordance with these principles. The difficulty of Catholic social teaching was that it did not correspond to any actual historical movement. Particularly in North America, there were no people in government, in industry or among workers who found this teaching in keeping with their actual interests and aspirations. Governments were committed to the party system and political representation; industry was interested in development and the increase of profits; and the workers sought to organize themselves in strong unions as the basis of their power in society.

Catholic social teaching was "idealistic" in the positive Catholic sense, inasmuch as it demanded faith, sacrifice and selflessness, and "idealistic" in the pejorative Marxist sense, inasmuch as it was a pure creation of the mind, outlining what ought to happen according to an abstract ideal of justice, and not a social theory, based on the actual historical experience of people struggling for emancipation. The "third way" beyond capitalism and socialism was not a concrete, historical political option in Western society. Catholic social teaching was used by American activist Catholics to win the support of the Catholic community for President Roosevelt's New Deal. Catholic social teaching has also been invoked by the Catholic parties of Europe and Latin America that advocate a restricted, government-steered capitalist economy and an extended protective legislation for workers; however, this was not a third way, but at best an attempt to humanize the capitalist system.

How, then, did Catholics follow the papal teaching? Catholic groups tended to read this teaching in ways that corresponded to their own material interests. The successful classes made much of the papal defence of private property, the condemnation of socialism, the repudiation of the class struggle and the summons to greater personal morality, while the workers and critics of society lauded in papal teaching the unmasking of industrial capitalism as the source of social injustices, the recognition of the exploitation of the proletariat, the approval of labour unions, the subordination of personal wealth and the production of goods to the promotion of the common good, and the duty of government to protect the poor and foster the well-being of the whole society. What the Church defined as "the third way," beyond capitalism and socialism, was no clearly defined option at all. It had no existence apart from the theory. The great majority of Catholics understood the teaching as a reluctant defence of capitalism; only a minority interpreted it as ecclesiastical support of labour activism.

The Depression Encyclical

Let us now turn to *Quadragesimo anno*, Pius XI's encyclical on the Depression published in 1931, which had such a profound effect on the Catholic church, including the Canadian bishops.

To extend Catholic social teaching to the new historical situation, Pius XI described the changes that had taken place in capitalism and socialism since Leo XIII's *Rerum Novarum* in 1891. Pius XI's account of the new capitalism was devastating. He showed that the system of free competition had produced giant corporations that wielded immense power, controlled the production and distribution of goods and the flow of money, and attempted through economic blackmail to gain control of national governments. Governments had become slaves of these corporations; they no longer protected the common good of society but served the economic ambitions of the corporations; they permitted themselves to be pushed into national conflicts that resulted in war or into the building of empires. Pius XI even foresaw that as the international corporations grew larger and assumed monopoly control over resources and production, they would create a new kind of world imperialism, one based not on political but on economic power, "the new imperialism of money." The pope clearly hinted at the economic theory that capitalism leads to imperialism, a theory that had not been found in Marx but was developed by J.A. Hobson, the British liberal scholar, and after him by Lenin, the creator of Russian communism.[10]

Since these passages from *Quadragesimo anno* are so remarkable and so little known, I will quote them in full.

> In the first place, then, it is patent that in our days not only is wealth accumulated, but immense power and despotic economic domination are concentrated in the hands of a few, and that those

few are frequently not the owners, but only the trustees and directors of invested funds, who administer them at their good pleasure.

This power becomes particularly irresistible when exercised by those who, because they hold and control money, are able also to govern credit and determine its allotment, for that reason supplying the life-blood, so to speak, to the entire economic body, and grasping in their hands, as it were, the very soul of the economy, so that no one dare breathe against their will.

This accumulation of power, a characteristic note of the modern economic order, is a natural result of unrestrained free competition, which permits the survival only of those who are the strongest. This often means those who fight most relentlessly, who pay least heed to the dictates of conscience.

This concentration of power has led to a threefold struggle for domination. First, there is the struggle for dictatorship in the economic sphere itself; then, the fierce battle to acquire control of the state, so that its resources and authority may be abused in the economic struggles. Finally, the clash between states themselves.

This latter arises from two causes: because the nations apply their economic power and political influence, regardless of circumstances, to promote the economic advantages of their citizens; and because, vice versa, economic forces and economic domination are used to decide political controversies between peoples.

You assuredly know, venerable brethren and beloved children, and you lament the ultimate consequences of this individualistic spirit in economic affairs. Free competition has committed suicide; economic dictatorship has replaced a free market.

Unbridled ambition for domination has succeeded the desire for gain; the whole economic life has become hard, cruel and relentless in a ghastly measure. Furthermore, the intermingling and scandalous confusing of the duties and offices of civil authority and of the economy have produced grave evils, not the least of which has been a downgrading of the majesty of the state. The state, which should be the supreme arbiter, ruling in queenly fashion far above all party contention, intent only upon justice and the common good, has become instead a slave, bound over to the service of human passion and greed. As regards the relations of nations among themselves, a double stream has issued forth from this one fountainhead; on the one hand, economic "nationalism" or even economic "imperialism"; on the other, a no less noxious and detestable "internationalism" or "international imperialism" in financial affairs, which holds that where a man's fortune is, there is his country.[11]

What did this scathing accusation and condemnation of monopoly capitalism mean? The passages above seem to indicate that free competition, unrestrained by just laws protecting society, would inevitably lead, by a struggle in which only the fittest could survive, to the formation of ever larger corporations that would eventually acquire monopoly control, suppress competition and exercise unrestrained power that even national governments could not control in the pursuit of their one aim: namely, to increase their profits. The reader has the impression that what was condemned here was the capitalist system, all the more so since Catholic teaching entertained little sympathy even for the entrepreneurial capitalism of the nineteenth century. The Church only approved of the earlier small-scale capitalism of family-owned enterprises, which produced reasonable wealth for their owners but operated with a responsible margin and did not yet seek to maximize profits by constant expansion and reinvestment of revenues. Pius XI seemed to say that capitalism inevitably led to the creation of an ever-smaller class of owners and managers, who exercised effective power in national and international affairs, organized the world economy for their own profit and relegated the rest of society, especially the workers, to a life of poverty and perpetual enslavement.

The reader is therefore surprised that despite this devastating analysis, Pius XI wrote, "Capitalism as such is not to be condemned," and "The system is not vicious by its very nature."[12] Capitalism only violated the moral order if economic activity were allowed to be governed by the sole principle of increasing profits. One has the impression that the pope was afraid here of the conclusion to which his own principles led. What Pius XI recommended in the present situation was government legislation to break the power of monopolies, restore free competition and keep it within proper bounds and finally to regulate the relation of capital and labour in accordance with the laws of justice.

The papal teaching on capitalism remained highly ambiguous. There were passages that revealed capitalism's systemic evil: they argued first that capitalism undermined spiritual values and made people preoccupied with material things, that is, the standard of living defined in terms of commodities; and secondly, that it led to the subservience of government to the interests of the large corporations and hence to the inevitable oppression of the vast majority by the corporate few. And yet there were other passages where the evils of contemporary capitalism were ascribed not to the system but to the economic greed of the rich. We read that the breakdown of the economic system in the Depression had been produced by the moral and spiritual failure of the bourgeoisie and, in a wider sense, by the breakdown of Christian morality in the Western world.[13]

While the systemic fault of capitalism was occasionally admitted, especially in the passages quoted above, in the long run it was the second fault, the spiritual one, that predominated in Catholic teaching. Papal statements and, as we shall see, the Canadian bishops repeatedly insisted that the Depression was first of all a moral failure. The crisis had come about because the modern world had abandoned God. What was demanded was a re-Christianization of society.

Pius XI admitted that "two things are necessary for the reconstruction of the social order, namely, the reform of institutions and the correction of morals."[14] This suggested that there was a mutual relationship between public institutions and personal consciousness, and that radical social change was brought about by the constant interaction between institutional changes and changes in people's perception of reality. Yet when Pius XI here spoke of the reform of institutions, he had in mind the state, not the economic system. We shall discuss precisely what the pope recommended for the reconstruction of society after we have looked at his description of the evolution of socialism.

Just as capitalism had undergone a change for the worse, so, Pius XI argued, had socialism. Socialism, he said, existed in two forms. There was the violent socialism that came to power in the Russian Revolution and now defined the international communist movement, and there was a more moderate socialist movement that repudiated recourse to violence, mitigated the class struggle and the abolition of private property, and — according to Pius XI — advocated "social programmes that strikingly approach the just demands of Christian social reforms."[15] Because of the religious persecution in Russia, Pius XI's condemnation of communism or revolutionary socialism was even more vehement than Leo XIII's repudiation of the socialism of his day. Communism in Russia had embraced a militant atheism, persecuted the Church and oppressed the Christian people; it had revealed itself as the enemy of God. In the rest of the world, communism pursued its twofold aim, "merciless class warfare and the complete abolition of private property."[16]

But what about the more moderate socialism that had rejected the communist position and pursued policies of social reconstruction that resembled Catholic social programmes? The importance of this question during the Depression cannot be exaggerated. Pius XI admitted that because of the similarity between democratic socialism and Christian reformism, the question being addressed to him from all sides was whether Catholics must still oppose the socialist movement or whether socialism could be accepted without loss of Christian principles and "be baptized in the Church."[17] It should be noted that in the Thirties, the authority of the papacy was so great that a decision of this kind would have been accepted by the Catholic bishops and the great number of the faithful not only in Italy, where the Church has always exerted great political power, but also in the rest of the Catholic world, where the Church had no direct influence on politics, except through its teaching that certain positions were irreconcilable with Christian faith.

Pius XI replied to the question in the negative. All the same, he clearly recognized that moderate socialism — he never used the term "democratic socialism" — did not wish to heighten class conflict to outright class warfare but sought rather to pressure public authority to limit the power of capital and prepare a new economic order. He also recognized that moderate socialism was no longer principally concerned with the public ownership of the means of production and hence no longer bent on the total abolition of private property; instead this socialism demanded simply that the social power wielded by the owners of industry, in violation of justice, be removed from them and taken up by those who exercise public authority in society. "If these changes continue," Pius XI wrote, "it may well come about that gradually the tenets of mitigated socialism will no longer be different from the programme of those who seek to reform human society according to Christian principles."[18] And he continued, "For it is rightly contended that certain forms of property must be reserved for the state, since they carry with them an opportunity of domination too great to be left to private individuals without injury to the community at large." While Catholic social teaching defended private property as in keeping with the natural law, private property was not an absolute. It was subordinated to the common good; and lest it endanger the common good, those who held authority in society must guide the use of this property and in special cases transfer it to public ownership. Pius XI also admitted that the socialist movement did not see itself in opposition to the Christian religion. What arguments, then, led him to an unqualified negative reply?

The arguments proposed were curiously brief. Since socialism was based on false principles, the pope argued, the mitigation of these principles did not modify their substance. In and by themselves, these principles would lead moderate socialism inevitably to its original radical form — including class warfare, the abolition of private property and the materialistic understanding of human life — and hence opposition to the Christian religion. Socialism, Pius XI wrote, seemed to be afraid of its own principles; it mitigated them for purely strategic purposes, but since it had not repudiated them in principle and had therefore ceased to be socialism in the proper sense of the word, it retained its bent to communism.

Socialism, Pius XI argued, remained foreign to Christian truth. It was materialistic because it wanted to build society without reference to God, the creator of humanity, and without obedience to the divine laws. Socialism denied that man's primary vocation on earth was to worship this God and enter upon the way of salvation. In this sense, one may add, all of modern society is "materialistic": socialism does not differ from liberalism in this. The modern pluralistic state leaves room for religious and nonreligious people.

Socialism, according to church teaching, was materialistic for a second reason. It hoped to reconstruct society through changes that belonged exclusively to the economic order. Socialism held that once the economy was freed from the competitive principle and production and distribution were rationally controlled in favour of the whole community, social life would be renewed. It neglected the spiritual values. It did not recognize that greed, selfishness, resentment and vindictiveness were vices that vitiated all societies, and that unless the material changes were accompanied by spiritual changes, they would not lead to the making of a more human society. And because socialism had an impoverished, purely materialistic understanding of man, it subordinated individuals entirely to the processes of production and the well-being of the collectivity. The single citizen lost the freedom that was connatural to the human person and became an instrument of the state machinery.

From this argument, put in the briefest fashion — less developed, in fact, than my own account of it — Pius XI drew the momentous conclusion that had an enormous impact on the Western world. He wrote, "Whether socialism be considered as a doctrine, or as a historical fact, or as a 'movement,' if it remains socialism, it cannot be brought into harmony with the dogmas of the Catholic church."[19] And a little further on, "If, like all error, socialism contains a certain element of truth, it is nevertheless founded upon a doctrine of human society peculiarly its own, which is opposed to true Christianity." "Religious socialism" and "Christian socialism" were expressions implying a contradiction in terms. "No one can be at the same time a sincere Catholic and a true socialist."[20]

This was a harsh judgment. The false philosophical principles of socialism invalidated any development that the socialist movement, under new historical circumstances, might undergo; the changes of theory and policy observed in this movement could not be taken at face value, for as long as the substance of socialism remained, the original false philosophical principles would emerge again and determine the future bent of the movement.

This argument is not convincing. In regard to capitalism, Pius XI had applied the opposite reasoning. For while the free market led inevitably to the survival of the fittest and hence prepared the economic dictatorship of the big corporations and the exploitation of the workers and the dependent classes, the system as such need not have been rejected because this powerful trend could be countered by reformist government policy. Pius XI chose not to apply to socialism a reasoning of this kind.

Let me add at this point that the Catholic church's official teaching retained this harsh and uncompromising condemnation until Pope John XXIII's encyclical *Pacem in Terris* (1963) made an allusion to Pius XI's argumentation and corrected it. In a section dealing with the cooperation of believers and non-believers in social and economic projects, Pope John wrote, "False philosophical teachings regarding the nature, origin and destiny of the universe cannot be identified with historical movements that have economic, social, cultural or political ends, not even when these movements have originated from these [false] teachings and have drawn and still draw inspiration from them."[21] The reference to the socialist movement was here quite patent. And why should one not identify the original false teachings with the movements? "For these teachings," the encyclical continued, "once they are drawn up and defined, remain always the same; but the movements, working in historical situations in constant evolution, are necessarily influenced by these historical situations and are, therefore, subject to changes, even of a profound nature." The socialist movement did not have an unchanging essence; it changed, it could even undergo profound modification; it must therefore be judged by what it was in the present and not by how it had defined itself in the past. For Pope John, it was through conversation and association that Christians had to decide in various historical situations whether or not the socialist movement adopted theoretical positions and pursued social policies in basic agreement with Catholic ideals. If the answer to this question was affirmative, cooperation was possible. This was in fact the position adopted by Pope Paul VI in his letter *Octogesima adveniens* (1971), where he recognized that many Catholics have come to identify themselves with socialist movements. The only forms of socialism against which Paul VI warned Catholics were those wedded to a total world-view or total world explanation and hence demanding of Catholics that they sacrifice their own philosophy of faith.[22]

Pius XI was being realistic when he warned, in *Quadragesimo anno*, that the nationalization of the means of production would lead to the concentration of political and economic power in the hands of the government, creating threats to the freedom of individuals and their associations. But was he right in regarding a state-owned and state-managed economy as the goal of socialism? It could be argued that what the pope condemned in his encyclical was actually indistinguishable from state capitalism. While demanding that public authority regulate the economy and protect the working class by just legislation, Pius XI invoked the ancient social "principle of subsidiarity" against excessive centralization. This principle, derived from the experience and vision of an organic society, defined as a grave injustice the transfer of functions that can be performed by a subordinate body in society to a higher and larger collectivity. The principle, which Pius XI called "fixed and unchangeable,"23 forbad governments to intervene in the running of the smaller social units that constituted society, whether of a political, economic or cultural kind, as long as these bodies were able to look after their needs and provide for adequate self-government. It limited the power of the state or any central government, of the headquarters of any social institution, to matters pertaining to the common good, that is, to matters affecting the bodies under their charge as a whole. At the same time, it allowed governments to intervene in the running of the subordinate bodies if these were unable to attend to their own affairs. This principle of subsidiary, which the Catholic church defended as a basic moral principle (even though in recent centuries it has not applied it to its own ecclesiastical life), constituted the moral barrier against the kind of centralization that Pope Pius XI saw as the inevitable consequence of socialism.

At the same time Pius XI recognized, in the same encyclical, that due to the decline of economic life produced by corporate capitalism, the subordinate bodies were unable to look after themselves and resolve their own problems. This warranted the intervention of public authority in guiding the national economy. Government should legislate regarding the use of wealth and resources, protect the working class against exploitation and establish strict laws governing the relation of employer and employees. Pius XI, we recall, even admitted that nationalization of private property was legitimate and in fact necessary when this property carried with it powers that were too great to be left to private individuals without danger to the community at large.[24] The principle of subsidiarity, which might well be translated as "small is beautiful," was actually balanced by a counter-principle, which could be called "big whenever necessary."

It was again only in the Sixties, especially in Pope John's encyclical *Mater et Magistra* (1961), that the balancing principle of socialization was clearly spelled out. Pope John here explored the meaning of "socialization."[25] This principle demanded that smaller social or economic units that were unable to provide adequately for their own needs enter into cooperative relations with others and seek greater coordination of their activities so that together, collectively, they would be able to resolve the problems of all. The principle of socialization limited the free enterprise of economic corporations when they failed to provide for the needs of the wider community; it limited as well the monopoly power of the giant corporations that planned production in view of increasing their own profit. The principle of socialization empowered the government to initiate cooperation and coordination in the national economy, widen the base of participation in the decisions affecting production and distribution, and guide the economic development of the nation if the needs of people were not being met.

The English translation of *Mater et Magistra* avoided the word "socialization," even though the appropriate cognate was used in the original Latin and in the official Italian translation published by *l'Osservatore Romano*. Since the English translator felt that "socialization" would be understood as "nationalization," he used a paraphrase, adequate in itself even if clumsy — "the multiplication of social relations." Socialization could of course include the nationalization of industries and services, but in general it referred to a wider process in society, even beyond purely economic matters, by which the separate concerns of subordinate groupings were coordinated through the multiplication of social relations and guided by appropriately higher authority structures. Small is beautiful, but big whenever necessary. Let me add that the avoidance of the word "socialization" in the English translation did not protect *Mater et Magistra* from severe criticism on the part of liberal thinkers in the Catholic Church: they called the encyclical "warmed-over Marxism," and created the slogan

"Mater si, Magistra no." One still finds Catholic teachers who emphasize the principle of subsidiarity without accompanying it by its balancing principle or dialectical complement, the principle of socialization.

Mater et Magistra initiated a significant change of emphasis in the Church's social teaching. Until that time, the popes defended the free enterprise system because they feared the all-powerful state; since that encyclical, the popes have become more afraid of the all-powerful transnational corporations. This is why they now put the primary emphasis on socialization, without of course neglecting the demands of subsidiarity. We have the following interesting passages in Pope Paul VI's *Populorum progressio* (1968): "Individual initiative alone and the mere free play of competition could never assure successful development. One must avoid the risk of increasing still more the wealth of the rich and the domination of the strong, whilst leaving the poor in their misery and adding to the servitude of the oppressed. Hence programmes are necessary in order to encourage, stimulate, coordinate, supplement and integrate the activity of individuals and of intermediary bodies. It pertains to the public authorities to choose, even to lay down the objectives to be pursued, the ends to be achieved and the means for attaining these, and it is for them to stimulate all the forces engaged in this common activity."[26] Still, in this process of socialization, the principle of subsidiarity must not be violated. "Let the authorities take care to associate private initiative and intermediary bodies with this work. They will thus avoid the danger of complete collectivization or of arbitrary planning, which, by denying liberty, would prevent the exercise of the fundamental rights of the human person."

Let us return to Pius XI's repudiation of socialism. The pope's decision to condemn socialization, including its democratic form, was a fateful event. In the first chapter we noted that in 1928, Stalin had declared democratic socialism to be the number one enemy of the Communist party, thereby preventing the collaboration of communists and socialists in opposing the rising fascism of Europe, unless the common action were under the direction of Moscow.[27] Pius XI's declaration, made in 1931, prevented the Catholics of Europe from allying themselves with the social-democratic parties in a common resistance against fascism.

Quadragesimo anno inoculated Catholics against the disease of socialism. The very word "socialism" began to frighten the Catholic people. Catholic men and women who belonged to socialist movements now had to choose between their religion and their politics. In Germany in particular, the policies of Stalin and Pius XI had devastating consequences: the social democrats were isolated in their struggle against Hitler and lost.

Was Pius XI forced into this decision? Since the Catholic church in the Latin countries was largely identified with the pre-capitalist classes, the remnants of the feudal order — landowners, craftsmen and peasants — and since the pope regarded as the principal enemy the secularization of society, it was almost inevitable that he would adopt such an uncompromising view in regard to socialism. There is a certain irony in the fact that the Church, which in the nineteenth century was a declared enemy of liberal society and struggled against the growing power of the bourgeoisie, now became the great defender of bourgeois society against the socialist movement. In the nineteenth century, as is well remembered, the bourgeoisie was secular, anti-clerical and to a large extent atheistic; but in the twentieth century, confronted with the growing power of the socialist movement and its iconoclasm, the bourgeoisie in many countries recognized the importance of religion in the stabilization of society and hence looked toward Catholicism as an ally. For reasons of religion and the defence of Christianity, the papacy was so preoccupied with the advancing secularization of society fostered by the growing industrialization, even in the traditionally Catholic countries, and so horrified by the brutal repression of religion in the Soviet Union and the militant atheism of the Communist party, that it did not occur to Pius XI to adopt a social policy that would help unite the enemies of fascism. As late as 1936, when Hitler had been in power for three years, Pius XI wrote an encyclical against atheistic communism, *Divini Redemptoris*, in which there is no hint of an awareness that the immediate threat to Europe, world peace and the basic standards of human justice would come from fascism.

From the perspective of Catholic social theory, Pius XI's decision to condemn all forms of socialism was by no means necessary. In fact, the arguments provided in *Quadragesimo anno* would have justified a very different conclusion. In this encyclical the pope recognized the evils of corporate capitalism, and demanded that public authority intervene to limit the power of the corporations and guide the economy in support of the common good; the same encyclical acknowledged that moderate socialism was no longer directly at odds with Christian teaching and proposed social policies surprisingly similar to those recommended by reformist Catholics. Therefore it could easily have reasoned, in consistency with Catholic teaching, that Catholics were free to join socialist parties as long as these did not escalate class conflict to class warfare, did not advocate the socialization of all private enterprises, but only of those that are necessary for a rational planning of the economy, and did not adopt anti-religious and in particular anti-Christian policies. Such a conclusion, it seems to me, was implicit in the arguments of the encyclical, even if this was not the conclusion that the pope in fact drew.

British Socialism

In England, Catholics did not regard the Church's official condemnation of moderate socialism as in any way applicable to the Labour party. Since the Catholics in England were to a large extent immigrants from Ireland and identified with the working class, Catholics had participated in the labour movement from the beginning; when the Labour party was founded in 1906, they had no hesitation in joining it. In the Thirties there were several Catholic Labour MPs in the House of Commons. English Catholics judged that Pius XI's condemnation of moderate socialism applied to the social democratic parties on the Continent, not to British socialism. This view was endorsed by the English Catholic bishops.

Cardinal Bourne, archbishop of Westminster, in an important speech given in Edinburgh in June 1931, a few weeks after the publication of *Quadragesimo anno*, expressed his view that the papal condemnation of moderate socialism did not apply to the Labour party. In fact he proposed a reading of this encyclical (similar, if not identical, to the one I proposed) that understood the pope to be permitting Catholics to join democratic socialist parties, provided certain conditions were fulfilled.

Since the class position of Catholics in England was so different from the historical situation of the Church in the so-called Catholic countries, it is interesting to look at Cardinal Bourne's reasoning in greater detail.[28] In his speech the cardinal recommended that Catholics enter political life in England; their presence was useful to the nation at large and their absence would constitute a real loss to the country. But to enter politics in England meant to join one of the three parties, Conservative, Liberal or Labour. What then should have been the attitude of a Catholic who chose one of these parties? In his adherence to any political party a Catholic had to rely on his own moral conscience, formed by Christian teaching. If a political party were based on principles that were clearly non-Christian, no Catholic would be justified in belonging to it. Happily, the cardinal held, at that time no political party defined itself through non-Christian principles. At the same time, no Catholic could ally himself or herself with any of these parties in an unreserved and non-critical manner. Cardinal Bourne then proceeded to offer his criticism of the three parties from a Catholic point of view. The Conservative party was in close and intimate connection with the Church of England, and since this church opposed the advancement of Catholics in England, the Conservative party, on issues such as the school question or family morality, easily adopted positions contrary to Catholic interests. In the Liberal party, Cardinal Bourne thought, matters were still worse. The Liberal party had tried to do permanent damage to religious education in England, and even if these efforts had for the time been overcome, Catholics had no reason to be grateful to the leaders of the Liberal party for their attitude toward the Catholic church. Even at that time, the Cardinal argued, there was considerable non-conformist Christian influence in the Liberal party, which accounted for its hostility to Catholic education. The Catholics in these two parties — Cardinal Bourne mentioned the late Duke of Norfolk in the Conservative and the Marquis of Ripon in the Liberal party — had courageously defended the Catholic viewpoint, although to no avail.

Passing to the third party, Bourne said this: "Doubtless we shall find in the Labour party some whose opinions are not in accordance with the teaching and the principles of the Catholic church. I suppose there are some who say that they are socialists in the technical sense — a thing which no true Catholic can be." (This was a literal reference to *Quadragesimo anno*.) In this party too, therefore, a Catholic must be a critical member. While he accepted in a general sense the policy of the party, he had to defend openly Christian principles when he thought they were being slighted. Recently, the cardinal continued, there were noble examples of this fidelity to conscience on the part of the Catholic Labour MPs.

"A question will now be asked me," Cardinal Bourne went on, "'Has the Holy Father's encyclical caused you to change your mind in any way?' On this point I am able to say that I see no reason whatever for changing my mind. On the contrary, I think the encyclical, if I understand it rightly, fully confirms this view." He then offered three final conclusions. First, in England a Catholic man or woman was free to join the political party that made the greatest appeal to his sympathy and understanding. Secondly, having done so, he or she had to be on guard against erroneous principles that, on account of the affiliations that affected these parties, were to some extent at work in them. Thirdly, he might never deliver himself, or his conscience, wholly into the keeping of any political party. Cardinal Bourne's reading of the encyclical, then, followed the arguments outlined by Pius XI and concluded that critical participation in democratic socialism was possible for Catholics, even though this was not the conclusion at which Pius XI arrived.

How did Catholics react in Canada when they were confronted in 1932 with the CCF, the new British-style socialist party? In Australia and New Zealand, with labour parties similar to the British one, the Catholic bishops followed the policy of the Catholic hierarchy of England. In these two countries, British dominions as was Canada, Catholics belonged largely to the working class and were strongly represented in the labour parties. Since Catholics in the English-speaking part of Canada were largely working-class and held a minority status in a Protestant land, they found themselves in circumstances similar to those enjoyed by Catholics in Britain and the other dominions. But since the Catholics in French Canada were not only the majority but also constituted a cohesive Catholic culture, the position of the Catholic church in French Canada resembled the position it held in the so-called Catholic countries. The official reaction of the Catholic church in this curious situation will be the topic of the next chapter.

3
The Official Catholic Reaction to Canadian Socialism

"When the CCF was founded in 1932, the reaction of Canada's Catholics was mixed." This, at least, is the view of Murray Ballantyne, who was at the time the editor of the *Beacon*, Montreal's English-language diocesan weekly. "The hierarchy," he continues, "was not unanimous in its reaction to this political development. Some members of the episcopate viewed it with considerable favour, others feared that its materialistic potentialities were highly dangerous."[1]

Catholic support for the CCF in those years is not easy to document. In the first place, the CCF was founded in western Canada, where Catholics were a small minority. And since the farmer, labour and socialist organizations that created the CCF were made up of men of largely British and Protestant background, there were few Catholics among them. This was true even of the radical farmers in Saskatchewan. As we shall see, in the Twenties the Conservative government of Saskatchewan adopted an openly anti-Catholic position (a strategy frequently used at one time by the Conservative party to get more votes in a Protestant land), which made the Catholic population look toward the Liberal party as its defender. The bigotry of the provincial government created a special loyalty of Catholics to the Liberal opposition, and when a third party, the CCF, was created in 1932, Catholics were wary of turning to a new political movement, especially since it had a marked Protestant, almost evangelical, flavour.

What about the Catholic reaction in the more industrial parts of Canada, such as Ontario and British Columbia? Very little is known of this. We do know that in August 1933, the *Beacon* published an editorial that expressed great sympathy for the CCF and suggested that of all the political parties of Canada, the CCF came closest to realizing the principles of Catholic social teaching.[2] When Henry Somerville, a Catholic social activist, returned to Canada from his native England in the fall of 1933 and assumed leadership of the *Catholic Register*, the diocesan weekly of Toronto, the paper began to defend the idea that the open attitude of English Catholics toward the labour party was valid for Canadian Catholics vis-à-vis the CCF, and that therefore Catholics were free to join the new party if it corresponded to their political views.[3] In a debate in the Commons, Henri Bourassa, a political thinker from Quebec, said he was not afraid of the word "socialist," that he saw much that was acceptable in the CCF, and that on several issues the new party represented the viewpoint of Catholic social teaching.[4] But whether and to what extent these sympathetic judgments by Catholic leaders of opinion corresponded to the views of Catholic working people cannot be asserted. The historical research has not yet been done.

It was not long after the parliamentary debate on the Woodsworth resolution, beginning 1 February 1933, that an official Catholic reaction was in preparation. On 9 March 1933, a group of thirteen ecclesiastics met in Montreal, under the auspices of the Ecole sociale populaire, to examine the new Canadian socialism. The Ecole had been founded by the Jesuits in 1911 to promote Catholic social teaching in the province of Quebec.[5] From the beginning, the Ecole betrayed a vehement opposition to socialism, even though socialist influence was minimal in Quebec. The small Socialist party that did exist regarded itself mainly as an agent of popular education and sponsored "workers' universities" for the unemployed, who were free during the day.[6]

Because of the positive reception the CCF was getting from many groups all over the country and the nationwide visibility it had obtained through the parliamentary debate, the Catholic leadership in Quebec felt that the time had come to formulate the Catholic response to the new party — in particular, one should add, from the Quebec perspective. The meeting of 9 March 1933, referred to in history books as "la journée des treize," was to spend the morning on the evaluation of the CCF programme and the afternoon on the elaboration of a reform programme for Quebec, reflecting specifically Catholic principles.

The Dominican Father Georges-Henri Lévesque, a social scientist who was later to play an important role in the liberalization of Quebec society, had been asked to prepare a report on the CCF and present it in the morning; but from the topic to be discussed in the afternoon it was clear from the beginning that his evaluation would have to be negative. Since this report became the model of all subsequent repudiations of the CCF on the part of the Church in Quebec and thus, indirectly at least, influenced the Catholic church in Canada in its entirety, we shall examine its argumentation in detail and discuss the issues raised in it.

The Lévesque Report

At the beginning of his report, Lévesque showed that the CCF, even though founded only in July of the preceding year, had become a significant force in Canada.[7] It brought together not only the various labour and farm groups in western Canada, but it was also joined by the United Farmers of Ontario and the Canadian Brotherhood of Railway Employees. On 7 December, Lévesque reported, an assembly of ministers of the United Church of Canada, held in Toronto, adopted a social programme similar to that of the CCF.[8] Then he named the League for Social Reconstruction, a group of intellectuals mainly from Toronto and McGill universities, which may not have had a formal link with the CCF but which cooperated with it and prepared policy statements for the use of the party. He also mentioned the famous debate in the Commons, which alerted the whole of Canada to the socialist programme of the movement. The leaders of the CCF, Lévesque claimed, were intelligent men, active and dedicated, who had prepared their nationwide campaign for years. They already counted on the support of a good number of MPs. And since the people, during those years of grave economic crisis, were pushed into extreme poverty and helplessness, the new programme for changing the economic system could well have appealed to them and laid the foundation for the rapid advance of Canadian socialism.

How shall we evaluate the CCF from a Catholic point of view, Lévesque asked. The leaders were claiming that the new party was socialist. It was therefore important for Catholics to decide whether this socialism fell under the condemnation of *Quadragesimo anno*. "There is socialism and socialism," the report continued. "There is the mitigated socialism of labour in England, which his Eminence Cardinal Bourne did not think he had to reprove; and there is the true, pure socialism of Belgium and France, which the Church has formally condemned."[9] British socialism, we are told, left out several principles of the socialist school and hence was not true socialism at all. What about the CCF? To solve this question it was necessary to examine how the new party was related to the three vices of socialism, namely, class warfare and violence, the abolition of private property and the materialist conception of society.

The Lévesque report did not attempt to give a historical account of the founding of the CCF. It did not analyze the different groups that joined in the national movement. This information was probably hard to find in Montreal, especially since francophone social thinkers in Quebec had no personal contacts with the western radicals. The report relied almost exclusively on the Calgary programme and the parliamentary debate initiated by Woodsworth in February 1933. The Regina convention, we must recall, had not yet taken place. The report drew heavily on the newspaper accounts cited in the parliamentary debate by the opponents of the CCF. Instead of trying to understand the new Canadian political movement, the report simply asked the three questions derived from papal teaching. This was the methodological shortcoming of the document. The report concluded that the CCF was dangerous territory for Catholics and represented the kind of socialism that fell under the condemnation of Pope Pius XI. As we shall see later, Murray Ballantyne, another Catholic social critic living in Montreal at the same time, came to the opposite conclusion.[10]

It should be added that a few years later Father Lévesque changed his mind about the CCF. In 1932 he had just returned from his studies in France and Belgium, where socially engaged Catholics vigorously fought against the socialist parties.[11] His outlook was largely determined by the recent teaching of Pius XI that it was impossible to be at the same time a loyal Catholic and a true socialist. This radical opposition to socialism characterized the attitude of the Quebec clergy. Some of the members of the thirteen, Father Lévesque now recalls, firmly believed that the CCF was a communist movement. They were not satisfied with the report's moderate, albeit negative, conclusion. The CCF was out of bounds at this time, the report argued; but if the party clarified or modified its position on the three crucial issues, it could well become open to Catholic participation.

Since the report was crucial in determining the attitude of the Quebec Church, and since, in all likelihood, it expressed the views of many Quebeckers as they looked beyond the borders of their province to the new political movement, we shall examine more carefully the report's threefold argumentation.

1.

In regard to the question of class warfare, the report admitted from the outset that the CCF defined itself as a democratic socialist party.[12] According to the Calgary programme, "the CCF is a lawful organization seeking its ends by democratic political methods. It does not advocate or make use of force...." Speaking on his resolution in the Commons, Woodsworth said, "We in our group are trying to bring about the end in view by peaceful and orderly means." The CCF, moreover, claimed it was wholly independent from Moscow. This was stressed by Woodsworth — "We have no connection whatever with Moscow — none whatever" — and repeated by Agnes McPhail, the farmer leader from Ontario. Since such formal statements were made many times, and since communist candidates had competed with socialist members in elections, there was no reason whatever to doubt the veracity of these words.

At the same time, the new party showed excessive sympathy for Moscow. Woodsworth had visited Russia and gave an affirmative report of his visit after his return. More than that, the CCF had recently intervened in favour of the communists arrested in Ontario. The discussion in Parliament revealed that the CCF members wanted to extend their tolerance even to members of the Communist International. Such tolerance, the report argued, manifested little respect for the primacy of the spiritual and the demands of good order. Lévesque concluded that while the CCF did not look upon violence as a normal means for achieving its end, one had to examine whether it possibly regarded violence as an exceptional means for bringing about radical social reconstruction. Here, the report said, we had reason to be suspicious. Introducing his resolution in the Commons, Woodsworth affirmed his party's peaceful intention, but then added, "It may very well be that force may prove inevitable, yes, if the attitude of certain gentlemen is persisted in and the people of this country are denied the right to self-expression and to the enjoyment of a decent livelihood.... If many take the position that we cannot do this thing constitutionally, and behind it is the threat that it will not be permitted to be done constitutionally, then none of us can answer as to what may actually take place."

The report understood these words as an ultimatum. Woodsworth here told the Canadian people that they would have to buy the remedy offered them by the CCF: we shall try to make you take the medicine by persuasion, but if you resist you will have to swallow it by force. It was true, the report continued, that Woodsworth claimed this inevitable violence to which his threat referred would not be unleashed by his own party; it would be produced by revolutionary forces foreign to its spirit. But this was an evasion: for where were there significant revolutionary forces in Canada except in the CCF?

Lévesque's suspicion was magnified in the light of the following quotations. A few months earlier, Woodsworth had made the following statement at Saskatoon: "Now how are we going to attain that power? I think that that is a practical question. There are a few people in our labour movement, as well as in the farm movement, who say that the only possible thing for us today is to win that power by force, to resort to force of arms, of violence or something of that kind. Of course, since the Dominion government has been taking such an active part in suppressing the advocates of open force we have not heard quite so much of that openly expressed. At the same time there are those who quite conscientiously and firmly believe that this is the only way in which we can obtain our ends. I am not so shocked as some people are at that because if it is right to obtain victory of one nation over another by means of force, it is right to obtain victory of one class over another by means of force." At Moose Jaw, Woodsworth made this statement: "The federal authorities control the military and the courts, and labour is not going to get what it wants until it in some way gets control of the military and the courts." And at London, he said this: "We have got to band together to bring these changes about. We will have to make the effort.... People shout at us that this is socialism, bolshevism. Maybe it is. What of it? Who runs this country, anyway?"

How could we interpret these quotations, the report argued, other than as expressions of Woodsworth's willingness to use force as an exceptional means of social revolution? Such an interpretation agreed with what was known of Woodsworth's past. We recall that he gave support to the revolutionary agitators of the One Big Union in 1919 during the Winnipeg strike, and claimed that in situations of this kind the use of violence is legitimate. When Woodsworth, in a speech in the House of Commons in 1932, demanded the release from prison of leading communists, he argued that there are situations in which the use of violence is legitimate — a principle recognized by all people — and that for this reason those who argued in favour of violent revolution should not be deprived of their civil liberties.

Angus MacInnis, the socialist member from Vancouver, the report continued, was even more ready to adopt violent means than Woodsworth. After referring to class struggle as a principle of social change "all down through history," he claimed that "every advance has been made through blood and tears." Appeals to cooperation between classes were useless because "it is absolutely impossible to have cooperation between the exploiters and the exploited. There is no cooperation between the wolf and the lamb, unless the lamb is inside the wolf. Nor is there cooperation between the workers in industry and the employer because of the inherent exploitation that must exist." At that point, the report argued, we had arrived at the revolutionary principles of Marx. In troubled times such as those, when the misery under which people suffered was so great, it was particularly irresponsible to speak of radical social change and revolution of consciousness, even if one had peaceful intentions, for people caught in suffering could easily develop hatred for the ruling class and yearn for violent revolution.

From all this, then, Lévesque drew the following conclusion. "To sum up our thought on this first point of violent class conflict, we believe that the CCF rejects violence as the ordinary means of arriving at its goal, but that it could easily make use of it by way of exception or fall into it even against its wish as a natural consequence of its influence on the people."

In arriving at this conclusion, the author had become the prisoner of his flawed methodology. Since he did not begin his report with an adequate account of the origin and nature of the CCF and offered no overview of the social programme proposed by the new party, he was unable to place the quotations into their proper contexts and thus interpret them correctly. In particular, he was quite unaware of the British connection of Canadian socialism. His principal sources of information were the proceedings of the House of Commons debate. The quotations of Woodsworth and other CCF leaders were simply drawn from speeches made in the Commons by MPs vehemently opposed to the Woodsworth resolution. These quotations were frequently derived from newspaper accounts or from notes taken by persons present at the occasion: they were thus quite unreliable. For instance, the quotation from Woodsworth at Saskatoon, cited in the Commons by G.D. Stanley, was drawn from the stenographic report taken by a person who attended the meeting.[13] When Stanley finished the quotation, with its reference to one nation triumphing over another by violence, Woodsworth jumped up in the House and demanded that Stanley read the entire quotation. He did not want the quotation to stand without its conclusion, which revealed his ardent pacifism. Stanley refused to read the entire passage. The Lévesque report used quotations presented by opponents without critical inquiry, even where Woodsworth or other MPs had registered their objections in the House.

Throughout the report the author permitted himself to be overly influenced by the parliamentary opponents of the CCF. Lévesque's interpretation of Woodsworth's "ultimatum" was derived from J.R. MacNicol's speech:[14] the same speech reported the words allegedly spoken by Woodsworth at London, based on a newspaper article.[15] The information and interpretation of Woodsworth's visit to Russia were taken from I.E. Lawson's speech, even though Woodsworth immediately protested against the misinterpretation;[16] and the account of Woodsworth's role in the One Big Union was derived from G.D. Stanley's speech, which we have seen provoked Woodsworth into clarifying his personal history.[17]

The report, moreover, did not appreciate the British and Protestant concern with the civil liberties of all citizens, including communists. For Lévesque, following the Catholic tradition (changed since his time at Vatican II), civil liberties were expressions of tolerance conceded by government, rather than rights in the strict sense. To be tolerant of those who aggressively criticize the basic structure of society is to be lacking in respect for public order and concern for social unity. In *Quadragesimo anno*, Pius XI recommended that governments "repress socialist organizations and efforts."[18] In the Catholic mind, at least until recently, the demand for the extension of civil liberties to all citizens was regarded as a dangerous policy, undermining public authority and social peace. In this context, the report concluded that Woodsworth's defence of civil rights for communists was based on a special sympathy the CCF had for the Communist party, even though Angus MacInnis, in the same parliamentary debate, had mentioned the attacks made by the Communist party against the Socialist party in British Columbia and later against the CCF.[19]

From Woodsworth's speeches it appears that he had no doubts regarding the dedication to democracy of his own party; what worried him instead was his doubt about the dedication to democracy of those who ruled the country at the time. Western history has shown, before the Thirties and frequently since then, that traditional political parties frequently favour democracy only as long as it protects the interests of the owning classes; as soon as the democratic process threatens gravely to undermine the power of the dominant groups, these parties become ready to drop democracy, introduce authoritarian methods, arrest the leaders of the emerging majority and establish their reign by violent means. It was not unreasonable to say, therefore, that if the CCF gained the enthusiastic support of the Canadian people and acquired the right to govern by democratic means, the resistance on the part of the old elite would have to be countered by legitimate force. If the army and the courts were used by the ruling groups to check the power of the new majority, whose contempt for democracy would then be responsible for the outbreak of violence? The CCF envisaged the possibility that after an electoral victory enlisting the great majority of Canadians in their support, their entry into legitimate power might have to be accompanied by a general strike and other demonstrations of majority support.

Radical social change through peaceful means, the CCF held, was the only chance of avoiding social chaos. Woodsworth feared that the opposition to social change on the part of the government might provoke revolts among the people most oppressed by the present system. "The question is not," Woodsworth said in a parliamentary debate, "whether we ought to have changes; the real issue is whether changes will be brought about in an orderly and peaceful fashion or whether matters will be allowed to drift until there is a crisis, possibly a catastrophe."[20] Even Puis XI, reflecting on the condition of society during the Depression, wrote that "unless efforts are made with all energy and without delay to put [these reforms] into practice, let no one persuade himself that public order and the peace and tranquillity of human society can be defended effectively against agitators of revolution."[21] These were rhetorical ultimatums designed to persuade reluctant governments.

The CCF recognized class conflict in society and wanted to engage in it. It wanted to make the people aware that the government ruled in favour of the owners of the large industrial and commercial enterprises; it wanted to convince Canadians that if all the disadvantaged sectors of society became united and organized, they would constitute the great majority in the country and acquire the power to create their own government by democratic means. The CCF was dedicated to democratic class struggle. The instrument of this war was to be mainly the ballot box. We mentioned above that the CCF differed from the Marxism then prevalent in its attitude toward the state and toward parliamentary institutions: while Marx, at least in his polemical writings, claimed that parliamentary democracy was the creation of the bourgeoisie, designed to promote capitalism and hence useless as an instrument of radical social change, British socialism had greater confidence in democracy. We also saw that while Marxists regarded the working class as the bearer of revolution, the CCF — according to its own modification of British socialism — held that the sector united against capitalism should include all workers of fist and brain, all employees, farmers and office staff, including possibly small producers and businessmen, crushed as they were by the large corporations.

The policy of the CCF to create solidarity among the exploited groups in Canada resembled Antonio Gramsci's notion of "the historic bloc." Who the bearer of socialism is must be determined in each historical situation by an analysis of the concrete conditions of oppression that delineate the revolutionary bloc. The CCF held that the great majority of Canadians would gain through the introduction of socialism. The CCF, then, did engage in a class struggle, but it was not class warfare; it aimed at establishing a new social and economic order in continuity with the political institutions and the moral traditions of the country. In my opinion, the Lévesque report was correct in one point: in emphasizing the social struggle, the CCF went beyond the ideal set down in papal teaching, where the conflict between labour and capital is to be settled by the submission of both sides to a common norm of justice.

2.

The second question regards the policy of the CCF in regard to private property. The Lévesque report recognized that it was difficult to assess CCF policy on this issue since several views were being defended in the new party and no definitive position had as yet emerged. There were extremists, we read, and these included M.J. Coldwell, the leader of the farmer/worker group in Saskatchewan; George Williams, president of the United Farmers of Saskatchewan; and Angus MacInnis of the Socialist party of British Columbia. In a speech recorded in the *Regina Leader* — the report again followed unreliable accounts cited by the parliamentary opponents of the CCF — Coldwell defined the policy of the CCF in this mannner: "Such a plan would mean the scrapping of the system of private enterprise. We have got to plan, and we must plan apart from the idea of ownership. Profits and ownership have to go. There is no way out until we have discarded them."

A more moderate view predominated among other CCFers. The report reproduced this quotation from Woodsworth's speech in the Commons: "I recognize that a great many object to the program which we have in view, in that it may undercut what is called the principle of private property. That may be quite true, but I suggest that the principle of private property has been unwarrantly extended.... It may very well be that my home is private property, that other things which I use and enjoy are private property, but the original idea of private property should never have been extended to the machinery by which modern production is carried on." Woodsworth was willing to recognize, the report argued, personal ownership of houses, things for individual use and some money. Article 3 of the Calgary programme made the same concession for the land owned and worked by farmers and for the homes owned by workers. Some CCFers were even suggesting that the new social system would increase the private property of ordinary working people: they would all own a home and have enough money to lead a life of modest comfort.

At the same time, according to the Calgary programme and the available speeches, the CCF wanted to socialize all the means of production and distribution, all transportation, stores, banks, natural resources and financial institutions. The United Farmers of Alberta even wanted to regard land as a means of production and hence transfer it to public ownership, even though this would be counter to article 3 of the Calgary programme. The report concluded that the dominant view in the CCF favoured the restriction of private property to a house, personal goods and a little money, and even this money, it said, would be heavily taxed. The CCF risked, therefore, weakening the private dimension of property to such an extent that it would disappear altogether, at least in practical terms.

At this point the report recalled the social doctrine of the Church. Church teaching defended the *private* dimension of property as providing independence and integrity of individuals in society. And to assure that the *social* dimension of property became operative for the whole of society, Church teaching did not recommend its nationalization, barring exceptional cases, but demanded that its use be guided by public law and controlled by appropriate associations representing the trades, even while leaving some room for private enterprise. The Lévesque report concluded: "We are convinced that even the moderate teaching of the CCF on private property is in opposition to the legitimate principle of private property."

The report, it seems to me, did not adequately appreciate that the CCF saw itself struggling mainly against modern corporate capitalism and, furthermore, missed the pragmatic nature of Canadian socialism.

The majority of farmers and workers in the prairie provinces were opposed to the capitalism of the large corporations and the power these corporations exercised on the government. The farmers in particular joined the radical movement to protect ownership of their farms, threatened by the foreclosure of their mortgages. They were joined by the hardworking people in these provinces who regarded contemporary capitalism, steered from eastern Canada, as the evil force that impoverished them, and made them lose their homes, shops and tools of work. The report's long quotation from Woodsworth on private property left out a significant sentence: after Woodsworth's remark that "the principle of private property had been unwarrantly extended," he said this: "We create an artificial body which we call a corporation, and then without imposing upon it any responsibilities, we give it all the privileges of a private person; without its having any soul, we endow it with immortality. I do not think we can allow an assumption of that kind to continue."[22] This raises a question that has never received proper attention in Catholic teaching. To what extent is a corporation "a person," and hence to what extent is it feasible to regard corporate property as "private property"? Nor did the report notice that the great majority of CCFers, with the exception of the socialists from British Columbia, did not adopt the Marxist view of surplus value, and hence did not think that all relations of employment in industry were inherently exploitative. In fact, the CCF defended small businesses and units of production. What the party opposed was modern capitalism: it wanted to break the back of corporate power, control the large corporations and replace the contemporary economic system by one that planned production and distribution in accordance with the needs of the people.

During the Depression, some radical Catholics in Quebec adopted almost the identical view. We shall see this when we examine the position of the Action libérale nationale.[23] However, these Catholics, following the Church's official teaching, claimed they did not repudiate capitalism as such but only condemned what capitalism had become in modern society, that is, "the abuse of capitalism."

The radical Catholic view was defended by Henri Bourassa in the parliamentary debate of February 1933. The influential French-Canadian thinker, journalist and politician thanked Woodsworth and the CCF for having brought forward the resolution and defended it so ably. He was particularly impressed by the speech given by A.A. Heaps from North Winnipeg, who offered "the most faithful paraphrasing of the recent encyclical of Pope Pius XI."[24] While Bourassa did not vote in favour of the Woodsworth resolution, for reasons we shall explain further on, he agreed with many of the points made in it. "I am absolutely in accord with my friends to the Left that the picture they have given of the present evils is not exaggerated. I am also in accord with them that the present political and economic system has proved a failure to correct those evils, and therefore that we must look for some remedy."[25] But was capitalism at fault? The answer to this question depends on what we mean by this. "If by capitalism we mean an association of five or ten individuals who pool their money to carry on a legitimate enterprise, and who by reason of the risks of this enterprise reap any benefits therefrom, then within certain limits which the state ought to fix, I admit that that sort of capitalism is legitimate."[26]

Such a small-scale capitalism, so often referred to in Catholic social thought, corresponded to pre-industrial society or the early stage of industrial production, small enough to keep owners and workers in a face-to-face relationship. Bourassa contrasted this small-scale capitalism with the modern corporate capitalism, with its fraudulent and exploitative style. Modern capitalism, he claimed, was controlled by financial brigands. The large companies, with the money owned by gullible subscribers, produced goods and made the public pay not only for these goods and the interest on the mortgage, but also for production costs, excessive interest and the high profit of the financial brigands themselves, who risked so little and contribute next to nothing to production. Modern capitalism was the abuse of capitalism. True conservatives, in whatever party, would oppose this modern system. "I am not afraid of the word 'socialism,'" Bourassa exclaimed. "It always amuses me when I hear cries of horror on both sides of the House the moment socialism is mentioned."[27] The position of the CCF on private property, Bourassa argued, was not at odds with Catholic social teaching.

Still, Bourassa would not vote in favour of the Woodsworth resolution. For one thing, it demanded too much power for the federal government, insufficiently reflecting the Canadian French/English duality and thus threatening the integrity of French-Canadian culture; and secondly, it seemed to regard the class of workers and farmers as the proper agents for remaking society and hence did not sufficiently protect the Catholic ideal of an eventual cooperation between the different ranks, classes and groupings in society.

The Lévesque report also overlooked the pragmatic nature of Canadian socialism. Its author noticed that CCFers openly admitted divergent views regarding private property in the party and that none of them had become official policy, but he did not appreciate that the formulation of such a policy depended on the support the party received from the Canadian people and on the political opinions of its members.

In his speech in the Commons, Woodsworth claimed that the CCF did not wish to introduce "bureaucratic state socialism."[28] We saw in our first chapter that by socialization the CCF did not only mean state ownership but also cooperative ownership, and public ownership held by municipalities, provinces and the federal government. What was of central importance for the CCF from the beginning, not only in subsequent years when it had become more respectable, was the planning of the economy. "We believe," Woodsworth said in the House, "that the first step to be taken for bettering the present conditions is to adopt a planned economy."[29] This non-doctrinaire approach made the party recognize that public ownership by itself does not assure benefits for the community at large; for industries owned by government could still be run for profit along capitalist lines, enriching the owner, in this case the state, and serving purposes (such as war) at odds with the common good. What counted was planning the economy in accordance with the needs and wishes of the people, and spending the surplus value produced by their hard labour in the service of the community at large. Seen in this perspective, the issue of ownership was secondary.

From the viewpoint of Catholic teaching, then, there was no reason to oppose CCF policy on private property, especially since Pius XI had just admitted that if a government wanted to guide the national economy for the well-being of the people, it may well be necessary to nationalize large corporations and financial institutions. "Certain forms of property must be reserved to the state, since they carry with them an opportunity too great to be left to private individuals without injury to the community at large."[30]

3.

This takes us to the third part of the report. Here the author concluded, "We must reproach the CCF for embracing, if not in principle at least in fact, a materialistic sociology." Since the party wanted to introduce a new social order and advocated radical political and economic changes, since CCFers even spoke of a revolution of consciousness, we had the right to ask them for a complete social programme. But, the report argued, what we got from them were only elements of an economic programme. What they offered us was an incomplete and truncated programme, devoid of spiritual values and a proper concept of humanity. While CCF documents and speeches did not deny the spiritual component of social life, they never mentioned it. They tried to persuade us that the social order could be remade through a mere change of the economic system. According to a sounder philosophy, the report argued, the economic changes must be understood as part of a broader, spiritual transformation of society. "This is why," the report concluded, "seeing that the political programme of the CCF restricts itself systematically to an economic programme, we do not hesitate to accuse the CCF of supposing that 'the human community has been constituted simply in view of its material well-being' and of presupposing, therefore, at least unconsciously, the materialistic conception of human society which forms the proper and deeply un-Christian character of true socialism." The principal reason Pius XI condemned socialism applied, therefore, to the CCF.

The Lévesque report recalled that in the view of Pius XI, the Depression was produced not simply by an economic crisis but also and especially by a moral disequilibrium. It was this moral element, Lévesque felt, that was not recognized by the CCF. He found this interpretation confirmed by certain incidents observed during the parliamentary debate: when speakers opposing the resolution reminded the CCF members that the Depression was a spiritual crisis, not simply an economic upheaval, their grave and well-founded words were greeted with sneers and laughter by the radicals in the House. "Is this not sufficient?" Lévesque asked. "After that," he continued, "one well understands why Mr. MacInnis calls Karl Marx 'his old friend,' and brags about 'his genius' and 'his profound teaching.'"

The third conclusion of the report was not well founded. Our account of Canadian socialism in the first chapter supplies ample evidence that the report was wrong. The four characteristics in terms of which we described the CCF movement — democratic, libertarian, populist and moral — certainly reveal the "spiritual" side of Canadian socialism. The report's third conclusion repeated two arguments against socialism constantly raised in Catholic literature: socialism is atheistic, and is based on a materialistic understanding of human life; hence it expects the emergence of a more humane society through changes in the economic system alone, leaving aside the spiritual transformation of persons. These accusations did not apply to the Canadian version of socialism.

While it is certainly correct to accuse mainline Marxism of atheism, it was nonsense to raise this issue in regard to the CCF. As a national movement and nationwide party, the CCF was open to believers and non-believers alike. It never occurred to any of the leaders to make hostility to religion an element of party philosophy. We have mentioned the presence of the old Methodist Social Gospel and the strong representation of the United Church of Canada in the CCF. We also mentioned the existence of a Christian socialist organization, the Fellowship for a Christian Social Order — closely related, through common membership, to the League for Social Reconstruction and more remotely to the CCF. In his speech in the Commons, CCF member Ted Garland, a practising Catholic, referred to the party's aim to establish "a Christian social order."[31]

In chapter 1 we saw that the CCF was heir to the Canadian Social Gospel, at least in the prairie provinces. Many CCF leaders had been Protestant ministers, and even though some of them had turned away from the church because of its identification with middle-class concerns, their zeal, passion for justice, moralism and sense of being on the right side continued to betray the evangelical heritage. Even the speakers who most vehemently opposed the CCF in the Commons never hinted at some sort of atheistic connection. On the contrary, they complained that the churches were too deeply involved in the new movement. G.C. Wilson claimed, "Today the churches are allowing their pulpits to be occupied by salad-faced college professors and new era economists" rather than preaching "the simple gospel of the Nazarene."[32] The suggestion of the report that the CCF betrayed "the deeply un-Christian character of true socialism" was unfounded.

Since Marxist philosophy was atheistic, the European socialist parties had to decide upon their attitude toward religion as a matter of public policy. Famous in this connection is a declaration by the largest and best-organized Marxist party prior to the First World War, the German Social-Democratic party, at Erfurt in 1892. This declaration recognized religion as a private affair. By doing this, the party criticized the public presence of religion in European society, that is, the constitutional relationship of church and state, including government support of church activities. The declaration also meant to assure Christian workers that they could become socialists with a good conscience; religion was their own private affair with no consequences for the political sphere. Today we find the same approach to religion in some of the socialist countries, for instance, Yugoslavia. Let me add that while Christians may be content with the separation of church and state and happy to organize their churches without the help of the government, they are unable to accept the idea that religion is a purely private matter. Since the Christian message reveals the structure of human existence, personal and social, or more simply, since religion declares God's will for human action, it will have public implications.

The CCF was never asked to make a public declaration on religion. This would not have fitted into the Anglo-American political tradition. Nor did it ever suggest that religion was a private matter in the sense in which this expression was used in Europe. Father Louis Chagnon and Archbishop Georges Gauthier — who, following the Lévesque report, condemned the CCF in public statements — accused the party of following the spirit of the Erfurt declaration.[33] This was, I think, untrue. Many CCFers, members and leaders alike, regarded their Christian faith as one of the factors that led them to socialism. They judged the contemporary social order in the light of Christian social teaching, found the present system wanting and then turned to a political movement with a programme that came closer to the Christian ideal of society. For the CCF, religion was private in the sense that it was as neutral in regard to religion as were the other Canadian parties; it was private, moreover, in the sense that each member followed his or her own conscience in the matter. But the CCF did not overlook the public impact of religion.

This takes us to the second meaning of the Catholic accusation that socialism is materialistic. In the words of the report, the CCF was based on a materialistic sociology. It presupposes that the only thing required for the creation of a just society is an economic system that produces sufficient goods and distributes wealth evenly among people, while disregarding the moral element — the virtues and the inwardness required on the part of men and women. This accusation, constantly raised against socialism in Catholic literature, deserves a more careful analysis. It may turn out that it is largely based on a misunderstanding of socialist thought. What this accusation overlooks is that socialist sociology is based on a special insight into the relationship of consciousness and society.

In liberal thought and in the dominant philosophies, consciousness is looked upon as independent of society; it can stretch and move in any direction depending on the creative spirit of the thinker. In socialist thought, on the other hand, consciousness is regarded as interrelated with society. Consciousness is grounded in social institutions. It does not float freely above the material conditions of life, but to a large extent reflects these conditions; at the same time, at certain historical moments, thanks to human creativity, consciousness is able to affect in turn the material conditions of life and thus have a transforming effect on human history.

This dialectical relationship between institution and consciousness was proposed by Marxism as well as by the cooperative movement from their very beginnings in the 1840s. These two movements argued that man's egotism or self-centredness could be overcome, not indeed by preaching higher values and demanding spiritual effort, but by involving men and women in new economic institutions that would summon forth cooperation and co-responsibility and hence would transform human consciousness. Egotism does not belong to human nature, both Marxists and members of the cooperative movement argued; egotism is rather the product of an economic system based on private property and self-promotion, and it can be transcended through the joint struggle, in solidarity, to build a new economic system based on sharing and cooperative planning. They insisted that public or cooperative ownership would be the key to a new consciousness and to the qualitative transformation of human life. This dialectical materialism, then, in no way neglected the spiritual dimension.

There are forms of socialism that opt for a mechanical, non-dialectical understanding of the impact of economic institutions on human consciousness. They underestimate the creativity of the spirit and therefore fully deserve the reproaches raised by church teaching against "materialism." Orthodox Marxism has, in fact, become mechanistic in this sense. It is, however, the strength of British socialism that it was never attracted to a materialism of this kind. From our first chapter we know that CCF socialism did not neglect the creativity of consciousness in the process of social revolution. On the contrary, CCFers used to argue that the Depression had created material conditions in Canada and the world that permitted morality to play a profound and irreplaceable part in the overcoming of capitalism.

At the same time, the CCF mocked Christian preaching and moral exhortation that demanded a change of heart while defending the existing economic system. They unmasked this sort of Christian morality as an ideology that legitimated the present system despite its injustices. They repudiated any moral preaching, whether religious or secular, that suggested that all the modern world needed was more love, more generosity, more sharing or, as many Christian leaders claimed, a universal return to God. They regarded such moral exhortation as totally illusory, a fraudulent attempt to defend the existing economic system and a denial of the dialectical relationship between consciousness and society. That is why the CCF members of Parliament chuckled and sneered whenever speakers in the Commons, arguing against socialism, invoked spiritual values and Christian virtues. The report did not read their derision correctly. The CCF, like all socialists, opposed Christian charity when it was recommended as a way of sidestepping the demands of justice.

Before leaving the topic of materialism, I wish to mention very briefly that in recent years Christian theologians, Catholic and Protestant, have taken this dialectical relationship between society and consciousness very seriously.[34] They have produced a Christian theology of the Left, critically aware of its political meaning, often known by such titles as "liberation theology" or "political theology." It focuses on the praxis of men and women, that is, on the manner in which people collectively deal with the real conditions of their lives. This theology acknowledges that ideas, ideals and spirituality are in fact part of this praxis of coping with life and improving it. Even an ecclesiastical document published in 1977 recognized that consciousness does not float freely above the human being's historical struggle but, however creative it may be, always remains grounded in particular socio-economic conditions and reflects one's concrete material circumstances.[35] If this is really correct, we have to ask what is the praxis that opens people to the divine mystery. The theologians referred to above argue that only a concrete commitment to human emancipation constitutes the appropriate praxis for understanding the Christian message and for receiving God in faith. Some of these theologians call themselves "religious materialists."

The examination of the Lévesque report leads us to the conclusion that it was hastily written, used its resources uncritically, revealed a total lack of contact with the CCF as a party and did not provide arguments that are wholly convincing. The great fault of the report was that it approached the CCF with the three papal questions in mind, instead of first making an effort to understand the birth of Canadian socialism in its own terms and out of its own history. The only valid contrast between the CCF and church teaching was in the area of class struggle. Canadian socialism advocated the use of class conflict as a lever for radical social change, albeit in a democratic context, while Catholic social teaching stressed the need for resolving class conflict in the search for a new, more just basis of cooperation. This point was well made by Henri Bourassa in the Commons. Still, Bourassa did not consider the difference great enough to make the CCF forbidden territory for Catholics. He understood that the CCF as a social phenomenon reflected the pragmatic socialist heritage of Great Britain. The parliamentary debate in February 1933, as Humphrey Mitchell told the House, was the Canadian equivalent, "ten years behind the times," of an identical debate in the British House of Commons on 20 March 1923, when Philip Snowden had moved a similar resolution to introduce a socialist economy in Great Britain.[36]

The Lévesque report, we recall, was written for the meeting of 9 March 1933, months prior to the Regina convention. After the convention and the publication of its manifesto, Lévesque reiterated his verdict in an article in *L'action nationale* of October 1933.[37] Henri Bourassa and Ted Garland expressed their displeasure and challenged the Dominican social scientist. Still, his report became the formal basis for the episcopal condemnation in February 1934. After a few years, Father Lévesque now recalls, the CCF softened its position — the amendments proposed by Woodsworth to the speech from the throne became more moderate every year — so that he eventually changed his mind. From 1939 on, he taught in his lectures at Laval University that the former condemnation of the CCF was no longer valid. He also persuaded Cardinal Villeneuve in 1943 to favour a statement by the Canadian bishops' conference, granting Catholics permission to vote for the CCF. But this anticipates later developments in the attitude of the Catholic hierarchy. We must return to the spring of 1933.

Warnings, Condemnations and Release

On 16 May 1933, the bishops of Quebec published a joint pastoral letter in which they condemned every form of socialism and defended the capitalist system. Socialists, they wrote, misjudging the role of freedom and private initiative in socio-economic organization, wanted to make the wealth and the well-being of individuals entirely dependent on the state; to bring this about they would transfer to the state, in a more or less total manner, the property and the control of productive capital. The bishops regretted the abuses of capitalism but defended the capitalist system as "the most suited to the people's inclinations and most appropriate for the well-being and economic progress of the nations."[38]

To illustrate the mood of the Quebec hierarchy at this time, we recall that in June of the same year Cardinal Villeneuve, archbishop of Quebec City, was so provoked by the unrest and upheaval among the workers of Quebec that he intervened in the affairs of the Catholic trade union, the Canadian and Catholic Confederation of Labour (CCCL), which had been founded in 1921 under the direction of ecclesiastical authority. After removing from office the duly appointed union leaders, he replaced them by A. Charpentier and J.-P. Filion, safe and obedient men chosen by himself.[39]

This fear of the labour movement and of socialism was not the only Catholic response in Canada. Among English-speaking Catholics, minorities as they were in a Protestant land and usually employed in low-paying jobs, there were positive reactions to the CCF. In the industrialized parts of Canada, English-speaking Catholics found themselves in conditions similar to those of Catholics in England. In August 1933, a few weeks after the Regina convention, the English-language weekly of the Montreal diocese, the *Beacon*, published an article on the CCF that followed the open approach of the English bishops and, in fact, went considerably beyond it in its sympathy for the new party.

The *Beacon* published the Regina Manifesto and, in an editorial, added a few Catholic reflections on the new party programme.[40] First it noted the strong bond of sympathy that Catholics committed to social justice must have felt toward the CCF movement. "We have approached the reading of the CCF programme with a natural interest, but no specially defined frame of mind. As we read Mr. Woodsworth's introductory speech and, with concentration, read the fourteen points and their development, clause by clause ... we seemed to sense a touch of sympathy and of fellowship, not necessarily because we agreed with all of its conclusions but because we had, as a result of our own struggle with the social question, a realization that before us was a set of proposals, issuing from a band of men and women ... who with high ideals and singleness of purpose had set themselves the task of finding for Canadians a way out of the economic chaos." The *Beacon* editorial argued that we were in need of a new order and that the most reasonable and persuasive proposal so far had been made by the CCF.

According to the *Beacon* editorial, there was nothing in the CCF programme that went against Catholic social teaching. "In the first place, while it provides for a lot of socializing, it contains nothing of the socialism condemned by Leo XIII. It does not abolish the principle of private property; there is in it nothing that interferes with the Catholic conception of the end of man in the realm of time or eternity. These are the two dangers against which Pius XI gives definite warning. For the rest the people can judge for themselves." The editorial strongly approved of the proposal to foster the cooperative idea. In this context, the editorial uttered a warning against too much state ownership. Here it was necessary to listen to the teaching of the popes, who argued that extended state ownership would enormously increase the power of government and endanger the freedom of individuals and the well-being of the network of small groups, communities and associations in the country.

The *Beacon* noted that "the socialization recommended by the CCF can be carried out without state ownership." To promote cooperation and social planning and to keep state ownership as limited as possible "in no way interferes with putting into operation the complete programme of socialization proposed by the CCF." What was most important, the editorial argued, was the planning of the economy. The *Beacon* was particularly impressed by the national planning committee proposed by the Regina programme, and it believed planning the economy through such an agency was even in keeping with the views of Professor J.M. Keynes. The *Beacon* recognized the pragmatic nature of CCF socialism. It quoted a revealing sentence from Woodsworth's introductory speech at Regina. "'In developing a constructive programme we face our most difficult task. We are passing through a hitherto untravelled land. We may make mistakes but we must go forward. Given the general direction we must proceed more or less by the method of trial and error.'" This, the *Beacon* argued, was the kind of radical party that could be trusted.

In the meantime, the CCF began to approach the Quebec public for support. A pamphlet published in French explained that a Catholic could well become a member of the new party.[41] Woodsworth himself cited papal encyclicals in the Commons and Bourassa supported him in this. The pamphlet also claimed that Bishop Duke of Vancouver had recently recommended a rather advanced social legislation that included the nationalization of public services.

It was at this time that Georges Gauthier, archbishop of Montreal, decided to intervene. In a sermon given in September, he warned Catholics against this new party that was trying to impose socialist measures on the Canadian people. He reprimanded the editors of the *Beacon*. In the issue of 24 November the diocesan paper carried a long article written by Father Louis Chagnon, SJ, a member of the Ecole sociale populaire and a participant in "la journée des treize," which tried to show that the CCF was advocating a socialism that fell under the condemnation of Pius XI.[42] His article was almost identical with the Lévesque report except for the inclusion of references to the Regina Manifesto. The article did not give an account of what the CCF was and what it stood for; it simply focussed on the three points — class conflict, private property and materialism — raised by Pius XI. One new item was the strange reference to the Erfurt declaration of 1891, which tolerated Christians in the German socialist movement because, it said, religion is a private affair. This was supposed to resemble the CCF position. The article quoted with full approval Lévesque's conclusion that the CCF advocated a moderate form of socialism but as such still fell under the condemnation of Pius XI. The only other new point of the article was that it promised that a reform programme, worked out by a group of

Quebec lay people, would soon be published, which would reflect the teaching of the Church and form a platform for political action to reform present economic order. We shall study this Catholic reform programme in a later chapter of this book.

The Canadian bishops met in the fall of 1933. They too made a declaration on the state of the Depression and the solution of the social question. They spoke of the suffering of the present hour, but added that socialism was not a suitable means to remedy the present misery. The declaration did not mention the CCF by name. This is what the text said: "It is important that the Catholics of this country be on their guard. Rarely do the new systems or parties which appeal for their confidence present themselves as complete error. They often include enough truth to give credibility to error. Catholics have the right to ask these systems and parties what happens in their bold programmes of nationalization to the principle of private property, whether the criticism and their radical claims are not in danger of provoking the class struggle, and if in the new society they wish to build there is not an exclusively materialistic conception of the social order."[43]

Was this an official warning against the CCF? It was certainly understood in this manner in Quebec. Since the bishops mentioned systems and parties, it was clear that they did not speak against the Communist party alone. Jean Hulliger, the author of a book on the social teaching of the bishops of Quebec and Canada, has argued that the episcopal declaration of the fall of 1933 warned Catholics against the CCF and its errors.[44]

There were, however, English-speaking Catholics who insisted that the bishops had not mentioned the CCF by name, for one thing; and in addition, they had formulated the warning in regard to the new parties in the form of three questions, without indicating how these must be answered in the case of the CCF. This was certainly the position of the Catholic diocesan paper of Toronto, edited by Henry Somerville; and eventually, after some fluctuation, it was the view defended by the *Prairie Messenger*, the Saskatchewan Catholic weekly, published by the Benedictines of St. Peter's Abbey. These papers insisted that Catholics were free to make up their own minds in regard to the CCF.

Early in January 1934, Henry Somerville wrote an editorial in the *Catholic Register* that declared the CCF was not socialist in the sense proscribed by papal teaching. He argued, "The basic decla-rations of the CCF were capable of an interpretation consistent with Catholic doctrine."[45] Somerville said the malicious use of the term "socialist" by the enemies of the party or even by extremists within it should be disregarded. He mentioned that the CCF de-rived its social philosophy largely from the British Labour party, not from Continental anti-clerical socialists, and urged that the open attitude displayed by Cardinal Bourne in regard to the Labour party should also prevail in Canada for this reason. It might even be recommendable, Somerville argued, that Catholics join the new party and work within it in order to prevent the radicals from exercising undue influence. As long as there was no pronouncement by Church authority against the CCF, a Catholic was free to join the organization. "The basic declarations of the CCF," he concluded, "are capable of an interpretation satisfactory to Catholics."

The same British model of responding to the CCF seemed to have been adopted by Henri Bourassa. We saw that in the original parliamentary debate of February 1933, Bourassa recognized the closeness between the CCF position and papal social teaching. He had reservations in regard to the party for two reasons: he was not wholly satisfied with their use of class conflict in their politi-cal strategy; and more concretely, as a leader in French Canada, he felt — and, one must admit, with justice — that the CCF pro-gramme had no sense of the dual nature of the Canadian reality and of the legislative power needed by Quebec to protect its national identity.

On 30 January 1934, he returned to the topic. In a speech that recommended, in view of the present economic crisis, the co-operation of all political parties in the reconstruction of the Canadian economy, he urged the traditional parties to accept the CCF as a respected partner in the dialogue. "I now turn to my friends on the Left. They are full of hope. Let me be frank and admit that there is much in them that is good. I commend this one thing to my young Conservative friends from Quebec: cease the campaign of slander which has been carried on by calling these men the agents of Moscow. To my Liberal friends in the province of Quebec, I give this further advice: do not raise your hands in horror and say, 'Oh no, we have nothing in common with these men from the West, these semi-Bolsheviks, these quarter-Communists.' When you make use of the papal encyclical to denounce the CCF, why do you not read that part of it which denounces the system that has been built, maintained and protected by the two great historic parties since Confederation.... Let us admit that there is much good in the programme of the CCF."[46]

While Henri Bourassa did not join the CCF himself, he seemed to think that there were good reasons for joining it and no special obstacles for Catholics committed to the Church's social teaching. This is how Bourassa was understood by Henry Somerville, who regarded the French-Canadian politician as an ally in the same cause. Somerville quoted Bourassa's speech in the *Catholic Register* of 15 February and explained that the view of this famous member of Parliament was identical with his own.[47]

On 16 February 1934, Archbishop Gauthier of Montreal finally published a long pastoral letter in which he condemned the CCF programme as irreconcilable with Catholic social teaching and declared that Catholics were not allowed to join or support the CCF.[48] His pastoral letter was a restatement of the Lévesque report, with additions taken from the Chagnon article published in November. Here a Catholic bishop for the first time attacked the CCF by name and openly joined the political campaign against Canadian socialism. This was a great blow to the future of the CCF in Quebec. Gauthier's position also influenced Catholics in the rest of the country even if, technically speaking, the prohibition to support and join the CCF applied only to those in Montreal. The shadow cast over the CCF by clerical voices in Quebec had now become darker. There was no strong Catholic voice in the country ready to respond to Gauthier. The CCF published a reply to the archbishop, *La CCF réplique* (written by Woodsworth's daughter, Grace McInnis, who knew French), that showed that none of the three points developed by him — class warfare, private property and materialism — offered an adequate description of CCF socialism, and that there was no reason why a Catholic committed to the social teaching of his church should not join the CCF.[49] But the CCF was not given a hearing in Quebec. When its leaders came to Montreal to deliver lectures — in English — on the basic harmony between their platform and Catholic social teaching, the French-Canadian press did not even report their presence, their speeches or ideas. And as if one condemnation of the CCF in Quebec were not enough, a year later Cardinal Villeneuve, archbishop of Quebec, spelled out his own condemnation in *La semaine religieuse* and repeated it periodically at various public functions.[50] One could not be a Catholic and a CCFer at the same time.

Outside Quebec some Catholics continued to defend the view that the CCF had never been condemned by the Church, except in Quebec, and hence Catholics were free to make up their own minds. The statement of the Canadian bishops in the fall of 1933 had been ambiguous. The faithful were warned against new political movements and parties, especially those whose programmes included large-scale nationalization of privately owned corporations, but the CCF was not mentioned by name. It is likely that the ecclesiastical statement had been composed as a compromise between the French- and English-speaking bishops. The Quebec hierarchy was intent on reproving the CCF not only because of its socialism but also because its secular spirit could undermine ecclesiastical power among the workers.

The English-speaking bishops, on the other hand, must have hated the idea of intervening directly in party politics, especially since the CCF was a Canadian grass-roots movement, free of anti-Christian bias. Condemning the Communist party seemed quite proper: that party had a foreign connection and was committed to an anti-religious ethos. But to condemn the CCF in the name of the Church was not consistent with the manner in which Catholic bishops in the Anglo-Saxon world understood their office. The joint statement of 1933 was a compromise, then; it could be read two ways. It allowed the Quebec bishops to say that the entire Canadian hierarchy had warned Catholics against the CCF, and it allowed the English-Canadian bishops, while in fact making it difficult for Catholics to support the new party, to insist that they had never disapproved of socialism or interfered in party politics.

Vast numbers of Catholics in English Canada believed that the Church had warned them against the CCF. They had read the condemnations by Archbishop Gauthier and Cardinal Villeneuve in the newspapers and felt that these men spoke not only for the bishops of Quebec but for the Canadian Church as a whole. In those days Catholics did not readily recognize the tensions and disagreements among their own bishops. Added to this was the anti-socialist fervour characteristic of the Church in the Thirties, a fervour inspired by Pius XI and gladly endorsed by the bishops in countries where the Church was identified with the ancien régime, feudal, bourgeois or a mixture of the two. Many Canadian priests believed that the CCF stood for a socialism that had been reproved by the Church, and instructed their parishioners accordingly in their Sunday morning sermons. Only a few Catholic thinkers, such as Henry Somerville, continued to argue that ecclesiastical authority had never officially condemned the CCF and that Catholics were free to support that party if this was their political judgment. It was certainly possible for Catholics to join the CCF in English Canada, but in many places this demanded a great deal of courage. Catholics were made to feel that by doing so they deviated from the authoritative view; and since they were a minority, they attached great importance to being united. The Catholics who did join the party and took an active part in it, especially in the rural sections of Saskatchewan, often had to go against the wishes of their parish priests. Some of these men and women went through much suffering because of their political convictions. On the whole, Catholic workers in the industrial unions were much less sensitive to Church teaching and less exposed to Church pressure; they often supported the CCF as they did their union without paying attention to ecclesiastical policy.

English-speaking Catholics, we noted, were a minority in Canada. They were largely working people who had few intellectuals among them, apart from the priests dedicated to higher education. For educational material and discussion of events, they relied on publications and reviews produced by American Catholics. Apart from the Canadian diocesan newspapers, educated Catholics read *America, The Commonweal* and other journals of opinion or edification published in the United States. Since that country had no equivalent of Canada's nationwide farmer/labour party, heir of British socialism, the Catholic discussion of social reform took a different direction altogether. There were no socialists among American Catholics. Even the socially committed American Catholics distinguished their political stance, whether radical or moderate, from socialism in any meaning of the term. The cultural dependence of English-speaking Catholics on their American co-religionists did not help them to gain insight into Canadian politics. It persuaded them, rather, to exclude socialism from their political horizon.

Toward the end of the Thirties, when the CCF, because of its comparative success, adopted less radical policies and adjusted itself to the gradualism to which the majority of Canadians were deeply attached, the Catholic vote increased. This is clearly shown by the voting patterns in Saskatchewan and parts of Ontario.[51] The Church's position in English Canada became increasingly unclear. The policy defended by the *Catholic Register* in Toronto, apparently with Archbishop James McGuigan's approval, differed from that of other diocesan papers of Ontario. Jeanne Beck's recent research in the Toronto archdiocesan archives has revealed that in 1938, Msgr. Ildebrando Antoniutti, the papal nuncio residing in Ottawa, was troubled by this public confusion and asked the bishops of Ontario to direct their attention to the CCF and clarify "its nature, its finality, its standing in regard to religion and the Church."[52] In his letter of reply, Archbishop McGuigan, in the name of the Ontario bishops, evaded the issue. "Considering the evils of the existing social order we feel...according to our present knowledge...that we could not possibly condemn this political party as holding a social doctrine opposed to or unacceptable to the teaching of the Church as revealed in the encyclicals. As the movement is nationwide... we respectfully suggest that the question be very carefully studied by a committee of expert representatives of various sections of the country. Meanwhile we do not think Catholics should be hastily condemned for joining the CCF nor should they be forbidden to do so.... This will avoid disunity, unfair criticism of the Church and confusion over our own social ideas."

By the early Forties, the CCF had gained strength in the western provinces and Ontario. It had modified its radical policy on nationalization; it allowed private property within reasonable limits; it gave assurances to the business community, especially small merchants, that they would thrive under a socialist government; it had, moreover, become involved in an open and often bitter conflict with the Communist party over control of unions.

Murray Ballantyne, then the editor of the Montreal edition of the *Catholic Register* (which had taken the place of the *Beacon*), became convinced that the time had come to appeal to the Canadian bishops to remove the shadow of suspicion from the CCF and give it the green light in a public manner.[53] He found an enthusiastic ally for this plan in Henry Somerville. Both editors approached their local ordinaries. McGuigan of Toronto, who had always supported Somerville, was quite ready to act. The then archbishop of Montreal, Joseph Charbonneau — later to become famous through his role in the asbestos strike in 1949 — was open to the suggestion and appointed a commission to study the matter. Since the commission looked upon the Canadian situation purely from the viewpoint of Quebec politics, it showed little interest in rehabilitating the CCF. Archbishop Charbonneau was then willing to study the matter himself. "Archbishop Charbonneau had been impressed," Murray Ballantyne reported, "by what he had read of the CCF leader, Mr. M.J. Coldwell.... The Archbishop asked me to arrange a meeting between himself and Mr. Coldwell. This took place at my house, when the Archbishop, Mr. Coldwell and Professor [Frank] Scott lunched with me. Several hours were spent in amicable discussion. No notes were kept, as the discussion was informal, but on both sides the talk was frank and friendly. No major point of disagreement was found. It seemed clear that, insofar as the leader and the national chairman of the party were concerned, Catholic participation in the CCF would be welcomed and there was nothing fundamentally irreconcilable in the two points of view."[54] After this meeting, Archbishop Charbonneau agreed to make a proposal to the plenary meeting of the Canadian bishops that they clear the way for Catholic participation in the CCF.

The Canadian bishops met in October 1943. We recall that in the year 1942, the membership of the CCF in Ontario had increased enormously. The labour movement, including the more conservative Trades and Labour Congress (TLC), began to express greater interest in politics and made overtures to the CCF for some form of association. The provincial election of August 1943 was a great victory for the CCF: prior to the election it had no seats in the House, but now it had 34. Would the next election lift the CCF into the seat of power? A feverish campaign of hatred and slander broke out at this time, sponsored by right-wing organizations but also supported wholeheartedly by the daily press. It was a hysterical campaign that sought to scare the electorate about the coming red menace, a totalitarian takeover by a political party as ruthless and deceitful as Russian communism and German nazism. In this uncertain climate, the Canadian bishops, on 14 October 1943, made their statement on political life in Canada.

In their declaration, the Canadian bishops appealed to the faithful and to all people in authority to promote the urgently needed social and economic reform. "As the authorized spiritual advisers of the Catholic people," the bishops declared that "the faithful are free to support any political party upholding the basic Christian traditions of Canada, and favouring the needed reforms in the social and economic order which are demanded with such an urgency in pontifical documents."[55] Archbishops McGuigan and Charbonneau were satisfied that this brief statement cleared the CCF in the eyes of the Catholic people. Because the CCF had not been mentioned by name in the warning issued by the Canadian hierarchy in May 1933, there was no need to mention it by name in this new policy statement, especially as naming the party might sound like an ecclesiastical endorsement of it. In a special paragraph, the bishops renewed their condemnation of communist parties, under whatever name (Labour Progressive at the time), thereby creating a clear distinction between international revolutionary socialism and Canadian democratic socialism, the latter being included among the acceptable parties in the preceding paragraph. As the episcopal declaration of 1933 was a compromise mainly between French- and English-speaking bishops, so was the present document.

Ballantyne and Somerville were greatly disappointed. The new declaration was far too obscure for them. Canadian Catholics would not understand that this ecclesiastical document expressed a significant change of policy. They devised a plan to publish the declaration, accompanied by an appropriate editorial, in several Catholic papers at the same time. On 23 October, the declaration and Somerville's editorial were carried by the Toronto and Montreal editions of the *Catholic Register* — papers of semi-official standing — and by *L'action catholique* and *Le devoir*, both of great influence in Quebec. The editorial comment was quite specific. It said that in this declaration, the Canadian hierarchy wanted to settle the question, agitated in some circles, of whether Catholics were free to support the CCF. Without mentioning the name of the party, lest their declaration be understood as political support of the CCF, the hierarchy had made it clear that Catholics were as free in regard to the CCF as they were in regard to the older parties. "In the early days of the CCF," the comment continued, "there was some misgiving among Catholics. Official and unofficial pronouncements of that party were capable of being interpreted as socialism in the sense condemned by the Church, and it was by no means clear for a time whether Communists would succeed in their endeavour to infiltrate themselves into dominant positions of the movement. For these reasons the bishops in several dioceses felt it their duty to warn their flock against the dangers that were apparent.... The situation is now clarified. The CCF has given all the guarantees that it could be reasonably expected to give, of no truck or trade with the Communists.... It may be said to be a matter of congratulations that there is such a party as the CCF to attract those voters who, as a recent election has shown, are dissatisfied with the older parties and who, in the absence of the CCF, might give their support to the Communists."[56] The comment then reminded the readers that the episcopal declaration recalled the duty of all Catholics to do what they could to hasten reform of the present social order, which suffered from serious ills that must not be regarded with complacency.

In this editorial comment Somerville probably paid so much attention to the Communist party, more than was demanded by the occasion, because this enabled him to explain the previous warnings of bishops against the CCF and to exploit the anti-Communist sentiment of Catholics at this time to produce CCF support.

The reaction to publication of the bishops' declaration and the editorial was vigorous and immediate. The CCF made up pamphlets of both statements. Members of the older parties, Ballantyne tells us, were shocked by the timing as well as the content of the declaration: "The professional defenders of capitalism and private enterprise were enraged by what they considered as little less than an act of treason. Reports from Quebec and Toronto indicated that both Cardinal Villeneuve and Archbishop Mc-Guigan were visited by important representatives of politics and business who argued that the bishops had made a disastrous, ill-timed and naive mistake. It was maintained that the bishops had in effect given a hand to revolutionary forces at the very moment when the citadel of free enterprise was in danger."[57]

Soon some smaller Catholic papers, among them the *Northwest Review* of Winnipeg and the *Catholic Record* of London, Ontario, challenged the interpretation given to the declaration by the *Catholic Register*. In their editorial comments they explained that the recent declaration was not at all a "clearing" of the CCF, but on the contrary a statement of principles that the CCF would have to meet if it wished to show that it merited "clearance." The comment of the *Catholic Register*, they argued, had no official standing but was just the private opinion of the editors. The same line was taken by the publication of the Ecole populaire sociale. Eventually even *L'action catholique* adopted this line. Ballantyne reports that according to Henry Somerville, this new interpretation gave much comfort to Mackenzie King.

The new interpretation gained credibility through incidents in British Columbia. Harold Winch, leader of the CCF in that province, made several revolutionary speeches, presenting a more radical image of the CCF, that were extensively reported in the press throughout the country. Ballantyne interprets these incidents as a sign that the radical CCFers in British Columbia, with their more doctrinaire approach to socialism, were upset by the possibility of greater Catholic participation in the party and possibly did their best to forestall it.[58] Archbishop Duke of Vancouver replied to Harold Winch. Preaching in his cathedral on All Saints' Day 1943, the archbishop complained that it was difficult to know how much national policy statements made by the CCF were worth, since the leaders in the provincial parties seemed to set their own, often divergent policies. In particular, he wondered how much weight one should attach to the stand the CCF had taken against communism. The question of Catholic participation in the CCF seemed as uncertain as it was before the bishops' declaration.

To clear up this confusion, Archbishop McGuigan issued a statement in the name of the Bishops' Committee for Social Action, carried by the Canadian Press on 6 December, in which he explained that while the word "socialism" had many meanings in the English language, the Catholic church used this word much more narrowly, to refer to a particular political system that it had condemned. This statement encouraged Ballantyne and Somerville to hatch another plan. They wanted to make public in the *Catholic Register* the events that had led to the bishops' declaration of 14 October and show that their interpretation of it corresponded to the bishops' intention. Before they sent the new editorial comment to the printers, they sought the approval of Archbishop McGuigan. This time the archbishop disapproved: "To avoid divisions among ourselves, I think we must be a bit cautious for the present." Ballantyne then decided to write an explanatory article, setting forth the meaning of the bishops' declaration and the subsequent controversy over it, which, after receiving the appropriate permission from Charbonneau, he published in an American Catholic publication, the *Commonweal* (3 March 1944). This article was later reprinted, without further commentary, in the Toronto and Montreal editions of the *Catholic Register* (15 April 1944).

Despite the efforts of Ballantyne and Somerville, the bishops' declaration and the fact that at that time great numbers of Catholics actually supported the CCF, there remained in the imagination of Canadian Catholics, primarily the French but also the English-speaking, a shadow of a religiously based doubt whether it was really all right for Catholics to join the socialist party. Did not the party carry the half-voiced disapproval of the Church? Catholics had been inoculated against socialism by repeated condemnations. The very word sounded dangerous to them, quite apart from its meaning.

If Canadian Catholics had been left alone by the bishops in the early Thirties, the pendulum might have swung the other way. Henri Bourassa, in the parliamentary debate of February 1933, said that he was not afraid of the word "socialist"; he understood its many meanings, in particular its meaning in the tradition of British labour. The English-speaking bishops at the time may have been wary of the new party, but they had no intention of making a public statement against it. Their people were, after all, mainly working-class. It was the initiative of certain French-Canadian bishops that led to the various ecclesiastical warnings against the CCF. The Quebec hierarchy, accustomed to intervening in the political life of the province, was engaged in a struggle against modern secularism and the dissolution of the cohesive, national religious culture of Quebec, and in this situation was quite unwilling to allow the leadership of a reform movement to pass outside the province into the hands of people over whom they had no control. They condemned the CCF as a foreign influence in Quebec. The ecclesiastical policy of the French-Canadian bishops spilled over into English Canada. The doubts and hesitations of the English-speaking bishops in regard to the CCF, which would have gone unexpressed, now flowed into ambiguous statements and warnings. It is largely due to these ecclesiastical directives that Canadian Catholics, despite their class position, came to respond so negatively to Canadian socialism.

As late as the mid-Forties, Father Eugene Cullinane, doing research on the Catholic attitude toward the CCF, came to the conclusion that the word "socialism" continued to summon forth doubts and fears among Canadian Catholics. "The mentality of most Catholics I have met across Canada," he wrote, "including the clergy, is infected with a terribly distorted view of the CCF reality. The result is that Catholics generally are afflicted with a deep-rooted though unconscious prejudice against the CCF. It is virtually identical with the kind of prejudice against Catholics found in the typical Ontario Protestant twenty years ago. Catholics by and large condemn the CCF for what it is not: they are enslaved by the tyranny of a single word—'socialism.' If I may generalize on the fairly large sample I have interviewed across the continent, then the overwhelming majority of Catholics are unconsciously banded together in a compact political unity based on an illusion."[59]

Historians may ask whether the reaction of the Catholic Church to Canadian socialism was an important reason why the CCF did not succeed, following the British and Continental pattern, in becoming the alternative to the government. In 1933 Catholics made up forty-five percent of the population. But did the bishops have that much power? There can be no doubt that the response of the Quebec bishops prevented the CCF from making significant inroads in that province and hence kept the party from becoming Dominion-wide in the true sense. But did the episcopal warnings, vague as they were, have a strong effect on the English-speaking working class? Neil Betten, an American labour historian, argues that the refusal of industrial unionism in the United States to espouse a socialist ideology was largely due to the strong Catholic presence in the labour movement.[60] That there was some restraining influence of Catholic teaching on the progress of the CCF is beyond doubt. But whether this was a determining influence or significant only in conjunction with other factors is something on which I would not hazard an opinion. I must leave this to historians with a comprehensive knowledge of Canadian history. What interests me in this book is above all the conflict of ideas generated by the Catholic reaction to Canadian socialism.

Part II
Catholics Against the Stream

4
Voices Crying in the Wilderness

In part I we examined the negative attitude of the Catholic church to Canadian socialism in the Thirties, and the half-hearted attempt by the Church in the early Forties to allow Catholics to support the CCF. In those days the voices of the bishops were powerful. The episcopal warning against socialism was heard by Canadian Catholics as an echo of papal social teaching. It is not surprising that the great majority of clergy and laity followed the directives given by the ecclesiastical hierarchy. Ecclesiastical obedience was the culturally demanded response in Quebec, where the Catholic church held a spiritual monopoly and where even reform movements that sought wide popular support had to define themselves in Catholic terms.

In English-speaking Canada the style of Church authority and the nature of ecclesiastical obedience were quite different. Here Catholics were in a minority: on the whole they were working people, many of whom had arrived in Canada only recently. They were exposed to prejudice and discrimination. Catholics were very often despised because of their religion. Mingled with the religious distaste for Catholicism was a certain racial contempt for the Irish and for immigrants from southern and eastern Europe as well as a certain sense of class superiority over workers and their families. In this situation it was not surprising that Catholics developed a strong sense of social cohesion and solidarity. They honoured priests and bishops as their spokesmen in a hostile environment. Catholics were willing to follow the directives of the hierarchy. Yet this ready obedience was not an attitude of submission to the powerful as it might have been in Quebec; it was rather an expression of solidarity with the Catholic community and the affirmation of Catholic identity in a Protestant land with a Protestant ruling elite.

Historians may be interested in the manner in which the Church's message regarding the CCF was actually passed on to the people. In addition to the episcopal statements we examined in part I, it would be necessary to study other forms of written communication, such as pastoral letters, diocesan publications, pamphlet literature and Catholic papers. One would have to study the sermons preached in the parishes and the more direct personal influence of the clergy on parishioners, especially those involved in the labour movement. What was the political message communicated at Holy Name breakfasts and other parish gatherings? How did the clergy in various locations influence the political climate and make the CCF appear as a dangerous party, the bearer of forbidden socialism? While it would indeed be interesting to study these channels of communication, the results would not be surprising to Catholics old enough to remember Catholic life prior to Vatican Council II (1962-65). They remember how the multiple mechanisms for creating unanimity in the Church were received as part and parcel of Catholic life. The willingness to be united and affirm a common public stance was nourished by nationalist feelings in Quebec, and in English-speaking Canada by a strong sense of solidarity in an unfriendly environment.

There were Catholic voices in Canada that went against the mainstream. Some Catholic papers continued to defend the position that Catholics were free to support the CCF. Some Catholics openly declared that the misery produced by the Depression demanded new and radical responses, and criticized the indifference to political struggle on the part of the great majority of church-going people. While the bishops called for social reform and endorsed the social reconstruction advocated by Pope Pius XI, their teaching did not back any existing political movement nor give rise to any concrete political strategy. Church teaching remained wholly abstract. The Catholic voices crying in the wilderness opted for a more radical approach to society, either by supporting Canadian socialism or by engaging in other forms of social protest against the capitalist system. It is these nonconformist Catholics that constitute the subject of part II of this study.

My special interest in the non-conformist voices among Catholics is not intended as an apologetical device to show that the Catholic church was not as committed to the defence of the status quo as is usually presumed. I am interested in these critical voices, just as I am interested in the socialist movements in Canadian society, because they represent significant countervailing forces that not only reveal the contradictions in the existing order but also disclose new possibilities for overcoming these contradictions in the future. Societies and churches are never as unified as they first appear. According to Max Weber, if we look closely enough at any society we find that the dominant structures that manifest its unity are accompanied by countervailing trends that register the alienation of the people and propose a new version of society, one that promises to overcome present misery.[1] Here societies (and churches) are seen as generating their own critique. While some countervailing trends are inspired by illusory ideas or even dangerous visions, others are based on a profound analysis of social evil and inspired by a rational imagination that reveals the as yet hidden possibilities of the present. It is from these movements that newness enters history.

It is of special interest to me, therefore, to show that the churches were not as unified as they presented themselves to society. They too were constituted by dominant structures and countervailing trends. While the Protestant Social Gospel and Protestant socialists in Canada have been studied, the much smaller circle of non-conformist Catholics has not received much attention. It is with them that I wish to deal in this and the following chapters.

Was there Catholic support for the CCF? Did Catholics vote for the new party? Did they occupy leadership positions in the movement? Did any Catholics speak out publicly in favour of the CCF? In the previous chapter we have referred to three Catholic diocesan weeklies that displayed considerable openness in regard to Canadian socialism: the *Beacon* in Montreal, under the editorship of Murray Ballantyne; the *Catholic Register* in Toronto, under Henry Somerville; and the *Prairie Messenger* in the province of Saskatchewan, published by the Benedictines of St. Peter's Abbey. The *Beacon*, we recall, published a positive editorial on the

CCF, for which it was censured by Archbishop Gauthier of Montreal. The *Catholic Register* defended the position, eventually endorsed by the *Prairie Messenger*, that the CCF programme contained many policies that were in keeping with Catholic social teaching and that Catholics were free to support the new party if they so chose — a position that was daring in the Church at that time.

Murray Ballantyne was part of a small group of Catholics in Montreal that supported the CCF.[2] Ballantyne, it must be pointed out, was an unusual Catholic. He came from a family with wealth and social connections. His father was Senator Charles Ballantyne, a prominent Conservative politician and a federal cabinet minister (1917-1921) under Sir Robert Borden. In the early Thirties, Murray Ballantyne was a student at McGill University, where he met Eugene Forsey and Frank Scott, was influenced by their social philosophy and allowed himself to be attracted by the ideas and policies of the League for Social Reconstruction. He became a Catholic during these years. A man of profound conviction, he wanted to apply his Catholic faith to the problems of society.

In an interview held many years later, Ballantyne recalled that as he saw the world collapsing around him, he strongly believed that the Catholic faith offered direction and power for social reconstruction.[3] He wanted the Catholic community, especially intellectuals, to become involved in the problems of Canada and, in the name of their faith, take an active part in society. He was greatly taken by the principles of the LSR and found that many of them resembled the social teaching of the popes. He was frustrated, however, by the widespread indifference of Catholics to the issues that troubled and preoccupied Canada. English-speaking Catholics in Canada, Ballantyne recalled, were untroubled, satisfied, unintellectual and paranoid about the influence of communism. He himself had learnt from Frank Scott, he told his interviewer, that communism was the unpaid bill presented to humanity for its social injustice. Ballantyne complained that few Catholics ever participated in associations and meetings of Canadian intellectuals that dealt with the problems of Canadian society. Catholics had so much to say, he felt, but were not using their faith as a source of practical wisdom. "We did not participate in national movements," he recalled. Religious training had conditioned Catholics just "to hang on for dear life," lest they lose their faith altogether.

This attitude of Catholics, we note, was largely induced by the lowly position assigned to Irish immigrants in a Protestant land and the defensive stance adopted by Churchmen intent upon protecting the Catholic faith against the cultural influence of the dominant classes. Ballantyne came from a very different background. The indifference of Catholics was recognized as such by some of the more progressive bishops at the time. As we shall see, Archbishop Neil McNeil of Toronto had invited Henry Somerville to come to Canada from England to promote adult education among Catholics, so that they could overcome the very attitudes criticized by Ballantyne. Living in the province of Quebec and in a largely French-speaking diocese under Archbishop Gauthier, Ballantyne felt doubly frustrated by the Catholic response to the Canadian political situation.

Ballantyne rejoiced when the CCF was founded. In his opinion, it was a party closely modelled after the British Labour party; it did not offer doctrinaire socialism but instead proposed pragmatic solutions for the ills of the present system; it had moreover a great deal of Christian inspiration. He thought that it might well be his role as editor of the *Beacon* to act as mediator between the intellectuals in the CCF and the Catholic community. But the *Beacon* soon got into trouble with Archbishop Gauthier. Ballantyne was aghast at the readiness of French-Canadian bishops to intervene in the political life of the nation. He felt they misunderstood the nature of the political process in Canada, and he used every opportunity to argue his case.

Ballantyne belonged to an anglophone group of Montreal Catholics that supported the CCF. When it became clear in the fall of 1932, after the condemnation of the *Beacon* and a sermon preached by Gauthier, that the hierarchy was planning to denounce the CCF, a few members of this group composed an outspoken memorandum, entitled *Catholics in the CCF*, in which they criticized the archbishop's political opinions and defended the Catholic involvement in the party.[4] The matter was of greatest importance to Joseph Wall, a member of the group and a labour organizer for the Canadian Brotherhood of Railway Employees.

The memorandum expressed outrage at the willingness of the Quebec hierarchy to become the defender of capitalism. It asserted that Catholic lay people had the right and duty to engage in political activities and promote economic views without direct ecclesiastical control. The authors insisted they had become active workers for the CCF because after years of talking to each other about fundamental principles of social reform in study clubs, they were now able to apply some of them in a concrete fashion. "The CCF programme provided us with an opportunity to make a beginning at least at carrying out the idea of the encyclicals." The CCF represented the first step in the direction of "a Christian social order."

Unfortunately, the memorandum continued, the critics of the CCF cried "socialism," and then all calm reflection would disappear. The opponents were painting a picture of Marxist nightmares that had nothing to do with the aims and purposes of the CCF, even if the new economic order did include a good deal of socialization. The authors declared that they would not allow themselves to be separated from men of good will, nor from common sense, by a mere word of disapproval. Catholics, they continued, cannot leave the support of the CCF to their brothers outside the Catholic church, be they Protestants, "as most of the leaders are," or non-believers. Catholics constituted such a large percentage of the population that if they joined the CCF, they could easily have affected party policy. Why was it, the authors complained, that we as Catholics were always looked upon as the right wing?

The memorandum, it appears, was signed by Joseph Wall, Madelaine Sheridan and G. Starkley. It was not, however, made public. The group decided to hand it to the apostolic delegate in Ottawa, but upon his refusal to deal with them, they sent it directly to Archbishop Gauthier. The group also got in touch with Henri Bourassa and Ted Garland in the hope that they might help avert a public denunciation of the CCF.

On 11 February Archbishop Gauthier, as we saw in the previous chapter, did condemn the CCF. In the name of his group, Joseph Wall made an appeal to the archbishop. The group wanted to know whether the public denunciation meant that Catholics could not become candidates for the CCF, or whether they could not work for the party, or whether they were even forbidden to vote CCF. The archbishop replied that his pastoral letter was sufficiently clear and that a Catholic of the position and calibre of Wall should know very well wherein his duty lay. While the Catholic group remained faithful to their political commitment, they were severely hindered in promoting the CCF in the Montreal area. Murray Ballantyne also refused to give up. He continued to appeal to his friends in the clergy, urging them to work toward a change of policy in the archdiocese. He allied himself with Henry Somerville; in fact, after discontinuing publication of the *Beacon*, he became the Montreal editor of the *Catholic Register*, where he was at least able to foster the idea that Catholics in Canada were free, if they so chose, to support the CCF. In the early Forties, we recall, Ballantyne and Somerville persuaded the Canadian bishops to lift the cloud of suspicion from the CCF.

Who was Henry Somerville? He was an English Catholic, a dedicated, socially concerned journalist who had been invited to Canada by Archbishop Neil McNeil to foster a new, more open social outlook among Ontario Catholics, who until then had remained cautious and aloof from the social and cultural mainstream. The spirit of Orange bigotry had affected its victims. Archbishop McNeil recognized that the industrial growth of Toronto and the liberal ideas associated with modern society were beginning to create a new climate in Toronto that in turn demanded a more positive, more active, more concerned approach on the part of Catholics. For this reason he had appointed Henry Somerville to exercise an apostolate of adult education in the archdiocese. Somerville did this mainly as editor of the diocesan weekly newspaper.

Henry Somerville was of working-class background, had participated in the Catholic Social Guild in England, and had taken an active part, as a journalist, in the common struggle for social justice. The great guide in all his activities was the Church's social teaching. He understood papal teaching as a middle road between contemporary capitalism and doctrinaire socialism. He criticized the chaos produced by capitalist production in the Twenties and Thirties, favoured the formation of labour unions, defended social legislation to protect workers and farmers — in short, he made himself the spokesman of the positions associated with Social Catholicism.

Somerville constituted an energetic one-man movement in Toronto. In the pages of the *Catholic Register* he published articles, columns and book reviews intended to educate Catholics about the burning social issues of the day. He examined social theories of religious and secular origins, introduced his readers to the social thought of contemporary thinkers and taught them how to analyze political events in a critical manner. He introduced them to social developments taking place in other countries and acquainted them with the ideas of socially concerned Catholics in the United States — especially those of John Ryan and other Catholics who supported the New Deal. Somerville presented an interpretation of papal teaching that demanded a new order and radical reform; he insisted that "socialism" had many meanings, some hostile to religion and therefore condemned by the Church, while others, pragmatic and open, were acceptable to Christians. In particular, he felt Catholics in Canada were free to support the CCF.

Fortunately, Somerville has found his biographer. In a doctoral thesis at McMaster University, Jeanne Beck has studied his life, his ideas, the policies he defended and the impact he had on the Canadian Church.[5] Jeanne Beck has tried to understand Somerville in the context of Ontario Catholicism. Her original intent was to write a thesis on the response of Ontario Catholics to the social misery of the Depression years. She eventually concentrated on Somerville himself, largely because this man had so far escaped the historians, even though he was an influential editor and had written many books and articles on social issues.

Somerville was a powerhouse of enthusiasm and energy. Yet in some way he remained curiously isolated. He influenced the Canadian bishops — he was listened to by Archbishop Neil McNeil and later by McNeil's successor, Archbishop James McGuigan — but it appears that he had no fellow workers or followers in Toronto, with whom he might have formed a group committed to study and public action. To many Toronto Catholics he remained an Englishman, a man with a different background and a different perception of their religion. At the same time, his involvement in the Catholic community and his concentration on the Catholic viewpoint isolated him from the cultural and political mainstream. He remained an unknown figure in the wider Toronto community.

What else was happening among Ontario Catholics? There was the work of Baroness Catherine de Hueck, a Russian emigrée, who had come to Toronto in the Thirties to establish friendship houses and foster religiously based social concerns, somewhat in the manner of the Catholic Worker, a radical social movement founded by Dorothy Day in 1933 in New York City.[6] Curiously enough, she seems to have been invited to Toronto by the archdiocese, following a request of the Mounted Police, to investigate communist influence among immigrant communities, especially those of Ukrainian, Polish and other Slavic origins, where communist agitators were allegedly at work.[7] But this was not her mission. As a vehement critic of capitalism, she was convinced that the Christian way lay somewhere in the middle between the Western system and Russian communism, but she believed that the contribution she could make was in the creation of a new socially concerned spirituality, based on love, poverty and cooperative labour. Her efforts eventually led to the formation in 1947 of a more organized community called Madonna House, at Combermere, Ontario, where men and women live out their dedication to God and God's world in prayer and work, pronounce through their lifestyle a judgment on capitalist society, and give witness through their own involvement to a new order of sharing and mutual assistance. Still, the movement Catherine de Hueck created was not close to the CCF.

What happened among Catholic workers, especially in the mining towns of northern Ontario and other industrial centres when the CIO began to organize labour in Canada in 1937? There were certainly Catholics among the union leaders. So far no research has been done on Catholics and the labour movement in Ontario.

There were, then, some positive responses to the CCF. Murray Ballantyne and Joseph Wall's small group in Montreal were examples of this. Were there others? Since in the early Forties the CCF gained strong popular support not only in Saskatchewan, where it was elected to form the government in 1944, but also in Ontario, Manitoba and British Columbia, where it became the official opposition, there must have been many Catholics among the voters.[8] Much of this history is still hidden. In my own research I found three stories that especially deserve to be told: the growing Catholic support in Saskatchewan; the radical movement l'Action libérale nationale in Quebec, a "purified version" of the CCF; and the radical social involvement of Catholics in Nova Scotia.

5
Catholic Support for the CCF in Saskatchewan

Since the CCF had a special character in Saskatchewan and produced a social movement that would ultimately sweep the province, let us look at the attitude of the Catholic population there to the new political party. George Hoffman, a Saskatchewan historian who has studied the Catholic reaction in the early Thirties, argues that there were several factors at work preventing Catholics from becoming supporters of the new socialism.[1]

There was first of all the loyalty of the Catholics to the Liberal party. We recall that the Conservative party in Saskatchewan had been the political party of the leading families, who entertained and promoted a purely Anglo-Saxon-Protestant understanding of Canada. They regretted the French presence in Saskatchewan and opposed the separate school system, which the Liberal party defended. Since the election of 1917, when the Conservatives stood for English as the only language of instruction, the political map of the province had been clearly drawn: the Conservatives were identified with the hard-line WASPs, while the Liberals were supported by the moderate WASPs, the French Canadians and the ethnic communities. In 1929, the Conservative party under J. T. M. Anderson came to power on a clearly anti-Catholic platform. The new government was strongly influenced by the Orange Lodge, of which the premier as well as some of his ministers were members. When the Ku Klux Klan began to operate in the province, there was evidence that money for its support had been received from sources connected with the Conservative party.[2]

Under these conditions, the Liberal party under James Gardiner became the defender of the Catholic population. The Liberals denounced the Klan and fought prejudice and discrimination, and as a result Catholics identified themselves with the Liberal party and supported it with fervour, as if defending their own religion. When a new party was formed in Saskatchewan, first a farmer/labour federation under M.J. Coldwell and later the CCF, the Catholics regarded it with suspicion. To them Canadian socialism was a WASP phenomenon and they were uneasy about its Protestant style; they preferred to support the Liberal party, which guaranteed Canadian pluralism and promised to protect the multicultural pattern of prairie life.

Since the Catholic population was an embattled minority in Saskatchewan, as it was in many parts of North America, it adopted a rather defensive attitude toward politics. Catholics involved themselves in politics to protect their own rights and gain advantages for their community; they were on the whole not interested in political philosophy and not ready to think of politics as a way of transforming society. Prior to the founding of the CCF, the important Catholic weekly of Saskatchewan, the *Prairie Messenger*, offered few comments on social issues and James McGuigan, then the archbishop of Regina (later of Toronto), paid little attention in his pastorals to the problem of the Depression. The Catholic community, Hoffman convincingly argues, looked upon the country as divided along religious lines.[3] It was not the conflict between rich and poor but between Catholics and Protestants that preoccupied them, and for this reason the socialist appeal to class conflict did not move them, even though the great majority of them belonged to the lower and most unprotected section of the population.

In addition to these local factors, there was the anti-socialist propaganda of the Church. Pius XI's encyclical *Quadragesimo anno* (1931), we recall, had just condemned socialism in all its forms, revolutionary and democratic, and insisted that believing Catholics could not be socialists nor support socialist parties. This anti-socialism was mediated through Sunday preaching and the Catholic press. Thus we read in the *Prairie Messenger* (21 January 1931) that the economic crisis in the province would not be improved by any policy "that savours of the methods employed in Russia, be that system called socialism, collectivism, communism or nationalization of the basic means of production." The paper argued here against the United Farmers of Canada, especially the

Saskatchewan section, which at that time advocated public ownership of the major productive forces. This anti-socialist stance was taken up, we recall, by the declaration of the Canadian bishops in 1933, after the foundation of the CCF at Calgary. It was later confirmed by a special pastoral letter of the Saskatchewan bishops in 1934, just prior to an important election in that province.[4]

"We do not hesitate to sound a note of warning," the Saskatchewan bishops said, "against all prophets of a new social order whose principles differ in any essential point from those upon which alone the Christian world-order can securely rest."[5] Following Pope Pius XI, the bishops held that the Depression was much more than an economic crisis — it was a moral crisis, caused by the greed, materialism and human selfish passion that had come to rule society. Because of these vices we had at that time the abuses of capitalism. The bishops demanded social reform, but they quoted in full Pius XI's insistence that one could not be a good Catholic and a true socialist at the same time and that religious socialism was a contradiction in terms. In this context, the Saskatchewan bishops repeated the warning uttered before by the Canadian hierarchy, which set the Catholic people on guard against the new parties that offered socialist solutions to the economic chaos. The pastoral letter was understood by people as a warning against the CCF, even though the party was not mentioned by name. The vagueness of the letter enabled Archbishop McGuigan to assert that the Catholic church had not interfered in provincial politics.

Such an assurance was made necessary a few months later. When two young students at Notre Dame College at Wilcox, Saskatchewan, joined the CCF young people's club in the town, the head of the college, Father Athol Murray, a vehement and outspoken opponent of the CCF, demanded that the students either withdraw from the club or leave the college altogether.[6] The incident became publicly known. Despite the increasing number of incidents in which Catholic clergy used their power to oppose the CCF, the party refused to look upon the Catholic church as an enemy. They hoped that eventually Catholics would vote for them. M.J. Coldwell wrote a letter to Archbishop McGuigan pleading with him not to interfere in provincial politics, to which the archbishop replied that "as head of the Catholic church in this province [he was] indeed anxious to keep the church independent of and outside all political parties.... [He was] determined not to be drawn into the political field."[7]

The bishops were not the only Catholic voices in Saskatchewan. It is instructive to follow the changes in policy of the *Prairie Messenger*. Prior to the foundation of the CCF, the *Prairie Messenger* engaged in anti-socialist propaganda and remained largely indifferent to social issues. It criticized the socialist influence among the farmers and later the farmer/labour group, and defended the view that the present world crisis was primarily a spiritual one.[8] After the encyclical *Quadragesimo anno*, the *Prairie Messenger* borrowed strong anti-socialist language from Catholic social thinkers in the United States.[9] When the CCF was founded in Saskatchewan, the paper warned the Catholic readers against it. While the *Prairie Messenger* acknowledged that the CCF did not favour violence, it regarded the new party with suspicion because it advocated extreme changes in society and endorsed Marxist principles.[10] The *Prairie Messenger* at that time, following Pius XI, regarded communism as "the natural offspring" of socialism.

At the same time the *Prairie Messenger* printed the speeches made by Henri Bourassa in the Commons. In these speeches, we recall, the French-Canadian politician complained that men opposed to social justice find it convenient to accuse the CCF of communism. He himself saw much good in the CCF. The new party had promoted many policies that corresponded to Catholic social teaching; it should by no means have been condemned, for it rendered an important service to the country. What Bourassa wanted to see was more stress on cooperation and less on class conflict. In two editorials, "Mr. Bourassa and the CCF" and "Our Stand in Politics," the *Prairie Messenger* slowly developed its own approach to Canadian socialism.[11]

The paper claimed that it was not identified with any one party in Canada and that it promoted Catholic social teaching, which it understood as a call to radical change, and which provided the norms for evaluating the programmes of all political parties, including that of the CCF. Hence to the extent that the CCF mitigated its stress on class conflict and the abolition of private perty, it became more acceptable to Catholics and had the sympathy of the *Prairie Messenger*. "A radical change, not palliatives, will have to come," argued the paper. Any party that followed the social teaching of Pius XI had the support of the *Prairie Messenger*. This policy, however, was not consistently carried through. Again and again, as in an article on Coldwell, leader of the farmer/labour group, the *Prairie Messenger* repeated that no Catholic could support socialist principles.[12] The *Prairie Messenger* reported the CCF's first national convention, held at Regina in 1933, and reprinted the manifesto without comment.[13] In the editorial "The CCF Teaches a Lesson," the paper expressed admiration for many of the social policies of the new party and acknowledged the intelligence of its leading personalities and its universally accepted commitment to British constitutionalism.[14] The CCF was in no way inspired by Russian communism. "We believe it is wrong to call the CCF red." "Many good citizens," the editorial went on, "some of our friends, belong to it." At this point, the editorial continued with less than consistency: the *Prairie Messenger* could not endorse the CCF because it was socialist and attacked not only the abuses of capitalism but the system itself. This, the newspaper believed, went beyond Catholic teaching. At the same time, the manifesto struck a sympathetic chord.

The *Prairie Messenger* was not able to maintain its open though slightly inconsistent stance toward Canadian socialism. The Canadian bishops and, a little later, the bishops of Saskatchewan uttered the warnings discussed above that Catholics should not fall prey to the false promises made by new political parties. In Quebec, Archbishop Gauthier condemned the CCF by name. In this situation the *Prairie Messenger* no longer expressed its sympathies. Yet the editors kept on making social issues the primary focus of the entire paper. The *Prairie Messenger* discussed the various reactions to the CCF throughout Canada, the negative ones from Quebec priests and bishops and the positive or neutral ones from other Catholics, such as the famous editorial of the Montreal *Beacon*[15] and the opinions of Henry Somerville. It recorded the positive verdict of the English Catholic bishops on British socialism[16] and reported at length Woodsworth's address at Humboldt.[17] The *Prairie Messenger* remained throughout in critical dialogue with the CCF, chiding it for being ambiguous in its land policy, its view of nationalization and its use of the word "socialism." When Ted Garland visited Humboldt, a largely Catholic community close to St. Peter's Abbey, where the *Prairie Messenger* was produced, the paper referred to his version of CCF policy as "the best application of the principles of the popes' encyclicals that has ever been undertaken by any political party we know of."[18] At the same time, the paper also noted that when Garland spoke to a largely Catholic audience, he denied being a socialist and claimed that no nationalization of land was intended, while when speaking at other places, he proudly regarded himself as a socialist and considered the public ownership of land as the logical outcome of the evolution toward socialism. In the Canadian context, the *Prairie Messenger* stood for an open approach. It never regarded the CCF as outlawed for Catholics, and it argued with the new party and suggested that Catholics might well wish to support it if certain ambiguities could be straightened out.

In its treatment of social issues, the *Prairie Messenger* often turned to Catholic social thinkers from the United States. In a previous chapter we have alluded to the confusion created among Canadian Catholics when they tried to apply the social teaching of American Catholic activists. While the Americans favoured the introduction of government legislation to protect farmers and workers, break the power of trusts and monopolies, and introduce insurance schemes of various kinds, they saw themselves fighting the abuses of capitalism. Even the more radical Catholics never thought of themselves as socialists. While there was a radical tradition in the United States, Catholics tended to stay away from it.[19] It appeared un-American to them. The radical populists in the United States, anticipating the farmers' movement in Saskatchewan, repudiated the capitalist system, but Catholics did not feel confident enough as Americans to join them. Reform Catholics in America supported the Democratic party. Yet when their books and articles were read by Catholics in Canada they caused confusion.[20] Since the American authors never referred to socialist movements or a labour party as possible options for concerned Catholics, the Canadian reader could easily get the impression that the British-style socialism of the CCF was simply out of bounds for Catholics.

The *Prairie Messenger* gave much space to reform-minded American Catholics. The editor of the reactionary Catholic weekly *Le patriote de l'ouest,* published in Saskatchewan, even wrote to the well-known Catholic social critic Father John Ryan, of Catholic University in Washington, D.C., whom Woodsworth had quoted in his celebrated speech in the Commons, and submitted to him for evaluation documents produced by the Saskatchewan farmer/labour group. Without knowing anything of the Canadian context and the trend and spirit of Canadian socialism, Ryan replied in highly doctrinaire fashion. "Obviously the programme is socialist," he wrote, "with one important modification, namely, the agricultural industry would be carried on by individual owners. Of course, I do not believe in socialism, even with this qualification, and it seems to be in contradiction with what the present Holy Father had to say about socialism in his encyclical *Quadragesimo anno.*"[21] This letter, first printed in *Le patriote,* was published in the *Prairie Messenger* and eventually made the rounds among the Catholic weeklies of Canada.

In his study of the Catholic reaction to the new politics in Saskatchewan, George Hoffman distinguishes three different attitudes.[22] There was first of all the negative view of those Catholics, probably at first the great majority, who regarded the CCF as irreconcilable with Catholic faith. The bishops were understood by many to have adopted this view. In an extreme form, this view was promoted by *Le patriote de l'ouest,* which waged a holy war against Canadian socialism. "On the whole the CCF is pure socialism," we read in one of its editorials. "Woodsworth and his professors have simply learnt from the doctrinaire socialism of Europe, which in turn sought inspiration from the old Jew, Karl Marx, the father of collectivism."[23] For the great number of Catholics the CCF was not to be considered seriously in terms of its relative merits and faults.

The second group mentioned by Hoffman were Catholics whose attitude to the CCF was open and critical. They were willing to listen to the new party; they voiced their criticism on issues where the CCF seemed to go beyond what to them seemed the good measure, but wanted to remain in conversation with it. This approach was represented by the *Prairie Messenger.* It is hard to know how much support this open attitude had among the Catholics.

Finally there was, even from the beginning, a small band of

Catholics who supported the CCF. Hoffman mentions several Catholic farmers who assumed some responsibility in the far- mers' organization and later in the new political party. In the early Thirties, Hector Roberge was the chief spokesman for Catholics who supported the CCF. He argued, as all Catholic supporters of the party have argued after him, that there was a basic congruity between the CCF programme and Catholic social teaching. "After a close study of the papal encyclicals and Father Ryan's book," he wrote, "I am convinced that the Catholic church does condemn socialism, but not the socialism of the Farmer- Labour party."[24] Roberge defended the CCF in the Catholic press and criticized the Quebec bishops, especially Archbishop Gau- thier, for their negative response. (However, in the late Thirties Roberge lost the confidence of his supporters, for unrelated reasons.)

Hoffman mentions several other Catholics in the third cate- gory: Frank Kellerman, a Catholic from Dana, who defended the CCF in the press; W.J. Boyle, who played a leading role in the farmer/labour parties in the early Thirties and who later, in the Forties, represented the Kinisino riding in the Saskatchewan legislature; Joseph Burton, who gained the Farmer-Labour nomi- nation in the Humboldt riding for the 1934 provincial election and was elected to the provincial legislature in a by-election of 1938; Ed Loehr, a Catholic who acted as Joe Burton's campaign manager in 1934; and Ted Garland, the Catholic Progressive MP from Alberta who campaigned in Saskatchewan, especially in ridings that had a large Catholic population.

The Catholic supporters of the CCF were an embattled minor- ity. They were made to feel that they were disloyal to the Catho- lic community and had adopted viewpoints considered suspect by the Catholic hierarchy. Even in the later Thirties and early Forties, when the CCF had modified its radical stance and adopt- ed the policies of social-democratic parties that aspired to be elected and form the government, and when the number of Catholic CCF supporters had greatly increased, there remained surrounding the CCF a certain religious taboo, which obliged the Catholics in the CCF to defend themselves. The *Prairie Messenger*, with its open approach, offered some support to these Catholics. The weekly showed interest in the social policies and political developments of the CCF and gave visibility to speeches made by party supporters that tried to show the Christian inspiration of Canadian socialism. Many of the Catholic CCFers had trouble in their parishes, where they were regarded as black sheep. In many instances this led to a certain bitterness. They began to relate themselves to the Church in a more remote way. Other Catholics did not want to give in to bitterness. They adopted the view that the CCF was the party that most adequately embodied Catholic social teaching and that consequently no one had the right to call them bad or disloyal Catholics.

Joseph Burton, a Catholic farmer from Humboldt who until the Depression had been identified with the Liberal party, became involved in the United Farmers and later in the farmer/labour group. He was a respected member of the Catholic community, a grand knight of the Knights of Columbus, in fact, and a state warden for Saskatchewan.[25] In 1938 he was elected as the CCF representative of Humboldt to the Saskatchewan legislature, where he remained until 1943. From 1943 to 1948 he was CCF Member of Parliament in Ottawa, and from 1952 to 1956 a member of the Saskatchewan legislature again, and in the cabinet. Throughout these years, but especially in the Thirties and Forties, Joe Burton had to defend himself against accusations of various kinds. In the legislature, he was taunted with the charge that as a Catholic he could not possibly be an authentic member of the socialist party, for everyone knew that no one could be a faithful Catholic and a true socialist at the same time.[26] Burton brought the papal encyclicals to Parliament, and by reading from them he showed that Catholic social teaching had repudiated modern capitalism, recommended the regulating influence of government on the economy and even allowed for nationalization under conditions of special need. He used the same arguments against Catholic critics who doubted his loyalty to the Church. He tried to show that the CCF more than any other party in Canada embodied Catholic social teaching. He dealt especially with the sore points, in particular with the question of private property and bureaucratic centralization, and emphasized in CCF policy those elements that favoured participation and cooperation on many levels and recommended various forms of public ownership.

For many Protestants in Saskatchewan, the Bible itself called people to become engaged in changing the social order. The Social Gospel, while not influential at the leadership level of the denominations, had considerable impact on the Protestant population. There was no equivalent Catholic movement at the time. Still, Joe Burton believed that the religious energies summoned forth by the biblical message could be made available to the social struggle. He was quite prepared to offer theological arguments. In an Easter broadcast in 1943, he offered several biblical arguments in favour of social involvement and argued against the use of the Bible in the defence of the status quo.[27]

While his treatment was brief, its content would have done honour to any theologian. Burton mentioned first that in the Old Testament the worship of God was inseparably linked to a social ethic that protected justice for the people — a social ethic, he added, that was not abrogated or mitigated by the coming of the new covenant. Secondly, Jesus Christ identified himself with the underprivileged, struggled against those in power who laid heavy burdens on the ordinary people and symbolized his social attitude by purging the temple precincts of the money-changers. Finally, Burton spoke of the biblical understanding of man's unity as body and soul. Because of the inseparable unity of body and soul, the Christian understanding of divine salvation could not refer to a purely spiritual process, but must have included the transformation of man's social existence. To serve the cause of salvation, then, had significant political consequences.

What are we to do with some of the embarrassing texts of the Scriptures? What about the saying of Jesus, "The poor you will always have with you"? What about the New Testament passages that praise poverty? What about the quotations that recommend patience, long-suffering and meekness? Burton denounced the ideological uses that had been made of these passages. Well-situated Christians easily reconcile themselves with present injustices and defend the status quo with biblical texts, according to which divine Providence has appointed some to wealth and others to poverty. They say that God attaches to poverty special spiritual blessings. What these passages mean in their context must be studied in each case, but the whole tenor of the Scriptures convinced Burton that God did not want his people to be poor, under-nourished, insecure, unemployed and estranged from society, with no access to the good things of life. While Christianity was vulnerable to ideological misuse, Burton believed, in line with the Protestant Social Gospel, that the Bible summoned people to commit themselves to social justice. In his public addresses and letters, Burton defended the view that the present economic system was at odds with Christianity.[28] He appealed to the Christian tradition not as a support for the inherited competitive order, but on the contrary for the reconstruction of this order in terms of cooperation, joint planning and fraternal community.

In this context it is appropriate to mention Ted Garland, a progressive politician from Alberta, who helped build up the farmer/labour group and later the CCF in Saskatchewan, especially in ridings with a strong Catholic population. Garland was a Catholic; he was born in Dublin, Ireland, in 1885, came to Canada in 1909 and eventually settled down to farming in Alberta in 1916.[29] In the years 1919-21, when the United Farmers of Alberta (UFA) were preparing to go into politics, Ted Garland took an active part in the movement. He was elected a member of the UFA executive and later, in 1921, a UFA member to the House of Commons, a position he retained for 14 years. In the House he became part of the ginger group of radical MPs who gathered around J.S. Woodsworth. He was an active participant in the founding of the CCF at Calgary in 1932, and at Regina in 1933. After his defeat in 1935, which he shared with the other members of the UFA, he was made national organizer of the CCF, a position he held until 1939.

In those early days, a Catholic who became a leader in the CCF was in an awkward position. If he wanted to remain an active member of his church, he had to argue that his political position was in keeping with Catholic social teaching. This is what Joe Burton did, and this is what Ted Garland chose to do. No one has yet collected and studied his speeches, articles and letters to get a complete picture of his political and theological positions. The few letters to which I had access revealed Garland as a Catholic activist who argued that Canadian socialism was in perfect accord with Catholic teaching and in fact a singular expression of Christianity.

In a long letter written in December 1934, Garland analyzed the three reasons why the Catholic church had condemned socialism and argued that none of these reasons applied to the CCF.[30] He offered policy statements made by radical farmers' groups and CCF conventions, supporting the family farm and hence the private ownership of land by the working farmer, as proof that the CCF did not intend to abolish all private property. To refute the second argument, he produced documentation that the CCF respected religion and in fact promised to do what no Canadian party had done until then: to defend the rights of ethnic and religious minorities and assure their religious liberty. Finally he argued that the CCF was committed to radical social change through parliamentary means, and that it had no connection whatever with the Communist party.

Of special interest in this letter was a theological argumentation, probably drawn from English Catholic journals, that showed that according to the ancient Catholic tradition, the goods of the earth were for all people, not only for those with money, and that the wealthy who distributed some of their goods to the deprived in fact surrendered what belonged to the poor by right. In this perspective, personal wealth was understood as a social reality. Private property was a privilege to which certain duties were attached, namely, to distribute the goods owned in superfluity for the sustenance of the poor. The Catholic tradition, Garland argued, was most sympathetic to the socialist vision. The people who did not want the present system to change disguised traditional Church teaching and accused as subversive and communist all critical social thought of the present.

Garland's letter presented the outline of a systematic defence, even though he was not in a position to expand the outline to a full-length study. I mentioned before that there was no Catholic intellectual at that time ready to defend the CCF; the only person who seemed to be studying the problem was Madelaine Sheridan, to whom Garland referred, one of the Catholics who took an active part in the CCF in Montreal and who made it her special task to collect Christian and Catholic texts advocating a socialist vision of society.

Throughout his career in the CCF, Ted Garland remained the official defender of the party against unjust Catholic accusations.

When J.S. Woodsworth argued with the Quebec hierarchy, he mentioned Garland as one of his colleagues and friends — identified with Canadian socialism, yet a faithful, practising Catholic.[31] When Cardinal Villeneuve, in November 1938, made another public statement renewing the Church's condemnation of the CCF, Garland wrote a letter of complaint to the apostolic delegate at Ottawa, in which he accused Cardinal Villeneuve of being unjust, of making unscrupulous use of CCF texts and of drawing the Church into the arena of party politics against the best Canadian tradition.[32] Garland asked that his letter of complaint be sent to the competent authorities in Rome and that the Catholic church in Canada set up a committee to study CCF policy in an impartial manner. Garland's letter was written firmly, but with the respect of a believing Catholic.

What response did Catholic voters give to the CCF in Saskatchewan in 1934? According to Hoffman's research, Catholics on the whole remained faithful to the Liberal party, even though a significant number did vote for the CCF, especially Catholics of Eastern European origin.[33] In the subsequent provincial elections of 1938 and 1944, the latter one a victory for the CCF, the Catholic support greatly increased.[34] According to one estimate, half the Catholics in the province voted CCF in 1944. Still, despite the bishops' declaration of 1943 and the shifting voting pattern, the CCF retained a certain stigma in the eyes of the faithful, churchgoing Catholics.

Father Eugene Cullinane

In the mid-Forties a Catholic priest and member of the Basilian Fathers, Eugene Cullinane, became a member of the CCF in Saskatchewan. He identified himself with the cause of Canadian socialism and defended the view that the CCF was more faithful to Catholic social teaching than any other political party in Canada.[35] This was a singular event. Catholic priests did not join political parties in Canada at that time. But since Cullinane felt that the Catholic church in Saskatchewan had identified itself, at least in an unofficial way, with the Liberal party, he decided to join the CCF publicly to show Catholics that they were free to choose a political party in accordance with their own perceptions of justice.

Father Cullinane soon became a public figure in Saskatchewan. For many Catholics who had supported the CCF over the years and found themselves looked upon as black sheep by their parishes and parish priests, Cullinane's public action was a source of joy and consolation. They were grateful to him. Other Catholics in Saskatchewan were distributed by the action of this priest. They complained to Philip Pocock, bishop of Saskatoon, in whose diocese Cullinane was active. They claimed to be scandalized at seeing a priest in politics, supporting a party and a philosophy about which the Church had so many misgivings. Responding to these outcries, the bishop of Saskatoon intervened: he forbade priests to get involved in politics. "We regret," the bishop wrote in a decree of 1948, "that it has become necessary to legislate that political activity of a partisan nature is strictly forbidden to all priests residing in the diocese of Saskatoon. Violations of this law will bring ecclesiastical penalties. This prohibition includes membership in any political party, active participation in political conventions, and speaking or writing in support of a political party . . . ." Cullinane, a man of obedience, intended to follow the new ruling, but when a letter he had written prior to the decree was published in a CCF paper, the bishop of Saskatoon ordered him to leave the diocese.

Who was Father Cullinane and what were his views? Eugene Cullinane was born in Michigan. He came to Canada as a young man to study at Assumption College in Windsor, where he eventually received his BA in 1928 and his MA in philosophy in 1931. The Depression touched his life profoundly. His own family was greatly affected by the economic disaster, and since his father had already died, it was his task as the oldest son to assume a position of responsibility. At that time he learned that there was something radically wrong with the current economic system. He was influenced by the labour priests in the United States who demanded social justice and the transformation of the existing order in the name of Church teaching.

In 1932, Eugene Cullinane entered the novitiate of the Basilian Fathers in Toronto; he remained in that city to pursue his theological studies until 1936. There he associated with various groups of people moved by the present misery and committed to radical social change. He was greatly impressed by the presence of Protestant ministers among the activists, and regretted the absence of Catholic priests. Yet some Catholics were moved by the social question and responded vigorously to the unjust system. Cullinane was particularly impressed by the teaching and the social witness of the great French thinker Jacques Maritain, who came to Toronto in those years. It seemed to him that Maritain's call for a new humanism provided a perception of the Christian message that directed the energies generated by genuine piety toward the struggle for social justice and the rebuilding of society. He thought Maritain was opposed to the free flow of economic competition, criticized the present capitalist order and advocated a more rational planning of production and distribution in accordance with the needs of the community. Later on in the Thirties, he saw Maritain exhibiting the extraordinary courage of supporting the Republican side in the Spanish civil war, while the body of Catholic opinion was wholly identified with Franco's cause.

At that time, Cullinane also met Catherine de Hueck, a charismatic woman of aristocratic background, a refugee from revolutionary Russia, who had committed herself to an apostolate of love and social witness, similar to the Catholic Worker movement developed by Dorothy Day and her friends in New York City. This movement created friendship houses in various cities of North America to help people in need and to initiate them into a new philosophy. This Christian philosophy, based on fraternal love, included a radical critique of the contemporary economic system. It denounced all large institutions because they acted in accordance with their own needs and the rules implicit in their organization, and not in accordance with the needs of ordinary people. The movement regarded the world as sinful and dehumanizing. What was needed was a new spirit of cooperation and simplicity accompanied by a firm, non-violent resistance against the powerful.

The Christian philosophy presented by Catherine de Hueck and Dorothy Day did not favour socialism. Socialism was also based on large organizations and thus could not be trusted. What was needed, in their eyes, was the multiplication of small self-help groups that would initiate people into a new spiritual style, enable them to produce for themselves the necessities of life and provide a pattern of cooperative living that eventually might be followed by society as a whole. Catherine de Hueck had witnessed in the Soviet Union the overwhelming power of a centralized government, and Dorothy Day, at one time a member of the Communist party in the United States, had turned away from large organizations as solutions of the social problem. The new Christian philosophy they developed was more in line with communitarian anarchism. It was a Catholic anarchism that despised the major economic and political institutions and sought the reconstruction of humanity through small groups, whose operation embodied a new logic of love and simplicity. To follow this road meant the pursuit of the life of poverty. The friendship houses lived from day to day, often begging for help, in the hope of feeding the unemployed and the destitute who visited them. In Toronto, Catherine de Hueck organized weekly meetings, under the title of Social Forum, in which socially concerned Catholics came together to express their disapproval of the present system and their hope in the regenerative power of a new, radical ethic. Maritain himself often attended these meetings. It was through these associations that Eugene Cullinane acquired a profound, religiously based social commitment.

After his ordination in 1936, Eugene Cullinane went to the Catholic University in Washington, D.C., to study sociology under professors who were regarded as leading critical thinkers within American Catholicism, especially Francis Haas and Paul Furfey. In his studies of sociology, he developed his own social ideals. He was greatly influenced by one of his professors, Goetz Briefs, a refugee from Hitler's Germany, a former member of the Catholic Centre party who was the author of a then widely read book, *Proletariat: A Challenge to Western Civilization*. Cullinane decided to write his doctoral dissertation on the CCF in Canada. In 1939, after finishing his course requirements at the university, Cullinane was sent to teach at St. Thomas College in Saskatoon, and was thus unable to work on his dissertation. When the war broke out, he became a chaplain in the Canadian Air Force. Immediately after the war, thanks to a gratuity from the Air Force, he began the research on his dissertation. For eight months he travelled across Canada to study the origin and the subsequent development of the CCF. Unfortunately he never had the time to write his thesis; he returned to St. Thomas College as professor of sociology and political science. Yet the outline of his thesis and the brief summary of his project that he submitted to Catholic University revealed that Cullinane had a profound knowledge of the CCF, and that his work would have been a major contribution to political theory in Canada from a Catholic socialist perspective.

Since Cullinane's thesis proposal was such a revealing document, I wish to discuss several of its more important points. Part I of the thesis was intended to deal with the socio-economic origins of the CCF: this was to include a study of the Canadian proletariat, and the regional character of this proletariat in the Maritimes, Quebec, Ontario, the prairies and British Columbia. By proletariat Cullinane seems to have meant the little people, the exploited people, who were dependent for their economic survival on the big system and threatened with being devoured by it.

Summarizing his findings, he made these remarks about the radical wing of the CCF in British Columbia:

> The British Columbia Section of the CCF has a Marxist background, and many confirmed Marxists of the old Socialist Party of Canada are to be found in its ranks. I have interviewed a number of them. I spent three hours with the "terrible" Mr. Harold Winch. He is not nearly so terrible as the daily press has made him out to be. He is not even so terrible as many CCF Easterners conceive him. Like all these Marxists out here, he has inherited, through Marx, much of that secularized Christian idealism which, if non-Christian, or even anti-Christian in its theology, is still powerfully Christian in its social ideology. Harold Winch was born into a Marxist home. Through the Depression he fought a heroic battle against overwhelming odds in defense of suffering and persecuted humanity. He himself has suffered much from the times. He is an admirable humanist, as fine and true as any I have seen on the temporal level — unenlivened, I mean, by the flame of the Spirit of Love. And, for all I know, it may be that very flame which raised him to such noble stature in the ranks of Canadian humanists. He is fighting in essentially the same cause and motivated by essentially the same idealism which impelled so many fine young Canadians I know to give up their life in the skies over Germany.

"We believe," he said to me with sincerity, "that we are going to give Christianity a chance to work." When and if Canadian history is properly written, Harold Winch will be numbered amongst those who have won the distinction of being a truly great Canadian.

Even here in this hotbed of Marxist Socialism, the CCF does not conform to that brand of "Socialism" condemned by Leo XIII and Pius XI. The Marxism has been tempered and modified by the influx of the movement of the Social Reconstruction Party, the Co-operatives, non-Marxist farmers, trade unionists, etc. They do not deny the right to private property: on the contrary they aim to eradicate those forces which, under Capitalism, have undermined and trampled upon that very right. They do not advocate the overthrow of the existing order by violence or force. They are democrats to the core and, from the very beginning, have engaged in a pitched battle with Communists on this fundamental point. And so far as the materialistic conception of society is concerned, they cannot even qualify as "Socialists" here. In fact, they are in spirit and truth much closer to the ideal of a Christian Social Reform party than anything Canada has yet produced.

The thesis proposal then reported on the Catholic reaction to the CCF. This is how Cullinane summarized his experience:

The mentality of most Catholics I have met across Canada, including the clergy, is infected with a terribly distorted view of the CCF *reality*. The result is that Catholics generally are afflicted with a deep-rooted, though unconscious, prejudice against the CCF. It is virtually identical with the kind of prejudice against Catholics found in the typical Ontario Protestant of twenty years ago. Catholics by and large condemn the CCF for something it is not; they are enslaved by the tyranny of a single word — "socialism." If I may generalize on the fairly large sample I have interviewed across the continent, then the overwhelming majority of Catholics are unconsciously banded together in a compact political unity based on an illusion (I suspect that this is not true of Nova Scotia due mainly to the enlightened leadership given the people by the priests of St. F.X.) [St. Francis Xavier University in Antigonish]. The result is that Catholics tend to fall into a mould of political and economic thought quite out of line with that of the encyclicals. Enslaved mentally by the tyranny of that awful word, they are virtually forced to devour with great avidity all the "anti-socialist" propaganda dispensed so generously and freely by the forces of reaction. And we come to the sad and tragic paradox where we find that Canadian Catholics, by and large, have divorced themselves from those constructive and creative forces about which Maritain has written so well, and which are the only hope we have of winning the peace. Outside of Joe Burton of Humboldt there is not a single Catholic in a place of influence or leadership in the Saskatchewan and British Columbia CCF movement. With rare exceptions the same is true all across Canada.

In part II of the proposed thesis, Cullinane searched for the key concepts by which to understand and account for the development of the CCF movement. He thought the two key concepts were "proletariat" and "humanism." The oppression to which the ordinary people of Canada were being exposed by a system that was intrinsically unjust gave rise to a counter-movement, a revolt, that was nourished and guided by a particular kind of humanism. There was first the self-interest of the proletariat seeking to better its economic condition: that gave rise to a revolt against monopolistic capitalism. Then there was an ethical element in the new movement, strongly connected with Christian faith, which led a revolt against the capitalist spirit of competition and individualism. And finally there was an attachment to British democracy that gave the movement an element of protest against all forms of totalitarianism. From the brief outline, it appeared that Cullinane understood the CCF as an original kind of socialism, a movement of protest carried forward by the exploited classes, based on a humanistic vision of society combining both Christian cooperative and British democratic elements. In this context it is worth recalling that for Max Weber, a movement of radical social change could be successful only if it was carried by a threefold motivation: by the self-interest of the participants (zweckrational), by a new set of values at odds with the dominant ethos (wertrational) and by strong emotional factors.[36] These three motivations were in fact described by Cullinane. The exploited people opposed monopoly capitalism for the sake of greater economic equality, they rejected the spirit of capitalism on the strength of a cooperative vision of society, and they stood against any form of state capitalism or bureaucratic centralism from an emotional commitment to the British democratic tradition.

In his thesis proposal, Cullinane argued against Friedrich Hayek's *The Road to Serfdom*, a successful book at the time, which presented a scholarly argument, persuasively written, against any form of social planning on the part of governments. Hayek argued that in Europe all programmes of social planning, whether inspired by socialism or fascism, contradicted the genius of free enterprise and ultimately led to the destruction of political freedom. This book, Cullinane told us, had been recommended to him by Catholic bishops and other highly placed persons in Canada as an argument against the CCF. The business community, he said, also cherished the book and publicized it widely. Cullinane thought that it was erroneous to make inferences from the European experience in regard to the future of Canadian socialism. In the first place, Hayek's thesis overlooked the fact that in the British tradition there existed a profound attachment to democracy, civil liberties and participation in decision-making that had no equivalent in most European countries. Secondly, Cullinane argued, the creation of the CCF took place at a point in Canadian history when people knew of the authoritarian socialism of Russia; and after the Second World War they felt an even stronger horror of the totalitarianism against which they had been willing to fight. Canadian socialism, then, situated itself within a regular freedom movement. Cullinane spoke of a veritable "passion for democracy" found in all ranks of the CCF, including the Marxist radicals in British Columbia.

According to Cullinane's thesis proposal, part III was to deal with the inner conflicts in the CCF. Cullinane held that neither the philosophy nor the policy of the party had been fully worked out. There existed various trends and tendencies, often in conflict with one another, out of which the CCF gradually clarified its self-understanding. That was how it appeared to Cullinane in 1946, when he submitted the proposal to the university. He examined the conflict within the CCF between Christian humanism and Marxist materialism, between security of ownership and state dependency, between democracy and state capitalism, and between cooperative and collectivist enterprises. From the outline it appears that Cullinane concluded that these conflicting trends were resolved in the CCF in favour of a humanistic socialism. Unfortunately this thesis, which could have been so useful, was never written. After Cullinane's speedy exit from Saskatoon in 1948, the notes he left behind were misplaced and never found again.

Let me quote the passage of the thesis proposal that reported on Cullinane's discovery of the Protestant Social Gospel:

> It appears to me that, since the Reformation, the Protestant conscience (and with it the Protestant ethic) has followed a somewhat circular movement. Under the influence of Calvin it broke from its original Catholic moorings and gave a tremendous moral impetus to the development of the Capitalist spirit, as Weber, Tawney and Fanfani have demonstrated so well. Under the influence of Wesley and the ever more apparent anti-Christian character of liberalism and capitalism, the Protestant conscience has gradually reversed its trend to the point where in our times it is in open revolt against liberalism and capitalism. Under the dynamic and inspiring leadership of J.S. Woodsworth, a Methodist minister who was a deeply religious man as well as an apostle of social justice and charity, the Protestant conscience in Canada is tending more and more to espouse Canadian "socialist" thought. This espousal is more in the nature of a spiritual marriage and, under the historical stimulus of the great depression, has given birth to that peculiarly Canadian and, I may say, purified "socialism" which is the ideology of the CCF.

Cullinane argued that the CCF was a socialist movement in keeping with Catholic social teaching, and in fact the one political party in Canada that sought to express a Christian vision of society. How did the CCF look upon the Catholic church? Here again Cullinane had interesting observations based on his extended research:

> CCF Humanism has inherited from Protestantism a latent hostility towards and a distrust of the Catholic Church. It has inherited from Marxism a pronounced hostility towards and dislike for the Catholic Church. This Marxist temperament is confined, in the main, to British Columbia — and to a relatively small section of the B.C. membership.
>
> Certain historico-temporal characteristics and policies of the Catholic Church tend to foster and intensify this prejudice. Keep in mind that the CCF movement is virtually a religious crusade to rescue the "man of common humanity" from the injustice and tyranny of "capitalism." Archbishop Gauthier condemned the

movement in 1934, and although the bishops of Canada in 1943 gave formal permission to Catholics to vote CCF, nevertheless the overwhelming majority of bishops and priests have remained hostile: they have used their clerical influence to keep Catholics from voting CCF. Not uncommonly a pastoral letter attacking "Socialism" has come out just before an election. Harold Winch told me that priests in B.C. time after time have actively participated in political campaigns to keep Catholics from voting CCF. A pastor here told me that the priests of the Archdiocese of Vancouver were ordered to preach against the CCF. The *B.C. Catholic* in previous years has refused to accept campaign advertising from the CCF, although it accepted and printed ads for the Liberal and Conservative parties: the same policy is being pursued in the current election. I have met several prominent men in the CCF who were defeated in elections by only a few votes: they are certain they would have been elected had it not been for the anti-CCF influence of the priests in their ridings. My own experience with the clergy proves that this open Catholic hostility exists, with a few notable exceptions, from Montreal to Vancouver. In the CCF mind this tends to identify the Church with the forces of exploitation and reaction. Marxists claim of course that the Church can't behave in any other way because it is the greatest property-owning corporation in the world and therefore an integral part of "Capitalism." They cite the wealth of the Quebec clergy and religious orders and the poverty of the Quebec people. In vivid contrast, and for the reason I have explained above, Protestant ministers have flocked to the support of the CCF and have helped fight its battles from the the beginning.

In the CCF Humanism there is a passion for democracy: it has the force of religious faith and conviction. But certain policies and sympathies of the historical Church tend to convince them that the Church is not only siding in with Big Business against the common people, but that she is, worst of all, fascistic in outlook and action. They cite the Vatican's sanction of Mussolini's conquest of Abyssinia, the Church's support of Franco in his revolt against the democratically elected people's government of Spain and the fascistic character of so many regimes in Catholic countries such as Portugal and the South American states. One CCF leader said to me the other night: "We may be misjudging Catholics, but it appears to me that the authoritarian character of the Church's doctrine makes it impossible for a real Catholic to be a real democrat."

In this situation Cullinane felt that what loyalty to the Catholic church demanded of him was to join the CCF in a public way. The Church stood for social justice. He also wanted to teach the Catholic people by example and make more visible the substance of Catholic social teaching. Since the Catholics in Saskatchewan presumed that the Church was backing the Liberal party and entertained suspicions in regard to the CCF, Cullinane felt that his public identification with the CCF would make Catholics take a new look at Canadian socialism and discover its affinity to Catholic social teaching.

In a letter written on 5 April 1948, Cullinane explained his reasons for joining the CCF to H.O. Hansen, a member of the Saskatchewan legislature. This letter was eventually published — at a time when the bishop of Saskatoon had just decreed that priests were not to get involved in party politics. As a result Cullinane had to leave the diocese. In the letter he provided theological arguments, against the common opinion in the Church at the time, for why a priest should take an active part in political life:

> Ordination to the priesthood does not disqualify or exempt us from the duties of democratic citizenship. If anything, it makes these responsibilities graver and more imperative. By the very nature of our calling, we are expected to lead the people to truth and virtuous living. The most effective way to do this — in fact, the only effective way — is by first setting a good example ourselves. The two great social virtues that it is our duty to teach are Justice and Charity. Included within these two great virtues are patriotism and love of country. I know of no other vocation or profession that makes such heavy demands upon us in this respect as does the priesthood. Not only as citizens, but as priests who are spiritual leaders of our flock, we are called upon to be model patriots and great lovers of our country and our people. In a democracy this means that we have to be model democrats (the word as here used has no connection with any political party). In our times there is no conceivable way of doing this without choosing one or other of the political parties, as conscience dictates, and giving it our whole-hearted support. This I have done.

The same letter provided arguments, with which we are by now familiar, for why Catholics are free to join the CCF. Cullinane emphasized the British heritage of Canadian socialism, recalled the difference between British socialism and the doctrinaire socialism of the Continent, cited at length statements made by the British Catholic hierarchy, defending the freedom of Catholics to join the Labour party even after the papal condemnation of socialism, and finally invoked the declaration made by the Canadian bishops in 1943, admitting in a general way the freedom of Catholics to support the CCF.

Then he gave the reasons why he had personally identified himself with the CCF. After a period of research lasting over eight months, during which he prepared his doctoral dissertation, he had come to conclusions regarding the origins, the public policies and the implicit philosophy of the CCF that impelled him to join it. "When I came to know it, I joined it," he wrote. "I did this for the following reasons."

1. Because, in my opinion, the CCF program and outlook comes closer than that of any other Canadian political party to realizing the great moral, social, political and economic truths on which God intended human society to be based.
2. Because, in my opinion, the CCF program and outlook is more in keeping with the Christian and democratic tradition than that of any other party in Canada.
3. Because the CCF is the only democratic political party in Canada which seems to realize what economic science is now able to prove — that the capitalist system, as we know it, carries within itself the seeds of its own destruction, and is already either a thing of the past (as in Europe), or in the final stage of its decay (as in Canada and the USA).
4. Because, alone possessing this realization, the CCF alone has an alternative democratic economic system to offer the Canadian people.
5. Because, drawing its strength mainly from the workers of the cities and the farmers of the plains, the CCF along with the Canadian national parties, has the independence, the freedom, the will, and the power necessary to challenge the invisible government of money in our midst, and so restore to the Canadian people democratic control of their economic system, which has for too long a time been concentrated in the hands of a small and irresponsible aristocracy of wealth.
6. Because the purification of democracy and the expansion of freedom, which all men of good will hope for and long for, can come

about only as the result of a new vision and a new leadership, evidence of which, in my opinion, is nowhere to be found in Canada — at least not concentrated and organized for action — except in the CCF.

During the brief years of his involvement with the CCF, Father Cullinane was not able to complete a book on Catholic political thought. All he published was a single pamphlet, *The Catholic Church and Socialism*, which was first distributed in Saskatchewan, later reprinted in other parts of the country and frequently used by the CCF to persuade Catholics to support socialism in Canada. The pamphlet demonstrated that the CCF had been slandered. Very largely due to high-powered propaganda, people had been made to link Canadian socialism with the kind of socialism observable in Russia, and Catholics had looked upon it as a political movement condemned by papal teaching. In reality, Cullinane argued, there was a radical difference between "the old revolutionary socialism" found in Russia and "the new democratic socialism" of the CCF. Distinguishing between the two, he actually proposed an original argument of considerable theoretical interest.

First of all, Cullinane described capitalist society as the work of the owners of productive property. They make profit and greed the law of economic activity. The system creates a class of workers, men obliged to work under inhuman conditions, threatened by insecurity, poverty and often hunger. The capitalist world is heartless. The owners of capital are able to dominate the government and use democracy as an instrument to promote their own interests. While they use the language of democracy and participation, they are actually the sole rulers of society. They look upon life in purely economic terms. They are men of empty heart, who make money their great divinity. Even if some of them occasionally go to church, their system is basically opposed to Christianity. Sometimes capitalists succeed in turning Christianity into a religion that protects their economic power. Pushing vast numbers of property-less people into poverty and often destitution and hunger, capitalism violates a basic element of justice, known from antiquity, namely, that man needs bread.

This capitalist system, Cullinane argued, had generated a revolt on the part of the workers, now that they had discovered strength in solidarity. "The builders of capitalism," he wrote, "were also, whether they knew it or not, the builders of communism." Communism is the violent reaction on the part of the workers to the greed of the owners. But since the workers have been wholly determined by capitalism, their violent reaction against the system tragically perpetuates the essential characteristics of the system. Communists think they can get out of the trap of capitalism, but since they are simply in reaction against capitalism, communism defines itself in the identical inhuman terms. Man is understood in economic categories. The heart remains empty. What inspires the workers is the desire to conquer the rulers and take their place. In particular, Cullinane showed that the individualistic concept of property, characteristic of capitalism, is reversed by communism into its opposite, the denial of private property and the surrender of all productive goods to the state. But this inversion of the old order does not give people access to the products of their labour, nor a share in the decisions regarding economic life. Since democracy has become the tool of the ruling class, communism inverts the democratic order and installs the dictatorship of the proletariat, thus continuing the principle of domination in society. And since religion has been associated with the ruling classes, communists simply suppress religion as the great illusion, thereby leaving the people as empty, economically oriented and insensitive to the spirit as they were in capitalism, when they were defined solely in terms of their productive power. The inversion of society favoured by communists does not correct the faults of capitalism, it simply prolongs them in a new key under a new system of domination. While an understandable reaction against the inherited order, communism remains just as inhuman a system, violating human nature and basically un-Christian, as was capitalism.

The socialism of the CCF, on the other hand, in line with other forms of humanistic socialism, was a reaction against the capitalist system that had introduced principles not derived from capitalism to correct its own basic errors. These principles, derived from Christian humanism, prevented socialism from simply assimilating the characteristics of the system it sought to replace. These principles included a profound appreciation of the human person, beyond its economic function; they also included norms of justice, freedom and cooperation not associated with capitalism, but derived from the Western democratic and libertarian tradition. For this reason, then, Cullinane argued, Canadian socialism negated the principle of private property not by advocating its direct opposite, state ownership, but by introducing a new concept of property, more in keeping with pre-capitalist tradition, that foresaw ownership on various levels of society, including some personal ownership — the use of which, however, would be determined by representatives of the people and accountable to them. Similarly, Canadian socialism negated the dictatorship of the capitalist class not by introducing the dictatorship of workers, but by affirming the democratic process, severed from its link with the former rulers, which would enable the people on all levels to cooperate in the creation of a just society. And finally Canadian socialism negated the false Christianity that served as a protection for the old order not by introducing atheism, but by seeking access to the original Gospel values that saved people from the emptiness of heart and the preoccupation with purely economic things, characteristic of capitalism as well as communism.

Thanks to these corrective principles, derived from traditions that preceded capitalism, Canadian socialism, along with other humanistic socialisms, was wholly different from communism and did not fall under the condemnation of the Church. While communism tragically defined itself simply as the reaction against capitalism and thus left people in the basic human vices of capitalism, the new democratic socialism liberated people from the inhumanity of capitalism by wedding them to values that were part of their heritage, however disguised; thanks to these values they perceived human life and society in a new light. Such a humanistic socialism was at once a material and a spiritual project.

No Catholic in Canada picked up these reflections of Father Cullinane. He did not have the time to develop them himself at greater length. On 11 June 1948, the bishop of Saskatoon decreed that priests may not take an active part in political life nor recommend political parties in their writings. When Cullinane's letter to Hanson, written prior to this date, was published, the bishop asked the superior of the Basilian Fathers to withdraw Cullinane from the diocese. The superior himself had complained several times that Cullinane's activity had caused anxiety in the community of priests. Cullinane's answer to this was that in a situation such as the present one it was the absence of anxiety that worried him.

After a year of teaching at St. Michael's College in Toronto, Cullinane was sent to teach at Rochester, New York. He returned to Canada — to Windsor, to be precise — in 1952, and got in touch again with the labour and cooperative movements. But the spiritual life of this remarkable priest began to move him to follow an even more radical vocation than the one he had chosen. He turned to the radicalism of the Catholic Worker, represented in Canada by the community founded by Catherine de Hueck, which had established itself by that time in Combermere, Ontario. There Christian men and women lived out their judgment on capitalism in the spirit of voluntary poverty, simplicity and trust, identified with the helpless and disadvantaged in society. They worked with their hands and surrendered themselves to the God of love as the author of human liberation. Father Cullinane joined this community of human hope. He did this not by rejecting his former political views, but by recognizing in them a call to a hidden life. It is to this beautiful and humble man that this study is dedicated.

6
Economic Radicals in Quebec

In a previous chapter we have seen that the CCF was repudiated by the Catholic church in the province of Quebec and that it did not succeed in gaining ground among French-speaking Quebeckers. The CCF found support among workers and intellectuals in English-speaking Montreal, including some Catholics. Yet the reason why the CCF made such little headway in French-speaking Quebec was not only the opposition of the Church. The new party presented a British image, British and Protestant, to the Quebec population. The CCF was not sensitive to the French reality in Canada. The founders of the CCF, living in western Canada, looked upon Canada as a British dominion and turned for inspiration to British socialism. They welcomed the minorities living in Canada and opposed all forms of discrimination. But the CCF failed to appreciate that for French Canadians, Canada was not a British land; it was rather the union of two civilizations, British and French, and in fact an unequal union with the British wielding power over the French.

Even the CCFers in Montreal did not grasp the French-Canadian perspective. In 1934, when the French-speaking members of the CCF asked for the right to be in charge of their own French-speaking organization, the provincial office refused to grant the request, a decision that prompted these members to leave the party.[1] Anglophones remained in charge of the CCF. Even though in the Forties and Fifties the number of francophone members of the CCF increased greatly, including such well-known personalities as Thérèse Casgrain,[2] until the mid-Fifties the meetings of the CCF in Montreal were carried on in English. It occurred to no one that this was strange.

175

The CCF, moreover, envisaged a strong federal government. The efforts of Quebeckers to limit federal powers and enhance the power of the provincial government were looked upon as provincial narrowness. The CCF did not recognize that Quebeckers understood themselves as a people. We recall that this was the main objection raised against the CCF by Henri Bourassa, despite his sympathy for its economic goals and his willingness to defend the party against its detractors. The CCF did not recognize that Quebec had its own intellectual history, social traditions and political heritage, and that if a new movement was to be successful it had to be in dialogue with this tradition and draw some inspiration from it.

While the CCF was rejected in the province of Quebec, it did act as a catalyst, sparking a reaction of significant proportion. In chapter 3 we discussed the 1933 meeting of the thirteen ecclesiastics sponsored by the Ecole sociale populaire, which condemned the CCF and, as a response to it, began to elaborate a reform programme based on Catholic principles. The reform programme proposed by the Ecole was placed in the hands of a group of lay leaders and intellectuals, who produced a second reform programme. More concrete than the first, it was to become the platform of a new political party, Action libérale nationale (ALN), through which a group of economic radicals, for the brief period from 1934 to 1936, achieved great popular support and political power. Yet the party was soon to disappear. Since this radical economic policy was sparked by the CCF, of which it was in a sense a purified version, it deserves our attention in this study.

To understand the impact of the "journée des treize," we must relate it to the political orientation of the Ecole sociale populaire. In his masterful and somewhat mordant analysis of the social and cultural situation of Quebec during its encounter with industrialization, Pierre Trudeau showed that the Jesuits who had founded the Ecole in 1911 and continued to be in charge of it were inspired by a nationalist perspective, in the narrow sense of the word: they sought to protect the province from modernity, defended the right of private property, adopted a vehement anti-socialist position, stressed harmony between the economic classes and promoted the ideal of an agricultural Quebec.[3] The Ecole advocated Catholic labour organizations and eventually, in 1921, successfully promoted the creation of Catholic trade unions, at odds with the entire labour movement in North America, that would place the main emphasis on cooperation and the spiritual formation of the workers. A.J. Bélanger has shown that during the Depression the Ecole continued to interpret the problems of society largely in spiritual terms. When Pius XI's *Quadragesimo anno* came out in 1931, the Ecole paid next to no attention to it.[4] It was only after the foundation of the CCF and its first impact on the country, including Montreal, that the Jesuits opted for a more vigorous response to economic disaster and universal misery. The proceedings of "la journée des treize," published as a booklet in the monthly series of the Ecole, under the title *Pour la restauration sociale au Canada*, represents the most progressive teaching ever endorsed by the Ecole. The publication of the booklet was a singular event with great impact on public life.[5]

The booklet contained three papers. One of these, Father Lévesque's report on the CCF, we have examined in detail in chapter 3. A second paper, written by Esdras Minville, dealt with the abuses of capitalism.[6] It is a remarkable and somewhat puzzling document. The paper offered a detailed critique of contemporary capitalism. Minville quoted the anti-capitalist passages of Pius XI and lamented that capitalism had moved into a new phase, in which free enterprise had given way to economic dictatorship. But why had such a deterioration of capitalism taken place? Minville argued that there were presuppositions in the earliest forms of capitalism that eventually led to the final monopolistic phase. He wrote of the individualism and the exclusive emphasis on personal freedom in capitalistic culture, accompanied by an easy but illusory trust that the mechanism of the market would protect the well-being of society.

In his critique of contemporary capitalism, Minville went beyond papal teaching; he echoed rather the classical socialist critiques of capitalist economy. He pointed to three corrupting trends. First, work and eventually the worker himself were understood as commodities. Capitalism violated the humanity of the worker and misunderstood the nature of work. Secondly, capitalism led to the concentration of wealth in the hands of the few and hence created an unjust society, in which ever larger sections of the population were pushed into poverty. And finally, capitalism led to the anarchy of production and hence did not satisfy the basic needs of the people. Minville's treatment of the alienation of labour and the anarchy of production was taken not from Catholic teaching but from socialist literature. What is puzzling about this article is that after such a devastating critique of capitalism, the concluding paragraph insisted, in keeping with the Church's teaching, that there was nothing intrinsically wrong with capitalism. While the weight of the argument had been that the present state of monopoly capitalism was in some sense implicit in capitalist principles from the beginning, the last ten lines of the article assured the reader that capitalism could be made to work again if the law of the market were subordinated to principles of justice. The reader is so unprepared for the closing paragraph that one suspects Minville added the conclusion to satisfy the demands of orthodoxy.

But it was the third paper of the booklet, Father Louis Chagnon's presentation, that developed a positive plan for radical social change in Quebec and a thirteen-point programme that, in its developed form, was to become the platform for a new political party.[7] At the outset of his paper, Chagnon recognized that the immediate cause of the Depression was "the sins of capitalism": something had gone wrong with the system. Later, the author felt obliged to repeat with the majority of Catholic critics that the Depression revealed the moral crisis of Western civilization, man's turning away from God and the concentration on material development. In any case radical reform had now become necessary; there was no time to waste. What counted was to engage in political action to introduce reforms in the institutions of society that would guarantee a more just distribution of wealth, the protection of farmers and workers, and the subordination of the large corporations to the common good of society. The paper began by rejecting the false solutions of communism and socialism, but then explained this did not mean that all forms of nationalization were to be rejected. On the contrary, in the present crisis it was the task of government to direct the national economy, transfer to public ownership — national, provincial or municipal — the corporations that had acquired excessive power, and subject to the strictest rules the major financial institutions such as banks and insurance companies. Chagnon developed the anti-capitalist side of Catholic teaching. We read that capitalism was not to be condemned as such and that cooperation between capital and labour must be defended, but the "abuses of capitalism" must be fought vigorously, namely, the concentration of power in the hands of the few and the operation of industries for the profit of the owners. Along with Pius XI, Chagnon condemned the present system as economic dictatorship. The enemy was monopoly capitalism. The requested reforms, Chagnon argued, would provoke not revolution but evolution. What was needed was a "human capitalism," a capitalism with a human face, "subject to the Christian law of justice and charity, socially managed, and directed by government action and the organization of professionals."[8] In this manner, said Chagnon, capital would be enabled to exercise its social function, namely, to promote a more just distribution of wealth and resources.

The paper then outlined the reforms that had become necessary. Farmers and workers would have to be protected through new forms of association, insurance plans and generous labour legislation. New powers would have to be conceded to governments, even though the state was not to be the only agent operative in the planning of the economy. What would ultimately have to happen was that the people themselves, represented in professional organizations, would find their interests promoted through an economic council distinct from the state, which would share with the state the responsibility for planning the economy. We recall that the CCF also spoke of a national planning commission,[9] responsible for steering the economy, but in line with the Fabian tradition this commission was to be made up of highly trained and dedicated civil servants, accountable to the elected government.

Chagnon's recommendation of an economic council fitted into the corporatist tradition of Catholic social thought, at which Pius XI hinted and which was to acquire great importance in French Canada. The organization of the medieval city-states became here the symbol for the social reconstruction or, more precisely, the "restoration" of modern society. According to the corporatist theory, professional organizations, bringing together people of different ranks and classes working in the same trade, business or profession, would represent the interests of these people and at the same time overcome the evils of class conflict. Corporatism wanted to unite employer and employees in the same organizations to assure simultaneously harmony between the classes and protection of the weaker partners. Chagnon argued that although an economic council could not be introduced from one day to another, the reforms recommended by him could be seen as steps in the direction of the corporate society.

We note in passing that corporatist theory was to assume great importance in Catholic teaching in French Canada.[10] The Ecole adopted it as its political response to the Depression and promoted it through its publications and the "semaines sociales," the church-sponsored yearly meetings to foster the spirit of social reform. The corporatist ideal was wholly abstract. It was not generated by people engaged in social conflict with the aim of remaking society; it was not connected with the political efforts of any of the social movements in Canada; and it did not give rise to any concrete social policies that could be pursued. We shall see that the lay leaders who reworked the programme of the Ecole removed the corporatist orientation. We also note that since in corporatism the people are represented through their professional and trade organizations, there seems to be little need for political representation in Parliament. Corporatist theory shows little interest in democracy. However, the Quebec proponents of corporatism strongly disapproved of any society in which the economic council was part of the state machinery: they called this "political corporatism" or fascism.[11] They objected to it because it granted excessive powers to government. Instead they advocated "social corporatism," which envisaged an economic council independent of the state, protecting pluralism in society and the distribution of power.[12]

There is no indication whether Chagnon's paper as published in *Pour la restauration sociale au Canada* was the actual text presented by him on 9 March 1933 or a later version. The meeting had given enthusiastic support to his effort, asked him to elaborate his ideas, engage in conservation with lay leaders in the province, and prepare a more detailed proposal for a meeting to be held on 9 March 1934. The published paper may well represent this second version. It includes a short programme of thirteen points, combining doctrinal positions and concrete social reforms, that summarized the content of the entire paper. Very briefly, it demanded the severe restriction of corporate capitalism, the protection of farmers and workers, and the application of the principle of the equality of the two races in the whole of Canada.

The ecclesiastical leaders decided to hand the programme to a group of lay intellectuals who strongly approved of its spirit; the latter group was to elaborate it as a viable political platform for the province.[13] These intellectuals were associated with nationalist organizations, especially with the Ligue d'action nationale and its publication, *L'action nationale*. These men produced a new programme in 1934. They replaced the corporatist orientation of the original programme with their own nationalist emphasis, according to which the oppression of Quebeckers by monopoly capitalism was not simply the oppression of a class, but the oppression of a people. Since the owning class that exercised the greatest power in Quebec was made up of "foreigners," nationalist sentiment could be harnessed for a movement of radical economic reconstruction.

The new programme received strong support from wide sections of Quebec society, from Church circles, intellectuals, businessmen and workers. In April 1934, Paul Gouin and several other politicians decided to leave the Liberal party, which formed the provincial government in Quebec, in complete disgust with Premier L.A. Taschereau's refusal to confront the economic problems and the human misery in the province. In June these men decided to form a new political party, Action liberale nationale (ALN), whose name indicated that it saw itself as a reform splinter of the Liberal party and in continuity with the nationalist spirit and political policy of Action nationale. The new party adopted the reform programme.[14]

To understand this turn to radical reform, we must recall at this point the strengthening of French-Canadian nationalism during the years of the Depression. While the misery caused by the collapse of the economy in Quebec was very similar to that in other provinces — mass unemployment, reduced income, bread lines, deprivations affecting most levels of society, especially the workers — in Quebec, capital and wealth on the whole represented by men the people regarded as "foreigners," mainly British.[15] The large corporations were owned by Americans, British or

Anglo-Canadians. The high positions in federal institutions were in the hands of Anglos. Small companies of industry and commerce were owned by Anglos as well as some French-Canadians and Jews. It was a situation in which economic inferiorization was linked to the remnants of colonialism and the oppression of a people. These conditions made it possible to link nationalist sentiment with the struggle against monopoly capitalism.

Several new nationalist associations were created in the early Thirties, each with its monthly publication, most important among them *L'action nationale*, the heir of the former *L'action française*, which had fostered nationalist sentiment in the past. These nationalists, as Pierre Trudeau so gloomily documents, wanted to defend the independence of French Canada by limiting its encounter with modern society, defined in terms of industrialization, commercialism and democracy.[16] They advocated the return to a rural Quebec. The farmers were the guardians of the traditional virtues. If they were able to produce enough food for the people of Quebec, they would help the province toward greater independence. But the nationalists also appealed to the French-Canadian manufacturers and businessmen: the French-Canadian middle class would do better if a strong government broke the power of the monopolies and weakened the role of small and medium-sized "foreign" competitors. The nationalists promoted the "L'achat chez nous" campaign, which asked Quebeckers to buy goods produced and sold in the province by French Canadians. The nationalists hoped that they could unite the various classes in Quebec, reconciling especially the workers and the middle class, to struggle against the remnant of the colonial system, make themselves more independent and create a country attached to its traditional Catholic values — basically rural but with small-scale industry scattered across it owned and run by French Canadians. Since these nationalists advocated a return to the land, they were often slow in favouring reform legislation for workers: they did not want life in the city to appear more attractive than the harsh existence in the country.

Some nationalists encouraged anti-Semitic sentiments.[17] They spoke as if the British were the owners of the large corporations and the managers of the powerful institutions, and as if Jews were the owners of the smaller industrial and commercial enterprises. Both British and Jews, it was argued, prevented French Canadians from laying hold of their own resources and their own powers. Yves Vaillancourt has shown that this form of anti-Semitism is a ploy of the petty bourgeoisie that seeks to expand its power through nationalism and that at the same time, in an attempt to attract popular support, disguises the fact that it too belongs to the owning class.[18] Nationalism is only too often a sentiment encouraged by the powerful elite to ensure the loyalty of workers and steer them away from a more systematic criticism of economic inequality.

Yet nationalism need not be narrow, nor serve exclusively the interests of the middle class. It expresses the vitality of a people that wants to liberate itself from the conditions of subordination, define itself through its own political and cultural activities, and enter into the modern age through a creative synthesis of industrialization and its own genius and inspiration. In a society where economic exploitation is mediated through a system of national oppression, nationalism often reveals radical and critical potential.

In 1934, the new party, the ALN, was able to commit the nationalist movement to the Catholic reform programme of the Ecole, thereby creating an economic radicalism acceptable to Catholics that had no parallel in the history of Quebec until the Sixties. The programme presented itself as anti-socialist, but its cutting edge was directed against monopoly capitalism.

The party programme, easily available today in English in Michiel Horn's collection *The Dirty Thirties*,[19] justified its opposition to monopoly capitalism by an appeal to Catholic social teaching and a reference to the New Deal of the Roosevelt administration. The first section of the programme dealt with agrarian reform. Even though industrialization was widespread in Quebec, and the movement from the land to the city had begun, the programme wanted to protect the farmer and if possible stop the influx into the cities. The second called for new labour legislation that was to guarantee the rights of workers, protect them against mishaps and insure them against unemployment. The third section dealt with the promotion of small industry and commerce in the province. The programme recommended the creation of a department of commerce — the corporatist idea of the Ecole had been abandoned — whose task it would be to explore the exploitation of Quebec's resources, promote industries in various parts of the province, look for markets outside Quebec and create jobs for the unemployed. The vision behind this programme was not that of a rural Quebec; it was more realistic. It envisaged a decentralized province, where agricultural communities would also be homes of small industries and where the isolation of the country would be overcome through the presence of manufacturers and commercial establishments.[20] The new Quebec was to produce such vital interrelations between the various sectors of society that cooperation in the building of a new and independent society would become possible.

However, the radical thrust of the programme was directed against the present form of corporate capitalism. It proposed "to destroy, by all possible means, the hold that the great financial establishments, the electricity trust and the paper industry have on the province and the municipalities."[20] It demanded an inquiry to determine whether it would be of interest to the province to nationalize the companies producing electricity. It proposed to combat the coal, gasoline and bread cartels, giving them state competition if necessary; to fight the milk trust by uniting in a closed association all the milk producers of the province; and to investigate the structure and financial methods of the public utility companies. The attack on the large corporations was accompanied by financial and political reforms. The programme called for a government investigation into the practices of banks and other financial institutions, and demanded that laws be made to protect the small investors and promote credit for small enterprises. The programme also required that cabinet ministers be prohibited from being shareholders in companies that obtain government contracts, and that ministers be prohibited from being directors of banks, trust companies, public utilities, insurance companies and railroads. The programme wanted to sever the secret and dishonest links of the provincial government to the capitalist class.

The response to the programme and the campaign of the ALN was extraordinary. The party, under the leadership of Paul Gouin, appealed to the people for support; they organized meetings all over the province, made radio broadcasts and started a new publication, *La province.* They were able to gain the support of the nationalist intellectuals and of their organizations and corresponding publications. They had an enormous impact on the entire province. In the election of 1935, the ALN gained 26 seats in the provincial parliament and thus significantly undermined Taschereau's Liberal government.

Yet the reform party did not last long. It was wooed by the newly elected leader of the Conservative party in Quebec, Maurice Duplessis, who, realizing that his own party could not unseat the Liberal government, persuaded his party convention to accept the reform programme of the ALN. Then he negotiated an agreement with Gouin and the other leaders of the ALN. Duplessis proposed the formation of a new party, the Union Nationale, in which Conservative and ALN leaders would work together and together stand behind the reform programme. Duplessis promised that he would invite some leaders of the ALN into his cabinet. Already after the 1935 election, when the ALN held 26 seats and the Conservatives only 16 (the Liberals held on to 46), it had become clear that Gouin was not a strong spokesman in the parliament. Duplessis became the powerful voice of the opposition. When at the next election, in August 1936, the newly formed Union nationale was swept to power with 76 seats, Duplessis excluded the leaders of the ALN from his government. Gouin withdrew from the party, and eventually most of the founders of the ALN abandoned the Union nationale. Duplessis not only betrayed these leaders, he also abandoned his commitment to the reform programme. He became the supporter of monopoly capitalism in Quebec. For the sake of immediate gains, he made Quebec even more dependent on foreign corporations: to attract the large corporations to the province, he promoted a peaceful, religious, tradition-minded Quebec, a source of cheap and compliant labour, shielded from troublemakers by a strict law-and-order administration.

This is the brief episode of economic radicalism in Quebec. It was a remarkable movement, the only time that the anti-capitalist side of Catholic teaching, joined to anti-colonial and nationalist sentiment, generated a movement that reached beyond clerical and lay intellectuals and found support among the great masses of people. It was destroyed by lack of political realism on the part of its leaders. The ALN could not shake itself loose from its origin in the circles of clerics and intellectuals. It was not born as a popular movement; it had been staged, if successfully, but the political leaders underestimated the seriousness of the struggle. Still, the ALN deserves attention as a radical response to the Depression, prompted by the foundation of the CCF.

The question arises of why the economic radicals of the ALN did not enter into serious conversation with the CCF and work out some sort of agreement. Joseph Levitt has dealt with this question in a master's thesis written for the University of Toronto.[22] On the surface, there were many similarities between CCF socialists and the radicals of the ALN. Both movements were opposed above all to monopoly capitalism, that is, to the capitalism then in existence. While the CCF adopted a socialist language and spoke of the eradication of capitalism, its main thrust was directed against the large corporations and the power they wielded over government. The agrarian radicalism of western Canada defended the family farm. The CCF's commitment to socialism was pragmatic; it would have been possible to make room in it for the struggle of the ALN against monopoly capitalism. Secondly, the Fabian spirit of the CCF that favoured the rational planning of the economy by a commission of experts responsible to government seems quite close to the rational planning recommended by the ALN. And finally, while the CCF did not hesitate to talk about class conflict, it did not define in classical socialist terms the underprivileged classes that must stick together in the struggle for power. The CCF preferred to speak of "the people," uniting farmers, workers and other systematically exploited groups, including small producers and businessmen, whose livelihood was threatened by the power of the monopolies. This would have formed an adequate basis for dialogue with the ALN. The economic radicals of the ALN realized this similarity. André Laurendeau, a Quebec journalist and political thinker, once called the ALN "the CCF of Quebec."[23]

However, there were also grave differences that prevented the CCF and the ALN from working together and forming a single movement in Canada. This is Joseph Levitt's conclusion, and it seems to me that he is correct. For one, the ALN was profoundly nationalistic: it opposed any attempt of the federal government to gain more power and wanted to strengthen the power of the provincial government, and some of its members even hoped that eventually Quebec would form an independent republic. The ALN wanted to define the identity of the Quebec people against the continent-wide trend of modernization, which they saw as materialistic, one-sidedly technological, Protestant-inspired and turning to secularism. As we indicated above, the ALN dreamt of a small-scale Quebec, with farms and small industries distributed throughout the province, with the emphasis not on material development but on family life and traditional values. The ALN was born out of a Catholic tradition, and it looked toward Catholicism as a defining element of Quebec society. Catholicism had political meaning for the party because it was one of the symbols that united Quebeckers of all ranks against "the foreigners" who owned and operated most of the major industrial and financial institutions of the province.

The CCF, on the other hand, while opposing the administration in Ottawa, favoured a strong federal government. They saw strong government as necessary to break the power of the corporations, plan the national economy and promote social development in all parts of the country. CCFers had little use for nationalism. They had the socialist suspicion that nationalism is a sentiment that undermines class solidarity and strengthens the middle class in its quest for power. Quebec nationalism seemed particularly narrow and parochial to them. CCFers, like most English-speaking Canadians, did not look on French Canadians as a people: they were simply a minority. In the CCF's opposition to French-Canadian nationalism there was, no doubt, a good deal of false consciousness: CCFers did not realize how British they actually were and how much their ideal of equality was a strategy for transforming other groups in accordance with their own image. The CCF hoped to overcome regional tensions in Canada by forming a strong, nationwide, farmer/labour movement that would be at home in all regions of Canada and eventually form a government that stood for regional equalization.

Secondly, the economic radicals of the ALN were not deeply attracted to democracy. They shared the Catholic suspicion of democracy as the dictatorship of the majority, overriding the principles of truth and justice. In particular, they regarded democracy in Quebec as a system that permitted the wealthy and powerful to make deals, buy their way into office and promote their own friends. Nor was the ALN horrified by the lack of civil liberties in Quebec. They did not warn their followers against fascism and dictatorship. They themselves did not supply any strong leader, but they did not object to the emergence of an authoritarian leader who would introduce radical social changes. The ALN stood in the elitist tradition: the movement was easily reconciled with the hierarchical structure of society and was not disturbed by the marginal position of minority groups. It gladly allowed the Church to exercise great cultural power and it looked upon the educated middle class as the natural leader of Quebec society.

The CCF, as we saw in chapter 1, was deeply committed to democracy, both in running its own party organization and in planning the Canada of the future. Its members passionately defended civil liberties, even when this interfered with party in-interests. They warned the world of the rise of fascism and discerned the seeds of fascism in Canadian society of the time. They fostered the ideal of an egalitarian society, defended minority rights in Canada and distrusted the inherited hierarchies. The CCFers were culturally Protestant while the ALN stood for the values of Catholic culture.

The CCF and the ALN could not get together. In the late Thirties, both radical movements almost disappeared in Quebec. Membership in the CCF dwindled away in the province, and the ALN movement was largely destroyed.[24] Under Duplessis, the critical voices in Quebec became silent.

7
Catholics in Eastern Nova Scotia

In Nova Scotia a group of Catholics reacted to the Great Depression in an original way that was independent of the CCF and the movements that led to its creation, even though it was close to it in spirit and, despite itself, eventually helped to bring about the victory of the CCF in industrial Cape Breton. In this section we shall study the Antigonish movement and the creation of the CCF in the steel and mining towns of eastern Nova Scotia.[1]

Eastern Nova Scotia is the home of a homogeneous group of Catholics, mainly Highland Scots with a minority of Irishmen blended in, who make up a substantial part of the total population and constitute a cohesive, popular Catholic culture to which there is no parallel in other English-speaking parts of Canada. In the rest of the country, English-speaking Catholics are ethnically more heterogeneous and represent minorities. The Catholic immigrants who arrived from continental Europe prior to and after the turn of the century did not settle in eastern Nova Scotia, with the exception of the industrial area of Cape Breton, and even there the influx was small. Eastern Nova Scotia remained essentially Scottish, Catholic and Protestant. Consulting the *Canadian Almanac* of 1931, we learn that of the six counties of eastern Nova Scotia, four had a Catholic population of over fifty percent: on the mainland, Antigonish, and on Cape Breton Island, Cape Breton County, Inverness and Richmond. There was a strong Catholic presence in the industrialized area of Cape Breton County, the cluster of towns around Sydney.[2]

The counties of eastern Nova Scotia were largely populated in the Thirties by farmers and fishermen, with the exception of Cape Breton County, with its miners and steelworkers. The people worked in primary production and the extractive industries. There was no production of goods to speak of. They depended for their survival on the land and the sea, unless they worked at the mines and steel mills of the industrialized part. There was no local bourgeoisie of small industrialists or successful merchants. The large companies that owned and directed the coal mines and steel production were British and they made their decisions regarding the branch plants in Cape Breton County in accordance with their wider international concerns. The rulers, the powerful, the men on whom the well-being of the people depended were all "foreigners." The result of this common dependency was an extraordinary sense of solidarity, grounded in kinship loyalty and religious sentiment, and strengthened by the growing poverty and a general feeling of impotence. In these parts the Depression had already begun in the Twenties.

The elite of eastern Nova Scotia was made up of lawyers, doctors, and priests, but they remained closely tied to the people: they were in no sense a ruling class. The kinship cohesion and religious sentiment the Scottish settlers had brought with them and developed over more than a century never gave way, as they do in most modern societies, to the emergence of distinct classes. Lawyers and doctors remained in solidarity with the people, and their children were often quite willing to leave the elite and marry farmers and miners. In this situation it was natural and generally accepted that priests assumed secular leadership in society.

We argue, then, that thanks to a combination of three factors, the Catholics of eastern Nova Scotia formed a community unique in the English-speaking parts of Canada: they constituted a largely homogeneous group, they made up a substantial section of the population and they were linked by an altogether unusual sense of solidarity. Under the pressure of prolonged poverty, inflicted by the powerful outside the province, they reacted to the Depression in a unique way. We shall examine two distinct but related forms of Catholic social action: the Antigonish movement operative among the farmers and fishermen, and the solidarity of the Catholic miners with Canadian socialism.

The Antigonish Movement

The Antigonish movement was a cooperative movement, based on a special kind of adult education, that sought to enlighten farmers and fishermen in regard to their economic helplessness and organize them as co-owners of new enterprises for the distribution and, in some cases, the production of goods. The creators of the movement were largely priests, and the system of communication used in promoting the cause was the network of Catholic institutions. Yet the movement assumed from the very beginning a non-denominational character; it was ecumenical before the word became current in its present meaning. The movement wanted to transform the conditions of people's lives and in this way their consciousness, whatever their religious affiliation. Still, given the division between Catholic and Protestant areas in rural eastern Nova Scotia, it was mostly in the strongly Catholic counties that the movement spread rapidly. Many Protestants were suspicious of it. Its success among Protestants came later and was more restricted. In the long run, the movement reached beyond Nova Scotia to the other maritime provinces.

The Antigonish movement was created by two imaginative and powerful personalities, Father J.J. Tompkins and Father M.M. Coady. They were usually referred to as Dr. Tompkins and Dr. Coady, since in that part of Nova Scotia, priests with a doctorate were addressed as "Doctor." Already before and during the Twenties, Tompkins, greatly disturbed by the growing depression and powerlessness of the region, devised a new philosophy of adult education, based in part on English and Scandinavian models, that envisaged a movement from the university to the people. He believed that people were intelligent enough, even when they had little formal education, to analyze the reasons for their poverty and organize for cooperative action. In a pamphlet written in 1920, entitled *Knowledge for the People*, he described a process that came close to what today, through the influence of radical educators such as Paulo Freire, is called consciousness-raising. Tompkins designated St. Francis Xavier University at Antigonish as the institution that should and could bring this education to the people.

According to Tompkins, the farmers and fishermen of Nova Scotia were exploited largely by commercial enterprises, which bought the primary products at low prices and sold them at higher ones in the cities. At the same time they demanded high prices for feed, fertilizer and equipment used in primary production, so that the farmers and fishermen lost at both ends. Cooperative ownership of trading companies would enable farmers and fishermen to sell their products on their own terms and purchase the goods they needed directly from the producers, at more advantageous prices. We can already see at this point that the analysis of exploitation blamed mainly the local merchants, without inquiring how their prices were related to the larger industrial and commercial corporations.

Tompkins's first attempt to create an extension department to propagate his adult education programme was unsuccessful. However, he was able to move ahead with the movement because he received the financial support of the Carnegie Foundation of New York City, a humanitarian society, that regarded his effort as a way of promoting self-help among the poor.

It was only in 1928, and effectively only in 1930, that the Extension Department of St. Francis Xavier University was founded, curiously enough with funds coming from the conservative Catholic Scottish Society, which was interested less in social justice than in staying the flow of emigration to other parts of North America. Dr. M.M. Coady was appointed as director. It was he who was most responsible for the rapid spread of the Antigonish movement in eastern Nova Scotia. With the help of his co-workers, he organized study clubs among the farmers and fishermen to teach them how to set up stores for buying and selling goods, cooperatively owned factories and mills, and eventually, when greater numbers were involved, credit unions or cooperative banks. Coady knew how to give people the confidence to make a new start and inspired them to organize their own study clubs and cooperative ventures. Each cooperative undertaking remained part of the movement, kept abreast of new ideas through the bulletin of the Extension Department and made financial contributions from its modest resources to help the department promote its educational task. The movement transformed people's lives, their economic situations and, more especially, their sense of self-worth and power; it initiated the participants into a new, more social self-understanding, thus laying the foundation of large-scale reconstruction. Nonetheless, the movement has not been studied a great deal.[3]

The Antigonish movement set men and women at odds with society. The two originators of the movement were "charismatic" personalities, in the Weberian sense of the term. They had power through their words and attracted people, men and women, who believed their social message and felt empowered to reorganize their labour. Tompkins and Coady articulated the misery experienced by Nova Scotians, gave a convincing analysis of the malfunctioning economy and offered a new vision of social organization that promised the good and abundant life. Their success was grounded in the oppressive conditions produced by the economic system. As we shall see, the Antigonish movement gave voice to a radical criticism of contemporary capitalism. The strong leadership knew how to create a grass-roots movement, made up of the economically underprivileged, that expressed an ethos at odds with dominant North American culture, at odds even with the dominant Catholicism, which understood religion as a source of consolation rather than a call to action.

In time, however, the Antigonish movement lost its radical character. Frank Mifflin defends the view that already in the early Forties, the movement ceased to challenge the social order.[4] Why? He gives several reasons. In part it was because the movement had been successful in changing the conditions of life for a great many people, and in part because the leaders had been willing, for the sake of greater institutional support, to soften their critical stance. The war alleviated some of the dire social need in the province. As well, the growth of the stores and credit unions demanded ever greater commercial and technical expertise, tending to exclude the ordinary people from directing their own enterprises. When it became necessary to hire salaried managers to run the cooperatives, the different social conditions under which the managers lived kept them from seeing themselves as participants in a radical social movement. Mifflin also mentions that at that time, the various cooperatives ceased to reserve a certain amount of money for the ongoing social mission of the Extension Department. The Antigonish movement, according to

Mifflin's study, became very largely a social service organization. It no longer initiated people into a new way of perceiving the social reality. While some students of the movement may wish to argue about the relatively early date that Mifflin assigns to the decline, all agree that such a change in fact took place.

What was the ideology of the Antigonish movement, especially in Coady's persuasive formulation? In *Masters of Their Own Destiny*, he offered an analysis of the ills of contemporary capitalism and presented the cooperative movement as one of the principal levers for the reconstruction of society. What went wrong, according to Coady, with the inherited capitalist system? The people lost power over their economic life.[5] Prior to the industrial revolution, production took place in the home and in small establishments. While there was a trend away from a domestic economy, the shops in which people made money by serving the interests of their owners were small businesses, responsible for small-scale production. What happened through the industrial revolution was the creation of large factories in which vast numbers of people were employed in large-scale production. The power of production slipped out of the hands of the people altogether. Still, distribution and consumption were left to them. But the organization of business enterprises, eventually on a large scale, took even that power away from them. The people became impotent participants in the economic order, subject to the will of a minority made up of owners of industry and business, who were ultimately to reduce them to total misery. Coady interpreted the Great Depression as the visible proof of the unworkability of the inherited economic order.

What had happened, according to Coady, was not due to ill will on the part of the owning classes. Rather, "an error had crept into the foundation of our economic structure."[6] To illustrate what an error was to ordinary people, Coady gave the example of a smokestack 150 feet high that had been built by careless workers. They built the foundation out of plumb and thus introduced an error at the base, scarcely visible to the naked eye, that would eventually be responsible for creating a leaning tower. Such a smokestack, Coady continued, could be held up by props and wires for a time, but eventually it would have to be rebuilt. After 150 years of industrial capitalism, we had come to the moment when the economic system had to be reconstructed.

What was the origin of Coady's theory? Neither he nor his older colleague, Tompkins, cited their sources. They mentioned the Rochdale foundation of mid-nineteenth-century England and sometimes referred to Scandinavian cooperatives, but the reader has the impression that Tompkins and Coady read more widely than they were willing to admit. The theory of alienation Coady proposed, even without mentioning the term, certainly recalls socialist literature. Marx himself, in his early writings, proposed a theory of alienation applicable to any and all social processes, whether economic, political or cultural.[7] Marx proposed a co-operative vision of society: society can be truly human only if people collectively, by direct participation, assume responsibility for the conditions of their lives. Such cooperative engagement transforms people's consciousness: they become the subject of their own history.

Coady presented his own ideas in the context of Catholic social teaching, yet went considerably beyond it. Papal social teaching, as mentioned above, clearly recognized that modern industrial capitalism and the business civilization derived from it permitted the economic interests of a limited class to determine the policies of government. Papal teaching repudiated the abuses of capitalism, the formation of trusts and the conglomeration of companies into economic empires, but these ills were not seen as flowing from an initial error in the system. In the view of Pius XI, they were due to the greed of the rich and the powerful. Coady and the Antigonish movement differed here from the papal teaching since they attributed the ills of the system to private ownership of the industries.

Yet how much the movement remained in line with the Catholic tradition appears when we look at the solution Coady proposed to the chaos and misery produced by capitalism. People must regain their power over the means of production and consumption, acquire a new consciousness in this process and then reconstruct the entire social order. Coady was convinced, however — and this put him plainly in the cooperative tradition — that people must begin the struggle by regaining the means of distribution and exchange, that is, by acquiring cooperative ownership of stores, businesses, banks, service agencies and so forth. "The [cooperative] ownership of such institutions is the natural means of eventually bringing back the control of the production to the people.... The ills of the social order must be attacked from the consumer's end."[8] The cooperative movement was the main lever for the reconstruction of society. Coady argued that the remaking of the social order must begin "from the fringes."[9] He thought that the cooperative movements in western Canada and Nova Scotia were the beginning, or at least could be the beginning, of a more universal transformation of Canadian society. He held that when these fringes became significantly wide and represented more power, the centre of society would undergo not only quantitative but also qualitative changes.

In line with this perspective, the Antigonish movement sought to protect those who still owned their means of production, however small their pieces of land or fishing boats might be, from becoming property-less wage-earners in larger farming companies or fisheries and thus joining the rural proletariat. Capitalism destroyed ordinary people in more ways than one. The present economic system, Coady wrote, by encouraging the ambitious to leave for the cities, constantly robbed the rural people of their natural leaders.[10] At the same time, Coady did not recommend socialism. He was committed to the principle that "small is beautiful."[11] He was not greatly interested in the labour movement since the unions did not lay claim to the co-ownership of industries. The unions, in Coady's view, perpetuated the competitive nature of society; and when the workers eventually succeeded in getting higher wages, they did not actually increase their buying power. Why? Because the institutions of consumption, over which they had no control, and which were often in collaboration with the owners of industry, would simply raise their prices, and the extra money spent by the owners on wages would return as increased profit on the consumption side.

The Antigonish movement, it is important to note, presented itself as politically neutral. This was a fundamental principle of the cooperative philosophy, even though in the 1930s the cooperative movement in England, after a long period of negotiation, joined the Labour party and identified itself with British socialism.[12] Coady was very insistent on the political neutrality of the

Antigonish movement. The leaders were allowed to vote but they were forbidden to support any party in public.[13] What were the reasons for this insistence on political neutrality? In the first place, the Extension Department still received financial help from the Carnegie Foundation. The movement was also helped by government grants. To guard neutrality here seemed important. In addition, since the critical ideology of the movement regarded capitalism as harbouring inner contradictions and favoured the social reconstruction of society, the movement was constantly accused of being socialist. Coady again and again denied this, fearing that any link to the democratic socialism of the CCF could undermine the movement's effectiveness.[14]

Coady went out of his way to show how his political philosophy differed from the socialism repudiated by papal teaching. He argued that the Antigonish movement did not stand for class war, was not opposed to private property and did not propose a materialistic concept of society. Still, his writings are full of curious contradictions. He insisted that "it would be a serious mistake to assume that the [St. Francis Xavier] programme is promoting or encouraging class strife."[15] At the same time he did oppose "the bourgeoisie" — which he defined as "those who live by dividends, rent and interest derived from economic institutions which they own and direct" — to "the masses," made up of primary producers, farmers and fishermen (who own their means of production), and workers (property-less labourers in factories, commerce and on the land).[16] Coady's language often suggested a polarization of society. "If the blacks got together," he wrote, "and demonstrated that they can set up a cooperative society, they could drive out all the white exploiters."[17] There were two sides in the struggle for justice, and they seemed to be decided in terms of ownership. The bourgeoisie, Coady argued, had blinded itself in regard to what was actually taking place in society. "It is a stupid rationalization on the part of the economically privileged to think that what has evolved in the Western world, and especially in America, is democracy. To identify democracy with the ability of a man or a small group of men to set up economic kingdoms which necessitate the subservience and, I might say, the slavery of the masses, is to indulge in a pure myth."[18] What he wanted to achieve through the cooperative movement was to "bring back the control of production to the people."

Coady also insisted he was not opposed to private property. In fact, very much like the leaders of the CCF, he demanded that more people, especially workers, become owners of property — say, a house and a garden. Yet when he did explain his social theory, he seemed to go far beyond Catholic social teaching. "A man owns what he has produced out of natural resources to which he has a title."[19] This applied to farmers, fishermen and craftsmen. But then Coady continued, "If a man uses others, and natural resources that are not his, then he exploits the workers if he regards himself as the sole owner." Why is that? First, because the resources are originally owned by all the people, and secondly, because the workers are the owners of what they produce with their hands. The owners of the industrial machinery cannot claim ownership of the goods produced. If they do, they exploit the workers. This theory goes beyond anything found in Catholic social teaching at the time.

While Coady was not a socialist, he did recommend the nationalization of a considerable section of the economy: banking and insurance companies, electrical power, transportation, systems of communication, medical services and steel and chemical industries.[20] Still, he defended the existence of a privately owned sector of the economy.

Since the Antigonish movement was largely made up of ardent Christians, its opponents did not accuse it of atheism. That would have been absurd. But the movement was accused of proposing a materialistic conception of society. Coady proposed a view of man's collective self-constitution that was indeed beyond traditional Catholic teaching. He believed that the economy is primary. The people produce food and necessities for themselves and by doing so they create their consciousness. "The basic problem of the world," he wrote, "is the creation and production of wealth."[21] This "simple materialistic statement," we read, has many ramifications, but it is "the storm centre" of social philosophy. Coady argued against idealists who believed that preaching the truth, including correct social theory, would produce changes in society. "The spiritual leaders — at least many of them — prefer to spend their time talking about abstract things like social justice, social charity, and democracy, that give them the feeling they are doing something to justify their existence, when in reality they are cute apologists for the privileged status quo."[22] It is impossible to introduce people to values and high ideas unless these grow out of the organization of their daily work. It is labour that produces consciousness. Coady cheerfully claimed, "Through credit unions, cooperative stores, lobster factories and saw mills, we are laying the foundation for an appreciation of Shakespeare and grand opera."[23] Unemployment, marginalization and wage labour had produced a depressed consciousness that no amount of teaching could overcome. It was only through the cooperative effort of making a living that consciousness would be significantly changed. By jointly solving their economic problems people would escape self-centredness and psychic paralysis.

A bare outline of this theory sounds a little more radical than Coady intended it. He was, after all, fully convinced that religion had a special role to play in the formation of consciousness. While he recognized that religion often promoted bigotry, divisiveness and idealistic illusions, and produced conformism and social immobilism, he argued nonetheless that faith, Christian faith, made people restless, critical, yearning for justice, concerned about their neighbours and eager to promote the common good of society. He suggested that religion reveals its radical features only if the people's consciousness is being modified by the cooperative organization of labour. Coady was no theoretician. He did not explore the relation of consciousness and society in any great detail. But his emphasis sounded dangerous to many Christians at the time and certainly went beyond Catholic social teaching. It is only in recent years that Christian theology has been willing to recognize the impact of labour on human consciousness.

Despite this partially disguised radicalism, Coady remained a Liberal politically, even though he never talked about it in public. The vision of society that appears in his writing was based on a balance of powers — he regarded this as a Catholic principle — between various sections of society: the cooperatively owned, the privately owned and the publicly owned sectors. Coady favoured the nationalization of the main natural resources and the main service agencies in the country. He advocated intelligent political activity on the part of the government to plan and promote the economy in the three sectors and, if I understand him correctly, to monitor the control of the means of communication, press and radio, presently in the hands of the economically powerful.[24] The cooperatively owned sector, Coady held, would be the source and foundation of the new direction: as soon as this sector achieved a significant size and a number of large corporations are publicly owned, the nature of society would undergo a radical change;[25] the cooperative sector would create a new consciousness among the participants and hold in check the other more individualistic and self-seeking forces in society.

In the early Thirties, the CCF proposed a programme that sounded more thoroughly socialist than those later in the decade; in the hope of winning electoral victories and becoming the national alternative to the established order, it modified its programme so that it actually came very close to proposing the mixed economy ruled by strong government that we find in Coady's writings. The CCF shared the same hope that these quantitative differences — significant enlargements of cooperative and public ownership — would lead to a qualitative difference of the whole of society. Yet Coady did not support the CCF. Still, he occasionally made remarks suggesting that democratic socialism would be the government of the future. In the early Fifties he wrote: "I think Saskatchewan is leading the way in Canada, perhaps New Zealand and Australia are also moving in that direction.... With all due respects to my American friends I really think that the U.S.A. will be the last country in the free world to get democracy."[26]

Let me say a few more words about the radical nature of the Antigonish movement. There can be no doubt that the movement was inspired by an alternative vision of society. Its leaders were well aware that the dominant culture, promoted by the major institutions of society, especially the economic institutions, made people feel ignorant and passive, preoccupied them with trivia, destroyed their self-confidence and generated dependency on expensive academics. The Antigonish movement was at odds with contemporary culture and called upon religion — to be more precise, the Christian religion — to help in the creation of a new cultural awareness.

The critique of the economic system proposed by the Antigonish movement had implications for the understanding of all institutional life. People become estranged from their own resources and cease to be masters of their own destiny whenever they are deprived of direct participation in the operation of their collective existence. Institutions are only sound if they retain their grass-roots character. Tompkins sometimes expressed his distrust of institutions in formulations that had an anarchist ring. "Beware of institutionalization," he used to say. "When a thing becomes over-institutionalized, it tends to become sterile."[27] What he meant, and what his friends and followers meant after him, was that an institution almost inevitably produces a full-time staff responsible for its operation, a bureaucracy in other words, which becomes removed from the concerns of the people, defines itself along organizational lines and makes decisions that foster the good of the institution rather than the good of the people for the sake of which the institution was created. The hesitation of the Antigonish movement (and all cooperative movements) in regard to socialism was due to distrust of political parties and their bureaucracies. The CCF itself, especially in Saskatchewan, kept alive the heritage of the cooperative movement and thus bore within itself resources of self-criticism that made it a party different from any other. The cooperative movement's demand for participation remains an abiding principle of renewal in the party and in society.

The Antigonish movement stood for a kind of social reform that in the terminology of contemporary political science is called "system-transcending." Since the movement tried to insert new principles into the present social and economic order, it was reformist; but since these principles were based on an alternative vision of society, they in some significant way transcended the present order, undermined it and prepared people for a more radical reconstruction of society.

How consistent were the leaders of the Antigonish movement in applying the principle of co-responsibility to the organization of the Church? Here they were conservatives. While Marx in his early writings gives as an example of alienation the institution of priesthood, which removes from ordinary people responsibility for worship and makes them dependent on the mediation of an elite,[28] Coady never applied his cooperative principle to the life of the Church. He was so deeply rooted in the Catholic tradition that the idea probably never came to him. The priest was for him the natural leader in the community who could help free the people from the false imagination created by the dominant culture.

One may ask furthermore whether there was not an inner contradiction between the movement's cooperative ideal and its refusal to endorse a socialist society, at least in principle. Its social analysis of the causes of exploitation focussed so much on the middlemen, visible to farmers and fishermen in the towns, that it neglected to examine how these merchants themselves were caught in the economic system defined by corporate capitalism. Moreover, whenever credit unions and cooperative stores were successful, they became practically indistinguishable from other large business or banking enterprises. A cooperatively owned company may remain true to its founding principles only in a non-competitive economic system where production is for use, not for profit. Hence to promote a cooperative movement while at the same time refusing to identify with the socialist party may well be a basic contradiction.[29]

The Antigonish movement was certainly the most original and the most daring response of Canadian Catholics to the social injustices during the Depression. It was based on an alternative vision of society, it was radical and went beyond the church teaching on several issues, advocated a religious materialism and introduced reforms in Canadian society that had explosive implications. Yet, as we saw, the movement also harboured paradoxes. Coady was not a theoretician. He was a radical and an activist deeply rooted in the Catholic tradition, and thanks to this religious identification, he was able to create a critical movement among basically conservative farmers and fishermen.

The question of whether the Antigonish movement was the Catholic church's response to communism has been raised.[30] I believe that Father Tompkins's pioneer work in the Twenties establishing cooperatives among farmers and fishermen was purely and simply the response of a gifted man to the helplessness and lack of organization on the part of the people of Nova Scotia. It is true that Catholics in Nova Scotia had been warned against the radicalism of the United Farmers and their union with the labour movement, but when this union dissolved in the early Twenties, the United Farmers declined and the cooperatives that had been supported by them also disappeared. In the rural parts of eastern Nova Scotia, especially in the Catholic counties, the radicals were no threat. One must add to this that Tompkins himself was not an instrument of ecclesiastical policy. He found himself at odds with his ecclesiastical superiors. He drew his philosophy of co-operatism from England and Scandinavia. Nor did he nor anyone else in the movement during the Twenties and Thirties engage in any red-baiting. The origin of the movement, I am inclined to argue, is therefore quite independent of communism.

At the same time, when we study the creation of the movement's organizational centre, the Extension Department of St. Francis Xavier University, the story becomes more complex. Tompkins had not met with early success. He had in fact once been removed for a time, though for reasons unrelated to the cooperative movement, from his association with the university and placed as a parish priest in a small fishing village. The friends of the cooperative movement were unable to move the university to adopt the new adult education programme. It was only at the end of the Twenties that the Catholic Scottish Society, strongly organized on Cape Breton, provided the necessary funds for its inauguration. To retain the cohesion of Scottish culture, the society advocated economic development in Nova Scotia and hoped that the educational facilities of St. Francis Xavier University reaching out to ordinary people — and here it specifically included farmers, fishermen and, for the first time, miners — would help them to improve the economic conditions of their lives.[31] It expressed the concern of many Catholics in eastern Nova Scotia over the radicalism of the miners in the industrialized part of Cape Breton. Some of the funds used in the creation of the Antigonish movement, then, coming from the Catholic Scottish Society and also, as mentioned above, from the Carnegie Foundation, represented an intention of helping farmers and working-men in order to make the present social order more secure. Yet this pressure, in my reading of the documents, did not influence the philosophy of the Antigonish movement.

But as soon as we leave the rural world of farmers and fishermen and turn to the industrialized part of Cape Breton, the Antigonish movement encountered and reacted to radical unionism and began to define itself as "the middle way" between liberal democracy and revolutionary communism. The St. Francis Xavier Extension Department opened an office in Glace Bay in 1932 in the hope of helping the labour movement there to remain non-revolutionary, democratic and congenial to religion. This takes us to the next topic of this section, the Catholic participation in the labour movement of Cape Breton in the Thirties.

The CCF in Cape Breton

Prior to the publication of Paul MacEwan's recent *Miners and Steelworkers*,[32] there was no book available on the labour movement in Cape Breton County, even though its history is one of the most troubled in North America. Six times between 1882 and 1925 the government sent in federal troops to smash the labour movement struggling for unionization and political power.[33] The first attempts to organize labour, MacEwan reports, united craftsmen and industrial workers, until the more radical miners of Cape Breton, working under inhuman conditions, succeeded after many attempts in creating an industrial union allied to a political programme. These labour struggles took place in the years 1909 and 1917. The new, more political unionism was less interested in consumers' cooperatives, favoured by the craft unions as an important means of struggling against exploitation of the workers. The industrial union was more socialist in orientation. Following the British model, its leaders favoured the creation of a labour party to act as the political arm of the labour movement.

For a brief time in the early Twenties, the politicization of workers as well as farmers led to a joint farmer/labour party, which was able to elect several members to the provincial parliament and constitute the official opposition. Yet this union of farmers and workers was not to last. The United Farmers declined in Nova Scotia as they did in the rest of the country. The farmers, moreover, were frightened by the outright socialist language of the labour leaders. The disappearance of the farmers as an organized force led to the decline of the cooperatives they had sponsored. This breakdown of organization among the farmers, as mentioned earlier, belongs to the background of the Antigonish movement.

The labour movement in Cape Breton, after temporary political success, came under brutal pressure from the companies, aided by the government. The workers were divided into radicals and moderates. The radicals advocated all-out opposition to the present system — sometimes, though by no means always, expressed in communist terms — and the moderates favoured more conventional collective bargaining, hoping that a more just and more generous government would force management to settle for better terms. The radicals were often able to win support among the workers, but in every case the government smashed their movement with violent repression. After 1925, the last invasion of Cape Breton County by federal troops, the labour movement was unable to produce significant results. Between 1925 and 1936, the rift between radicals and moderates within the unions absorbed the attention of leaders and workers. There was much agitation and strife among the workers, many of whom adopted a revolutionary rhetoric, idealized the events that had taken place in Russia and gladly called themselves communists.

It was during this time that the Catholic Rural Life Conference extended its interest to the industrial workers and began to call itself the Rural and Industrial Life Conference. This yearly conference, sponsored by the diocese of Antigonish since 1924, was primarily concerned with the plight of farmers. After 1930 the newly founded Extension Department was asked to plan and organize the conferences. In order to convince the 1932 conference in Sydney that the Church should adopt a more open and sympathetic approach to the labour struggle, a priest had invited Alex MacIntyre, a former communist labour leader, blacklisted by the Besco mining and steel company and now unemployed, to address the assembly on the labour movement in Cape Breton.[34] His speech became famous among the men and women associated with the Antigonish movement. He told the audience that the clergy were identified on the whole with the interests of the owners of industry, and hence with the powers that exploited the workers and their families. He told them that the widespread

Catholic prejudice against the radical miners, as materialists, communists and atheists, was largely based on ignorance, for it was the so-called materialist workers, communists included, who were moved to compassion by the misery of the workers and were ready to give their lives for the well-being of others. He suggested that the Church, by its indifference to the well-being of the workers — despite the papal encyclicals — was in fact driving the workers into communism and contempt for religion. MacIntyre exhorted the conference to change its attitude toward the labour movement.

The actual relationship of the Catholic church to the labour movement in Cape Breton has not been studied in detail. It is true, of course, that the Catholics of the rural areas, and especially Antigonish, the seat of the diocese, on the mainland, were frightened by the radicalism of the labour movement. Yet they were united to the labourers by kinship loyalty and hence in the hour of dire need, the Church organized help for the hungry strikers and their families. In 1925, when the longest and most painful strike of the miners ended in violent repression and humiliation of the workers, Bishop James Morrison of Antigonish asked the Catholic parishes in his diocese to send the strikers food and money.[35] Still, on the whole, the Church in rural areas was cautious. When the workers in the early Twenties created an Independent Labour party and later joined with the United Farmers, *The Casket*, the diocesan weekly of Antigonish, warned Catholics against this third provincial party.[36] The Church appeared as the defender of the traditional parties. In the industrialized area of Cape Breton, however, there was always a minority of priests who identified with labour and its struggle against oppression. Their story has yet to be written.

Here is an example. When in 1936, at a time when the steel workers were not yet fully organized, Father "Mickey" MacDonald used his leadership position in the parish to help the workers organize and defended their action from the pulpit with papal citations, J.H. Kelly, managing director of the steel plant, complained to Bishop Morrison about the priest and claimed that he had interfered in the business of the company beyond the scope of the Church's authority. Yet Bishop Morrison, despite his cautious style, did not interfere with Father MacDonald's activity. While it may well be true, as Alex MacIntyre asserted, that the Church as a whole identified itself with the established order, this group of priests who identified with the workers were accepted by them as brothers in the common struggle.

The Rural and Industrial Life Conference of 1932, profoundly touched by MacIntyre's speech, resolved to support the labourers of Cape Breton in their struggle for social justice. Alex MacIntyre was hired as a full-time organizer. In addition to the usual study clubs and cooperative stores, the Extension Department decided to open a labour school in Cape Breton. The staff prepared workers to become labour leaders and play an active role in the union. They introduced them to the principles of modern economics, existing labour legislation and the principles of social justice. Here the anti-communist trend of Catholic teaching was a significant element. The Extension Department wanted to steer the workers, especially the Catholics, away from revolutionary politics that seemed attractive to many of them because of their utter frustration. The labour school promoted an evolutionary approach to the labour struggle. Following the principles of Catholic teaching, it taught the workers not to regard the quest for their own class interest as the lever for the reconstruction of society, but rather to understand their struggle as a quest for social justice that the government ought to honour and the owning classes should accept. In the Catholic tradition of that time, the labour struggle did not aim at the conquest of the exploiters by the exploited but at the submission to the demands of justice by all sections of society. Behind the labour struggle, in the Catholic tradition, stood the vision of an organic society, based on the cooperation of the classes and united by a common set of values.

How influential was the Extension Department in Cape Breton County? This is a difficult question. It is easy to show that it was very influential in organizing cooperative stores and credit unions. But what about the effect on the workers' movement? From my conversations with old-timers in Cape Breton who remember the struggle of the Thirties, I have the impression that the labour school helped many to gain greater self-confidence at public meetings, but that it had no definable influence on the labour movement. The positions the workers took in the labour movement were determined by the conditions of their lives and forces within their own ranks.

It should be said at this point that religious affiliation did not play a significant role in the labour movement of Cape Breton. Labour solidarity was stronger than religious ties. While in the rural areas of eastern Nova Scotia, the division of the Scots into Catholics and Presbyterians had political consequences, in Cape Breton County — which was evenly divided, some towns having a Protestant and others a Catholic majority — there was unity in the common cause. At least this is how Cape Bretoners describe it; detailed studies have not yet been undertaken. In the mines there were tensions based on religious affiliation over job opportunities and promotion, but these apparently never affected the common opposition to the bosses. The conflict within the labour movement was between militants and moderates, especially during the years 1909 to 1917 and again between 1925 and 1936.[37] This division did not involve a religious factor, aligning Protestants against Catholics, or Christians against atheists. The Scottish workers of Cape Breton remained so linked to the country people that they rarely adopted a hostile attitude toward their churches. Even when they called themselves communists, they were not usually committed to atheism in an ideological sense. And while the churches as a whole, Protestant or Catholic, did not join the struggle of the labourers and sided, as churches usually do, with the government and the ruling groups, there was always a significant number of Presbyterian ministers and Catholic priests in Cape Breton County who passionately endorsed the cause of labour. In this social context, therefore, the Extension Department did not exert any specifically "Catholic" influence on the labour movement.

What was the condition of labour in Cape Breton in the early Thirties? After 1925, the union that had spearheaded the more radical movement fifteen years earlier and with whom the mining companies had come to an agreement was regarded as soft and too obliging to management. It seemed that when a miner left the pit as a union leader and sat at his desk in shirt and tie, he became a gentleman, polite and yielding to company pressure. The frustrated workers formed a new union but the companies, aided by government, supported the old one and refused to deal with them. This set the stage for a profound division of the labour movement, with dire consequences for collective bargaining and for the political influence of labour in the community. For years — since the early Twenties, to be exact — the workers had been unable to elect representatives to the provincial legislature.

By 1936 the miners were exhausted. They decided to bury their old conflict, become reconciled in the old legitimate union and present a more united political force in the area.[38] We recall that by this time the CCF had been founded in Calgary, in 1932. Yet the party was still generally unknown in the East. The Regina Manifesto had been read by Nova Scotian labour leaders, and some had even endorsed it as their personal platforms.[39] But the CCF was not organized anywhere east of Montreal. The newly reconciled miners of District 26 were the first labour union to join the CCF, and since no statutory provisions had been made for such affiliations, the party decided to follow the rules of the British Labour party. Not all the workers were behind the move; some locals did not pay their membership dues. The communists among them fought the CCF as a counter-revolutionary force. Still, with the arrival of the CCF, Cape Breton labour presented a more united front than it had done since the early Twenties and was able to elect representatives to the provincial parliament and to the House of Commons in Ottawa.

Was the reconciliation of the workers and the creation of a democratic socialist movement in Cape Breton in any way due to the influence of the Antigonish movement? I think not. From my conversations, I gather that the Extension Department was associated by the workers mainly with the cooperative stores and credit unions. To Catholics, the Extension Department also symbolized the Church's concern for labour and allowed them to link their political struggle with their religious commitment. But it had no direct influence on political developments.

Since our interest here is the reaction of Catholics to Canadian socialism, we take notice of the Catholic participation in the labour movement of Cape Breton from the beginning, and in particular of the strong Catholic presence in the newly founded CCF of Nova Scotia, a presence unique in Canada. Cape Breton County was the only strongly Catholic area that elected socialist representatives to Parliament, beginning with the miner Clarence Gillis, a labour leader steeped in Social Gospel, Catholic style. The CCF members elected to the provincial legislature, Donald MacDonald in 1939 and Michael MacDonald in 1945, were Catholics of the same tradition. This ready identification of the Catholic workers with Canadian socialism deserves special mention because in the rest of Canada, the Catholic church had uttered warnings against the CCF. The bishop of Antigonish did not repeat the general ecclesiastical caveat. The supporters of the CCF in Cape Breton did not use the term "socialist" as did CCFers in Saskatchewan, and Cape Bretoners, even when linked to revolutionary politics, were not interested in ideology. They were culturally conservative, remaining close to the customs and religion of their kinsfolk. Their identification with socialism, whether democratic or revolutionary, was an act of class protest against a system that made them and their wives and children suffer.

In the strongly Catholic areas of Nova Scotia, the CCF leaders tried to show that Canadian socialism, more than the traditional parties, corresponded to the ideals outlined in Catholic social teaching. Clarence Gillis sought the support of the people by quoting the papal encyclicals and arguing that the CCF was in accord with the philosophy of the Antigonish movement.[40] In a letter to Dr. Coady — which might contain a touch of flattery — Gillis wrote: "Most of my ideas and principles were formed on the basis of the cooperative movement, and all my thinking is in this direction.... I think you can be quite proud of the many young people who got their start through you and the cooperative movement."[41] After his election to the House of Commons in 1940, Gillis wrote an article entitled "Miners Stand United" for *The New Commonwealth*, the CCF weekly at Regina. There he made this observation: "In addition to the political and industrial movements, the miners of Nova Scotia recognized the value of education, and when St. Francis Xavier Extension Department inaugurated their movement to bring the university to the people and laid down the programme of adult education in the establishment of credit unions and cooperative stores, the miners of Nova Scotia became part of that organization, and today are marching forward and are practically taking over, under the guidance of the Extension Department, the economic resources of the province."[42] In the Commons, in his first speech on unemployment, on 4 June 1940, Gillis affirmed the value of the cooperative movement, saying: "The people of Nova Scotia are making a wonderful effort to solve their own economic problems by cooperative action. They have already established 180 credit unions, 43 stores, 17 lobster factories, 7 fish plants, 8 community industries and some 10 other cooperatives. The total number of cooperative organizations in the Maritimes is 422."

In the memory of the old CCFers, today often NDPers, those early years after the foundation of the party in Nova Scotia were a period of victorious struggle and unity among the workers. They recall that the workers participated in three parallel movements: the political movement of the CCF through identification with the party, the labour movement through the support of their union and the cooperative movement through credit unions and cooperative stores. This is how Gillis described it, and how David Lewis and Frank Scott understood it in their book, *Make This Your Canada* (1943).[43] So it has remained in the memory of Donald MacDonald, a labour leader of the late Thirties, elected to the legislature in 1939, who later became president of the Canadian Labour Congress. This is how it appeared to other labour leaders I have interviewed. Paul MacEwan, NDP member of the legislature and historian of Nova Scotia, received the same impression of the early years of the CCF as the result of his studies. This memory of unity may be a little exaggerated. Many workers remained committed to revolutionary politics. The cooperative movement did not publicly support the CCF at all. Still, at the end of the Thirties and the beginning of the Forties, when in the whole of Canada the CCF made considerable strides and appeared, following the British pattern, to become the recognized alternative to the government, the workers of Cape Breton experienced more hope and less importance than they ever had, and jointly supported a movement to revolutionize the social order.

Afterword

The story of Canadian socialism and the Catholic reactions to it raises interesting questions, especially at this time when world capitalism is again showing signs of impending crisis. The issues that emerged in the Thirties are being taken up again in the contemporary context. The Christian churches have again become the place where the inherited order is being critically examined, where a growing number of men and women demand a new economic order based on cooperation and participation, and where even ecclesiastical leadership is rethinking its own attitude toward socialism.

In the preceding chapters we have mentioned several times that in the Seventies, the official teaching of the Catholic church underwent a remarkable shift to the Left. Already in the Sixties, the popes began to emphasize anew the principle of socialization, repeated their warnings against the international imperialism of money (the power of transnational corporations), insisted on a rationally planned economy and approved the cooperation of Catholics and socialists — including, under certain circumstances, Marxists. In his 1971 letter *Octogesima adveniens*, Pope Paul VI recognized that many Catholics have become enormously attracted to socialist movements, that they find in these movements ideals and aspirations they share precisely as Christian believers, and that they see in these movements the current of history in which they want to play an active part.[1] Pope Paul recalled that discernment was needed in this. Not all socialist movements are acceptable. The pope argued that Catholics are not able to participate in socialist movements that are wedded to a total philosophy, to a complete world picture — the various Marxist orthodoxies would belong to this category — because

212

Christians receive their total world picture from Jesus Christ. Still, *Octogesima adveniens* rehabilitated the word "socialism" in Catholic parlance. Robert McAfee Brown, the well-known Protestant theologian, called this change of position from Pius XI to Paul VI "the Catholic journey" to the Left.[2]

This shift in papal teaching has been largely due to the influence of the Latin American Church, which, at the 1968 bishops' conference at Medellin, Colombia, announced its solidarity with the poor of the Third World and proclaimed the Gospel as a radical and even revolutionary message.[3] At the 1971 synod of bishops in Rome, the representatives of the world episcopate endorsed this new perspective. In a document entitled *Justice in the World*, they recognized that gigantic injustices have built around the world a network of domination and oppression that keeps the greater part of humanity from sharing in the building of society and from having access to its wealth.[4] In the face of this worldwide misery, the synod affirmed that the Christian message is good news for the poor, that the salvation brought by Christ and preached by the Church includes the liberation of people from the oppressive conditions of their social existence and that the life of the Gospel includes, as a constitutive element, active commitment to the transformation of society.

This new approach affected the teaching of the Canadian Catholic bishops. In a series of remarkable documents, the Canadian bishops have introduced the Catholic people to a critical perception of their country and its relation to the rest of the world. The bishops have spoken out on concrete issues such as world hunger, the development of the Canadian North and the liberation of the native peoples; more than that, they have provided critical directives for a Catholic approach to the problems of Canadian society. It is not an exaggeration to say that the nature of Church teaching has undergone a change. In the pastoral letter *From Words to Action* (1976), the bishops demand that Catholics re-read the scriptures to discover in them God's call to social solidarity, that they listen to the victims of society and speak out against their exploitation or exclusion and that they analyze the social causes of these injustices. The bishops ask that Catholics engage themselves in social and political action in order to remove these causes from society.

The same pastoral acknowledges that the capitalist system will no longer do: it widens the gap between the rich and the poor, especially between rich and poor countries, and it allows the decisions regarding resources and production to slip into the hands of an ever shrinking elite. The bishops recognize that this new social reading of the Gospel is only accepted by a minority of Catholics at this time, but they call this "a significant minority" because they call the entire Church community to greater fidelity.

In a subsequent pastoral, entitled *A Society to be Transformed* (1977), the Canadian bishops describe the plural responses of Catholics to the needs of society. Some Catholics, the bishops say, still believe that present capitalism can be reformed and engage themselves in reform programmes of various kinds. While the bishops do not give concrete examples, they may have in mind the reform groups in the Liberal and Conservative parties and the political action of the New Democratic Party. Other Catholics, the bishops continue, do not believe that reform of the present system is the answer and hence participate in socialist movements. While again they do not mention the specifics, what the bishops probably have in mind is the socialist presence in the NDP and the solidarity and assistance extended by some Canadian Catholics to Third-World socialist movements with strong Catholic participation. The bishops mention a third group of engaged Catholics, committed to projects that lie beyond capitalism and socialism. While they do not tell us what groups they have in mind, it is likely that they refer to movements such as the Catholic Worker that represent Catholic forms of communitarian anarchism, cooperative movements that look to the replacement of private ownership by joint ownership as the key to a qualitative transformation of society; and to the environmental movement, which seeks to slow down industrial growth and thus differs from both capitalism and socialism. But whatever people's concrete choices, the Christian life, the pastoral argues, demands critical engagement.

This turn to the Left has been endorsed by Pope John Paul II, the pope from Poland, himself a citizen of the Second World.[5] While the pope has accused the Eastern European communist regimes of governing through a bureaucracy dominated by a small elite, of violating the civil liberties of their people and of treating Christians as second- or third-class citizens, he has not questioned the socialist economic system. Yet when Pope John Paul becomes a critic of the Western nations, he focusses almost exclusively on the capitalist economy. He argues, like his predecessors, that capitalism structures a growing sector of the population into poverty. He holds, moreover, that in the present system workers are exploited because their labour gives them no title to ownership or participation in decision-making. And finally, he argues that capitalism has harmful cultural consequences, of which he particularly stresses consumerism or, in Marx's terms, commodity fetishism. While as a defender of Church discipline and intellectual conformism, Pope John Paul appears a conservative, a study of his social teaching reveals that he stands behind the recent Catholic shift to the Left.

This shift does not mean that the Catholic church has come to endorse a socialist position. The official documents, papal or episcopal, can be read in a socialist or a non-socialist way. They all argue, in one way or another, that in a world of scarcity the production and distribution of goods cannot be left to market forces but must be rationally planned in accordance with justice. But the documents do not say whether this responsible planning should take place in a socialist system that is open to participation, new ideas and human freedom, or in a capitalist system where the industries, privately owned in part, are operated in accordance with directives worked out by a democratically elected government.

Let me add immediately that a similar shift to the Left is observable in the directives of the World Council of Churches and national church councils such as the Canadian Council of Churches, as well as in social policy statements produced by the major Anglican and Protestant churches. If we are to believe these documents — Anglican, Protestant, Catholic — there must exist today, in proportions unequalled in the past, a visible and vocal Christian Left — a minority to be sure, but nonetheless a significant number of engaged Christians who raise the same issues that preoccupied Canadians in the Thirties and early Forties — the socialist question.

Notes

Part I
Chapter 1   Canadian Socialism

1. The best-known works dealing with Canadian socialism are, in alphabetical order: Ivan Avakumovic, *Socialism in Canada* (Toronto: McClelland and Stewart, 1978); Gerald Caplan, *The Dilemma of Canadian Socialism* (Toronto: McClelland and Stewart, 1973); William Christian and Colin Campbell, *Political Parties and Ideologies in Canada* (Toronto: McGraw-Hill Ryerson, 1974); Samuel D. Clark et al., eds., *Prophecy and Protest* (Toronto: Gage Educational Publishing, 1975); Gad Horowitz, *Canadian Labour in Politics* (Toronto: University of Toronto Press, 1968); Seymour Martin Lipset, *Agrarian Socialism* (Berkeley: University of California Press, 1971); Kenneth McNaught, *A Prophet in Politics* (Toronto: University of Toronto Press, 1963); Desmond Morton, *NDP: The Dream of Power* (Toronto: A. M. Hakkert, 1974); Norman Penner, *The Canadian Left* (Toronto: Prentice-Hall Canada, 1977); Walter Young, *The Anatomy of a Party: The National CCF* (Toronto: University of Toronto Press, 1969); Leo Zakuta, *A Protest Movement Becalmed* (Toronto: University of Toronto Press, 1964).

2. For a text of the Calgary programme, see Young, *Anatomy*, pp. 303-4. The subsequent quotations are taken from these pages.

3. At a meeting at the Church of All Nations in Toronto, on 12-13 January 1932, a group of activist Christians committed themselves to socialism. "The teachings of Jesus Christ, applied in an age of machine production and financial control, mean Christian socialism." See Roger Hutchinson, "The Fellowship for a Christian Social Order" (ThD thesis, Toronto School of Theology, 1975), pp. 31-2.

4. *Hansard*, 1 February 1933, p. 1687.

5. See pp. 110-1, 123-4 below.

6. See pp. 175-88 below.

7. Young, *Anatomy*, p. 45.

8. Ibid., p. 43. See also Penner, *Canadian Left*, pp. 200-2.

9. For the text of the Regina Manifesto, see Young, *Anatomy*,

pp. 304-13.

10. Ibid., p. 304.

11. Ibid., p. 305.

12. *Hansard*, 1 February 1933, p. 1688.

13. Arguing in the Commons, Woodsworth used as an instrument of political analysis J. A. Hobson's theory of imperialism; see Penner, *Canadian Left*, pp. 204-5. Once he lamented, "We have our own song, 'Britiannia Rules' — and I am not at all sure it is preferable to 'Germany Above All'"; ibid., p. 205.

14. See Lipset, *Agrarian Socialism*, especially two essays: Joan Bennet and Cynthia Krueger, "Agrarian Pragmatism and Radical Politics," and John Richards, "The Decline and Fall of Agrarian Socialism"; also Penner, *Canadian Left*, pp. 171-8; Norman Pollack, *The Populist Response to Industrial America* (Cambridge: Harvard University Press, 1962); and Paul Frederick Sharp, *Agrarian Revolt in Western Canada* (New York: Octagon Books, 1971).

15. Lipset, *Agrarian Socialism*, p. 22.

16. Ibid., p. 28.

17. T. B. Bottomore, *Critics of Society: Radical Thought in North America* (New York: Random House, Vintage Books, 1968), p. 45.

18. C. B. Macpherson, *Democracy in Alberta* (Toronto: University of Toronto Press, 2nd ed., 1968); William Lewis Morton, *The Progressive Party in Canada* (Toronto: University of Toronto Press, 1950); G. J. Schmitz, "The Paradox of Prairie Radicalism" (MA thesis, University of Saskatchewan, 1974); Nelson Wiseman, "A Political History of the Manitoba CCF-NDP" (PhD thesis, University of Toronto, 1975).

19. In his *The Life of a Prairie Radical: William Irvine* (Toronto: James Lorimer, 1979), pp. 141-64, Anthony Mardiros argues that at the beginning, Social Credit appeared to offer a radical critique of society, so that CCFers in Alberta thought the new movement could be joined to theirs.

20. Hans H. Gerth and C. Wright Mills, eds., *From Max Weber* (New York: Oxford University Press, 1946), pp. 183-4.

21. See Schmitz, "Prairie Radicalism."

22. This is the position defended by Bennet and Krueger in

Lipset, *Agrarian Socialism*, and by Schmitz, "Prairie Radicalism."

23. See especially Kenneth McNaught's indispensable *A Prophet in Politics*.

24. We follow here the analysis of Penner in *Canadian Left*, pp. 180-5, and the longer treatment in his PhD thesis, "The Socialist Idea in Canadian Political Thought" (University of Toronto, 1975), pp. 329-60.

25. Penner, *Canadian Left*, p. 181.

26. Ibid., p. 182.

27. The CCF kept up this type of class analysis. In *Make This Your Canada* (Toronto: Central Canada Publishing, 1943), p. 105, David Lewis and Frank Scott speak of four groups — industrial workers, white-collar workers, professional workers and farmers — that constitute a bloc facing the owners and controllers of industry and finance. The structure of exploitation, they argue, creates a fundamental unity between factory, farm and office, even if this identity of interest is often obscured by conflicts set in motion by the nature of capitalism.

28. Penner, *Canadian Left*, p. 183.

29. Ibid.

30. Quoted in Penner, "Socialist Idea," p. 347.

31. Woodsworth wrote this during the Winnipeg strike of 1919. It was cited against him in subsequent trial relating to the strike, and again by a Conservative MP arguing in the Commons. Woodsworth repeated the sentence at that time so that it could be recorded officially. See Penner, *Canadian Left*, p. 185.

32. See pp. 101-5 below.

33. Martin Robin, "The Social Basis of Party Politics in B.C.," in Bernard Blishen et al., eds., *Canadian Society* (Toronto: Macmillan of Canada, 1971), pp. 290-300.

34. McNaught, *Prophet*, p. 90; Penner, *Canadian Left*, p. 42.

35. Dorothy G. Steeves, *The Compassionate Rebel: Ernest E. Winch and His Times* (Vancouver: Booy Foundation, 1960), pp. 94, 105, 203-4.

36. Ibid., p. 87.

37. For Father Eugene Cullinane's evaluation of Harold Winch, see pp. 163-4 below.

38. See Penner, *Canadian Left*, pp. 60-7.

39. Ibid., pp. 58-9.

40. The following is taken from Penner, *Canadian Left*, pp. 143-60.

41. Ibid., p. 147.

42. Ibid., p. 148.

43. Ibid., p. 149.

44. Irving Martin Abella, *Nationalism, Communism and Canadian Labour* (Toronto: University of Toronto Press, 1973), p. 221.

45. See Michiel Horn, "The League for Social Reconstruction and the Development of a Canadian Socialism," *Journal of Canadian Studies* 7 (1972): 3-17.

46. See Margaret Cole, *The Story of Fabian Socialism* (London: Heinemann, 1961).

47. Ibid., p. 18.

48. Horowitz, *Canadian Labour*, pp. 24-9. Penner (*Canadian Left*, pp. 75-6) argues that the socialism brought by British immigrants was not exclusively Fabian, but in fact largely Marxist, especially before the First World War. Still, Horowitz's argument, that British socialism was part of the social reality of the Dominion, where men with Scottish or English accents were not regarded as foreigners, seems to stand. See also Martin Robin, *Radical Politics and Canadian Labour* (Kingston: Industrial Relations Centre, Queens University, 1968), pp. 275-7.

49. See Robin, *Radical Politics*, pp. 165-7; and Paul MacEwan, *Miners and Steelworkers* (Toronto: Samuel Stevens, Hakkert, 1976), pp. 104-5, 110.

50. Horowitz, *Canadian Labour*, p. 24.

51. Penner, *Canadian Left*, pp. 33-4, 178. In particular, he refers to J.S. Woodsworth, William Irvine, Salem Bland, W. Ivens and Henry Wise Wood.

52. McNaught, *Prophet*, p. 81.

53. Richard Allen, *The Social Passion* (Toronto: University of Toronto Press, 1973), p. 17.

54. Ibid., pp. 71-9. See also Stewart Crysdale, *The Industrial Struggle and Protestant Ethics in Canada* (Toronto: Ryerson, 1961), p. 29.

55. See Hutchison, "Christian Social Order."

56. Ibid., pp. 31-2.

57. R.B.Y. Scott and Gregory Vlastos, eds., *Toward the Christian Revolution* (Chicago: Willett, Clark, 1936).

58. Hutchinson, "Christian Social Order," pp. 106-28.

59. See for example Young, *Anatomy*, pp. 212-3.

60. Hutchinson, "Christian Social Order," pp. 73-6.

61. *Quadragesimo anno*, n. 109. See note 6 for chapter 2 below.

62. *The New Era*, 2 March 1938.

63. Michael Harrington makes the distinction between "socialism from above" and "socialism from below" central in his study *Socialism* (New York: Saturday Review Press, 1970), especially in the chapter "Revolution from Above," pp. 154-86.

64. Lewis and Scott, *Make This Your Canada*, p. 147.

65. Ibid., p. 150.

66. This letter was addressed to J. J. Tompkins; see George Boyle, *Father Tompkins of Nova Scotia* (New York: P.J. Kennedy, 1953), pp. 155-6.

67. Lipset, *Agrarian Socialism*, p. 244.

68. See note 63 above.

69. Young, *Anatomy*, pp. 155-6.

70. Ibid., p. 156.

71. See page 166 below.

72. See Young, *Anatomy*, pp. 144-5.

73. See note 13 above. For J. A. Hobson's theory of imperialism, see Irving Zeitlin, *Capitalism and Imperialism* (Chicago: Markham, 1972), pp. 65-84.

74. James Luther Adam, *On Being Human Religiously* (Boston: Beacon Press, 1976), pp. 173-87. See also Ernst Troeltsch, *The Social Teaching of the Christian Churches* (New York: Harper & Row, Harper Torchbooks, 1960), pp. 371, 670.

75. *Quadragesimo anno*, n. 95.

76. See pp. 191-204 below.

77. Young, *Anatomy*, p. 56.

78. Daniel J. McDonald, *The Philosophy of the Antigonish Movement* (Antigonish: Extension Department, St. Francis Xavier University, 1942).

79. Salem Bland, *The New Christianity* (Toronto: University of

Toronto Press, 1973), pp. 14-33.

80. Friedrich Engels, "Socialism: Utopian and Scientific," in C. Wright Mills, ed., *The Marxists* (New York: Dell Publishing, Laurel Editions, 1962), pp. 72-80.

Chapter 2 Papal Teaching on Socialism

1. See Alexander Roper Vidler, *A Century of Social Catholicism: 1820-1930* (London: S.P.C.K., 1964).

2. For the use of the term "red Tory" in Canada, see Gad Horowitz, *Canadian Labour in Politics* (Toronto: University of Toronto Press, 1968), pp. 20-23.

3. David O'Brien, *American Catholics and Social Reform* (New York: Oxford University Press, 1968), pp. 47-69.

4. Horowitz, *Canadian Labour*, pp. 10-19; William Christian and Colin Campbell, *Political Parties and Ideologies in Canada* (Toronto: McGraw-Hill Ryerson, 1974), pp. 76-115.

5. Pierre E. Trudeau, *The Asbestos Strike* (Toronto: James Lewis & Samuel, 1974), pp. 16-18. "French Canada demands a leader.... Our survival urgently requires a leader, with our tradition in his bones, strong in our faith, clear-headed, determined, high-spirited. May Providence bring him forth!" *L'action nationale*, 5 January 1935; quoted in ibid., p. 17. See also Joseph Levitt, "The CCF and French Canadian 'Radical Nationalism,' 1933-1942" (MA thesis, University of Toronto, 1963), pp. 47-8; and M. R. Oliver, "The Social and Political Ideas of French Canadian Nationalists, 1920-1945" (PhD thesis, McGill University, 1956), p. 321.

6. *Quadragesimo anno*, n. 3. The encyclicals referred to in this book may be found in several collections, including William J. Gibbons, ed., *Seven Great Encyclicals* (New York: Paulist Press, 1963); and Joseph Gremillion, *The Gospel of Peace and Justice: Catholic Social Teaching since Pope John* (Maryknoll, N.Y.: Orbis Books, 1976).

7. Ibid., n. 4.

8. *Rerum novarum*, n. 15.

9. *Quadragesimo anno*, nn. 82-87.

10. See Irving Zeitlin, *Capitalism and Imperialism* (Chicago: Mark-

ham, 1972).

11. *Quadragesimo anno*, nn. 105-9.
12. Ibid., n. 104.
13. Ibid., n. 132.
14. Ibid., n. 77.
15. Ibid., n. 113.
16. Ibid., n. 112.
17. Ibid., n. 117.
18. Ibid., n. 114.
19. Ibid., n. 117.
20. Ibid., n. 120.
21. *Pacem in terris*, n. 159.
22. *Octogesima adveniens*, n. 31.
23. *Quadragesimo anno*, n. 79.
24. Ibid., n. 114.
25. *Mater et magistra*, nn. 59-67 and passim.
26. *Populorum progressio*, n. 33.
27. See page 111 above.
28. Cardinal Bourne's address of 20 June 1931 was published years later in the *Prairie Messenger*, 13 March 1935.

Chapter 3   The Official Catholic Reaction to Canadian Socialism

1. Murray Ballantyne, "The Catholic Church and the CCF," *Canadian Catholic Historical Association* 30 (1963): 33.
2. See pp. 119-21 below.
3. See pp. 122-4 below.
4. See pp. 110-1 below.
5. See pp. 176-7 below.
6. Robert Rumilly, *Histoire de la province du Québec*, vol. 33 (Montreal: B. Valiquette, 1961), p. 164. Rumilly mentions the names of twelve of the participants: Mgr. E. Lapointe, Mgr. Charbonneau, Mgr. Desrauleau, Mgr. Lebon, Abbé Yelle, Père Forest, Abbé P. Perrier, Père Leon Lébel, Abbé J. Bertrand, Père G.-H. Lévesque,

Père Chagnon and Père de Léry.

7. The report was published as "Pour la restauration sociale au Canada," in *L'école sociale populaire* 232-3: 18-37.

8. This information was undoubtedly taken from a speech in the Commons by R. K. Anderson (*Hansard*, 9 February 1933, p. 1945), who claims that "the United Church of Canada on Dec. 7, 1932, in their report presented to the Presbytery of that city, moved a resolution, which was passed, that the Church adopt some such programme as that of the CCF." It is not clear precisely which meeting this refers to. Earlier in the year a group of radical churchmen had committed themselves to a Christian socialist position. See page 50 above. The Toronto conference of the United Church, which adopted a radical social policy, took place in the spring of 1933.

9. Lévesque, "Pour la restauration," pp. 20-1.

10. See page 141 below.

11. This remark and the following ones are taken from a letter written by Father Lévesque to the author and dated 10 April 1978.

12. Since the report is fairly brief, page references are not given for each individual argument. The use made in the report of the parliamentary debate of February 1933 will be discussed below.

13. See *Hansard*, 9 February 1933, p. 155.

14. *Hansard*, 2 February 1933, pp. 1719-20.

15. Ibid., p. 1720.

16. Ibid., pp. 1745-6.

17. *Hansard*, 9 February 1933, p. 1953.

18. *Quadragesimo anno*, n. 95.

19. *Hansard*, 2 February 1933, pp. 1736-7.

20. *Hansard*, 1 February 1933, p. 1693.

21. *Quadragesimo anno*, n. 62.

22. *Hansard*, 1 February 1933, p. 1692.

23. See page 175-88 below.

24. *Hansard*, 2 February 1933, p. 1723.

25. Ibid., p. 1724.

26. Ibid., p. 1726.

27. Ibid., p. 1727.

28. *Hansard*, 1 February 1933, p. 1688.

29. Ibid., p. 1690.

30. *Quadragesimo anno*, n. 114.

31. *Hansard*, 2 February 1933, p. 1714.

32. Ibid., p. 1729.

33. See page 121 below.

34. See Gregory Baum, *Religion and Alienation* (New York: Paulist Press, 1975), pp. 213-23.

35. "Le marxisme, l'homme et la foi chrétienne: déclaration du conseil permanent de l'épiscopat français [17 July 1977]," *Documentation catholique* 75 (no. 1724, 1978): 684-90. See Gregory Baum, "The French Bishops and Euro-Communism," in Baum, ed., *The Social Imperative* (New York: Paulist Press, 1979), pp. 184-202.

36. *Hansard*, 9 February 1933, p. 1981.

37. This and the following information is taken from the letter by Father Lévesque referred to in note 11 above.

38. Jean Hulliger, *L'enseignement social des évêques canadiens* (Montreal: Fides, 1957), p. 192.

39. Rumilly, *Province du Québec*, p. 176.

40. The *Beacon* editorial of 25 August 1933, printed as a flyer by the CCF of Saskatchewan, is in the author's possession.

41. Rumilly, *Province du Québec*, p. 197.

42. Chagnon's article in the *Beacon* was published in Saskatchewan by the *Prairie Messenger*, January 1934.

43. Hulliger, *L'enseignement social*, pp. 192-3.

44. Ibid.

45. Jeanne Beck, "Henry Somerville: Catholics and the CCF," *Chelsea Journal* 2 (September/October 1976): 262-3.

46. *Hansard*, 30 January 1934, p.110.

47. Beck, "Somerville: Catholics and the CCF," p. 263.

48. The pastoral letter was reprinted in Saskatchewan in the *Prairie Messenger*, 14 and 21 March 1934.

49. Joseph Levitt, "The CCF and French Canadian 'Radical Nationalism,' 1933-1942" (MA thesis, University of Toronto,

1963), pp. 16-18.

50. Walter Young, *The Anatomy of a Party: The National CCF* (Toronto: University of Toronto Press, 1969), p. 211.

51. Seymour Martin Lipset thinks that because of the modification of CCF policy, the Catholic church dropped its hostility to the new party in 1936; *Agrarian Socialism* (Berkeley: University of California Press, 1971), p. 172. Nonetheless, he believes, the Catholic vote rose very slowly, except among Ukrainians, who supported the CCF in great numbers (ibid., p. 210). Catholics tended to remain loyal to the Liberal party. Nelson Wiseman goes so far as to relate the 1943 declaration of the Canadian bishops, clearing the CCF for Catholics, to the 1944 victory of the party in Saskatchewan; "A Political History of the Manitoba CCF-NDP" (PhD thesis, University of Toronto, 1975), p. 56. In Ontario , the Catholic vote for the CCF rose fairly rapidly in the industrialized parts; see David Cameron, "An Electoral Analysis of Democratic Socialism in Ontario" (MPh thesis, University of Toronto, 1965), graph on p. 56.

52. Beck, "Somerville: Catholics and the CCF," pp. 263-4.

53. Ballantyne has published the story of his and Somerville's involvement in clearing the CCF in the detailed account, "The Catholic Church and the CCF."

54. Ibid., p. 39.

55. Ibid., p. 41.

56. The text of the bishops' declaration, together with Somerville's editorial, published as a flyer by the CCF in Saskatchewan, is in the author's possession.

57. Ballantyne, "Catholic Church," p. 42.

58. Ibid., p. 43.

59. Quoted in Lipset, *Agrarian Socialism*, pp. 210-11.

60. Neil Betten, *Catholic Activism and the Industrial Worker* (Gainesville, Florida: University Presses of Florida, 1976), pp. 1-16.

Part II

Chapter 4   Voices Crying in the Wilderness

1. See Gregory Baum, *Religion and Alienation* (New York: Paulist

Press, 1975), pp. 170-2.

2. The information on Ballantyne is taken from Jeanne Beck's PhD thesis, "Henry Somerville and Catholic Social Thought" (McMaster University, 1977), especially pp. 400-2.

3. Ballantyne was interviewed by Sister Louise Sharum at Combermere, Ontario, on 31 July 1974. A transcript of the tape was made available to Jeanne Beck, whose account in her thesis I follow here (see preceding note).

4. The information on Joseph Wall's group and the memorandum is drawn from Beck, "Catholic Social Thought," pp. 375-7. The complete documentation is found in the Ballantyne papers, Redpath Library, McGill University.

5. Beck, "Catholic Social Thought." See also idem, "Henry Somerville and Social Reform: His Contribution to Canadian Catholic Social Thought," *Canadian Catholic Historical Association* 42 (1975): pp. 91-108; and idem,"Henry Somerville: Catholics and the CCF," *Chelsea Journal* 2 (September/October 1976): pp. 259-64.

6. So far no study of Catherine de Hueck's achievement has been undertaken.

7. Beck, "Catholic Social Thought," p. 335.

8. In the election of 1943, the CCF took eleven out of the twelve ridings in northern Ontario that had a predominantly French and Catholic population. See David Lewis and Frank Scott, *Make This Your Canada* (Toronto: Central Canada Publishing, 1943), p. ix.

Chapter 5   Catholic Support for the CCF in Saskatchewan

1. George Hoffman, "Saskatchewan Catholics and the Coming of the New Politics," in Richard Allen, ed., *Religion and Society in the Prairie West* (Regina: Canadian Plains Research Centre, University of Regina, 1974), pp. 65-88. This article is the revision of Hoffman's "The Saskatchewan Provincial Election of 1935: Its Political, Economic and Social Background" (MA thesis, University of Saskatchewan, 1973). The following quotations are from the published article.

2. Hoffman, "Saskatchewan Catholics," pp. 67-8.

3. Ibid., p. 69.

4. James C. McGuigan, Pastoral Letters and Circular Letters, n. p., n. d., pp. 217-27.

5. Ibid., p. 219.

6. Hoffman, "Saskatchewan Catholics," pp. 75-6.

7. *Regina Leader-Post*, 23 May 1934. The CCF made a flyer of Coldwell's letter and McGuigan's response to convince Catholics that the Church had no objection to the new party.

8. Hoffman, "Saskatchewan Catholics," p. 70.

9. Ibid., pp. 72, 78. The *Prairie Messenger*, edited by the German-American Benedictines of St. Peter's Abbey, reflected the social ideals, at once conservative and reformist, of the Centralverein, a German society in St. Louis, Missouri. For an analysis of these ideas, see Philip Gleason, *The Conservative Reformers* (Notre Dame, Indiana: University of Notre Dame Press, 1968). Occasionally, prior to the founding of the CCF, the *Prairie Messenger* published very reactionary statements made by American Catholics. The issue of 4 February 1931 records an address by an American vicar-general, given to a group of 500 unemployed. "Is there any obligation on the part of the poor? In the first place should you people be filled with self-pity, feeling that the world owes you a living without any obligation on your part? You know that in many cases your condition of poverty is brought about because you have not assumed an obligation toward your brethren. If you had been earnest in doing your part for those who are depending on you, your sense of responsibility would have made you more industrious, enabled you not only to hold a position but to take advantage of every opportunity to advance yourself in order to protect that position as far as humanly possible." The *Prairie Messenger* of 21 October 1931 reports a refutation of egalitarianism offered by an American Catholic bishop. "Difference in wealth has existed in every age. Christ solemnly declared that 'the poor you have always with you." Pain, sorrow and hardship will ever follow a man from the cradle to the grave amidst disappointments and delusions . . . . The right of property, according to the tenets of the Church, is based on the immutable, eternal laws of God."

10. *Prairie Messenger*, 7 December 1932.

11. *Prairie Messenger*, 15 and 22 February 1933.

12. *Prairie Messenger*, 31 May 1933.

13. *Prairie Messenger*, 26 July 1933.

14. Ibid.

15. *Prairie Messenger*, 23 May 1934.

16. *Prairie Messenger*, 18 May 1934 and 13 March 1935.

17. *Prairie Messenger*, 27 June 1934.

18. *Prairie Messenger*, 22 November 1933.

19. David O'Brien, *American Catholics and Social Reform* (New York: Oxford University Press, 1968), pp. 31-4; and idem, *The Renewal of American Catholicism* (New York: Oxford Univeristy Press, 1972), p. 185.

20. As an excellent example of this confusion, see a series of articles carried by the *Prairie Messenger* (8, 15 and 22 February and 8, 15, 22 and 27 March 1933), entitled "A Socialist and a Catholic Discuss Socialism." Reprinted from the U.S. weekly *The Catholic Visitor*, it looks at social and political issues exclusively from the American viewpoint.

21. Hoffman, "Saskatchewan Catholics," p. 75.

22. Ibid., p. 77.

23. Ibid., p. 74.

24. Ibid., p. 78. The *Prairie Messenger* was willing to publish some of Roberge's statements and letters, and at times argued with him. See for example the edition of 5 April 1933.

25. Gregory Baum, "Joe Burton: Catholic and Saskatchewan Socialist," *The Ecumenist* 14 (July/August 1976): pp. 70-7.

26. Ibid., p. 73.

27. Ibid., p. 75. See also *The Commonwealth*, 28 April 1943.

28. Baum, "Joe Burton," p. 76.

29. The following biographical notes on Ted Garland are taken from a letter written to the author by Professor Anthony Mardiros of the University of Alberta in Edmonton.

30. The letter — dated Gleichen, Alta., 6 December 1934 — is addressed to a Catholic correspondent in Toronto who wonders how a Catholic can be a socialist. Archives, National Library, Ottawa.

31. See page 114 below.

32. The letter, addressed to the Most Rev. I. Antoniutti, is dated Calgary, Alta., 2 January 1939. Archives, National Library, Ottawa.

33. Hoffman, "Saskatchewan Catholics," pp. 79, 87.

34. See note 51 for chapter 3.

35. The following section on Father Eugene Cullinane is based on an extended interview I had with him on 26 April 1976. Father Cullinane gave me four documents: his thesis proposal, submitted to the Catholic University of America in the summer of 1946 and entitled "The Cooperative Commonwealth Federation: A Sociological Analysis of its Origins and Ideology," including an outline and preliminary notes made after several months of research; an eight-page pamphlet, originally written by him as an article for *The People's Weekly*, called "The Catholic Church and Socialism," distributed widely by the CCF in Saskatchewan; a letter, dated 5 April 1948, he had written to H. O. Hansen, MLA, who had asked why Cullinane, as a priest, had joined the CCF; and the Saskatchewan diocesan bulletin of 11 June 1948, which forbad priests to engage in political activity of a partisan nature.

36. This is an inference from Weber's fourfold distinction of action motivation, applied throughout his work, between traditionalist conduct and three kinds of action that can make people deviate from the inherited norm. See for example Max Weber, *Basic Concepts in Sociology* (New York: Citadel Press, 1969), pp. 59-62.

Chapter 6   Economic Radicals in Quebec

1. Joseph Levitt, "The CCF and French Canadian 'Radical Nationalism,' 1933-1942" (MA thesis, University of Toronto, 1963), p. 8.

2. Thérèse Casgrain, *A Woman in a Man's World* (Toronto: McClelland and Stewart, 1972), pp. 118-25.

3. Pierre E. Trudeau, *The Asbestos Strike* (Toronto: James Lewis & Samuel, 1974), pp. 28-31.

4. André-J. Belanger, *L'apoliticisme des ideologies québecoises: 1934-1936* (Quebec: Presses de l'Université Laval, 1974), p. 309.

5. Trudeau, *Asbestos Strike*, p. 29.

6. "Pour la restauration sociale au Canada," *L'école sociale populaire* 232-3: 5-17.

7. Ibid., pp. 36-64.

8. Ibid., p. 44.

9. Regina Manifesto, section 1; text in Walter Young, *The Anatomy of a Party: The National CCF* (Toronto: University of Toronto Press, 1969), pp. 304-13.

10. Belanger, *L'apoliticisme*, pp. 307-27.

11. Ibid., p. 314.

12. It would be interesting to compare the social corporatism of Quebec with the non-partisan social philosophy of western Canada, expressed by Henry Wood and William Irvine, which also sought to replace the party system by a form of group representation. See Anthony Mardiros, *The Life of a Prairie Radical: William Irvine* (Toronto: James Lorimer, 1979), pp. 98-108.

13. Who were some of these intellectuals? Robert Rumilly in *Historie de la province du Québec*, vol. 33 (Montreal: B. Valiquette, 1961), p. 197, mentions the following names: V. E. Beaupré, R. Chalout, A. Charpentier, W. Guerin, A. Laurendeau, E. L'Heureux, E. Minville, J. B. Price and A. Vanier.

14. Apart from Patricia Reid's MA thesis on the ALN at Queens University in 1970, the movement is briefly described in Rumilly, *Province du Québec*, vol. 34, pp. 56-7. Yves Vaillancourt, "Les politiques sociales et les travailleurs, cahier 2: Les années trente" (mimeographed; 1975), pp. 149-67. See also Herbert F. Quinn, *The Union Nationale* (Toronto: University of Toronto Press, 1963), pp. 48-62; and Patricia G. Dirks, "The Origins of the Union Nationale" (PhD thesis, University of Toronto, 1974).

15. Quinn, *Union Nationale*, pp. 43-7.

16. Trudeau, *Asbestos Strike*, pp. 9-13.

17. Levitt, "Radical Nationalism," pp. 50-1.

18. Vaillancourt, "Les années trente," pp. 125-7.

19. Michiel Horn, ed., *The Dirty Thirties* (Toronto: Copp Clark, 1972), pp. 669-75.

20. Dirks, "Origins," p. 238.

21. Horn, *Dirty Thirties*, p. 672.

22. Levitt, "Radical Nationalism."

23. Ibid., p. 8.

24. Ibid., p. 46.

Chapter 7 Catholics in Eastern Nova Scotia

1. Much of the material in this chapter has been published in my article "Social Catholicism in Nova Scotia," in Peter Slater, ed., *Religion and Culture in Canada* (Waterloo: Wilfrid Laurier University Press, 1977), pp. 117-48.

2.

Counties	Population	Catholics
Antigonish	10,073	8,736
Cape Breton C.	92,419	49,558
Inverness	21,005	14,949
Richmond	11,098	8,801

Cities & Towns	Population	Catholics
Sydney	23,089	11,360
Dominion	2,846	2,134
Glace Bay	20,706	10,705
New Waterford	7,745	5,553
North Sydney	6,139	2,420
Sydney Mines	7,769	3,744

Canadian Almanac and Directory (Toronto: Copp Clark, 1931).

3. On the Antigonish movement, see: Moses M. Coady, *Masters of Their Own Destiny* (New York: Harper & Row, 1939) and idem, "The Social Significance of the Cooperative Movement" (Antigonish: Extension Department, St. Francis Xavier University, 1961); Alex Laidlaw, *The Man from Margaree: Writings and Speeches of M. M. Coady* (Toronto: McClelland and Stewart, 1971); Mary E. Arnold, *The Story of Tompkinsville* (New York: The Cooperative League, 1940); George Boyle, *Father Tompkins of Nova Scotia* (New York; P. J. Kenedy, 1953); Alex Laidlaw, *The Campus and the Community* (Montreal: Harvest House, 1961); Jim Lotz, "The Antigonish Movement: A Critical Analysis," *Studies in Adult Education* 5 (October 1973): pp. 97-122; Gregory Baum, "Moses Coady: Critique of Capitalism," *Chelsea Journal* 3 (September/October 1977): 229-231, 260; Frank Mifflin, "The Antigonish Movement: A Revitalization Movement in Eastern Nova Scotia" (PhD thesis,

Boston College, 1974); Robert Sacouman, "Social Origins of the Antigonish Movement" (PhD thesis, University of Toronto, 1976); Daniel McGinnis, "Clerics, Farmers, Fishermen and Workers: Religion and Collectivity in the Antigonish Movement" (PhD thesis in progress, McMaster University).

4. Mifflin, "Revitalization Movement," pp. 120 ff.

5. Coady, *Masters*, pp. 17-29.

6. Ibid., p. 122.

7. "On the Jewish Question," in T. B. Bottomore, ed., *Karl Marx: Early Writings* (New York: McGraw-Hill, 1963), pp. 3-31.

8. Coady, *Masters*, p. 79.

9. Laidlaw, *Man from Margaree*, p. 25.

10. Coady, *Masters*, p. 122.

11. "Small is beautiful," used as the title of E. F. Schumacher's celebrated book (New York: Harper & Row, 1973), characterizes the philosophy of the Antigonish movement. The complementary principle, "Big whenever necessary," affirmed in Catholic social teaching, received less attention.

12. George D. H. Cole, *A Century of Cooperation* (London: Allen & Unwin, The Cooperative Union, 1944), pp. 103-19.

13. Mifflin, "Revitalization Movement," p. 95. In the early Forties, Mifflin reports, a Liberal politician accused Alex MacIntyre of the Extension Department of promoting the CCF. Coady reacted vehemently. He investigated the charge, found it based on rumour alone and only then informed his co-worker.

14. Ibid., p. 96.

15. Coady, *Masters*, pp. 120-38.

16. Ibid., p. 134.

17. Laidlaw, *Campus and Community*, p. 26.

18. Ibid., p. 28.

19. Ibid., p. 47.

20. Ibid., p. 114.

21. Ibid., p. 47.

22. Ibid., p. 26.

23. Coady, *Masters*, p. 68.

24. Ibid., p. 23.

25. Ibid., pp. 120-38.

26. Laidlaw, *Campus and Community*, p. 25.

27. See the paragraph entitled "Beware of Institutionalizing," in Tompkins's pamphlet *The Future of the Antigonish Movement*, quoted in Boyle, *Father Tompkins*, p. 146.

28. "Economic and Philosophical Manuscripts," in Bottomore, *Marx: Early Writings*, p. 130.

29. This view is defended by Gary Webster in "Tignish and Antigonish: A Critique of the Antigonish Movement as a Cadre for Cooperation," *The Abegweit Review* 2 (September 1975): 94-102.

30. George Rawlyk has suggested that the promotion of cooperatives by the priests of Antigonish was largely a reaction to the advances made by the radical farmers during the period in the early Twenties when the farmer/labour party was able to elect representatives to the provincial legislature. See "The Farmer-Labour Movement and the Failure of Socialism in Nova Scotia," in Laurier LaPierre, ed., *Essays on the Left* (Toronto: McClelland and Stewart, 1971), p. 36. The available evidence suggests to me that the radicals were on the decline in the Twenties.

31. A letter written by the Catholic Scottish Society to St. Francis Xavier University, expressing their wish that "extension work" be established among the miners, is quoted in Peter A. Nearing, "*He Loved the Church· The Biography of Bishop John R. MacDonald* (Antigonish: Casket Printing & Publishing, 1975), p. 36.

32. Paul MacEwan, *Miners and Steelworkers* (Toronto: Samuel Stevens, Hakkert, 1976).

33. Ibid., p. 142.

34. Nearing, *John R. MacDonald*, p. 46. The impact of Alex MacIntyre on the Antigonish movement is examined in McGinnis, "Religion and Collectivity."

35. Nearing, *John R. MacDonald*, p. 27.

36. The topic is studied in McGinnis, "Religion and Collectivity."

37. MacEwan, *Miners and Steelworkers*, p. 27.

38. Ibid., pp. 195-205.

39. Ibid., p. 173.

40. Jean Hulliger, *L'enseignement social des évêques canadiens* (Montreal:

Fides, 1957), p. 196.

41. Letter of 25 March 1955, Archives, National Library, Ottawa.

42. *The New Commonwealth*, 20 September 1940, p. 3.

43. "The first major union to affiliate [with the CCF] was District 26 of the United Mine-Workers of America in the fall of 1938. The miners of Nova Scotia had benefitted greatly from the cooperative and credit union movement in that province. They had obtained an insight into the workings of the economic system through the educational work conducted by the Extension Department of St. Francis Xavier University. Political action through the CCF followed naturally." David Lewis and Frank Scott, *Make This Your Canada* (Toronto: Central Canada Publishing, 1943), p. 128.

Afterword

1. *Octogesima adveniens*, n. 31. See note 6 for chapter 2.

2. Robert McAfee Brown, *Theology in a New Key* (Philadelphia: Westminster Press, 1978), p. 27.

3. For the important section of the Medellin conclusions, see Joseph Gremillion, *The Gospel of Peace and Justice* (Maryknoll, New York: Orbis Books, 1976), pp. 445-76.

4. Ibid., pp. 513-14.

5. See Gregory Baum, "The First Papal Encyclical," *The Ecumenist* 17 (January/February 1979): 55-9; and idem, "A Pope from the Second World," ibid. 18 (January/February 1980): 22-26.

Bibliography

Abella, Irving Martin. *Nationalism, Communism and Canadian Labour.* Toronto: University of Toronto Press, 1973.

Allen, Richard. *The Social Passion.* Toronto: University of Toronto Press, 1971.

Avakumovic, Ivan. *Socialism in Canada.* Toronto: McClelland and Stewart, 1978.

Baum, Gregory. *Religion and Alienation.* New York: Paulist Press, 1975.

Baum, Gregory. *The Social Imperative.* New York: Paulist Press, 1979.

Bélanger, André-J. *L'apoliticisme des idéologies québecoises: 1934-1936.* Quebec: Presses de l'Université, Laval, 1974.

Betten, Neil. *Catholic Activism and the Industrial Worker.* Gainesville, Florida: University Presses of Florida, 1976.

Bland, Salem. *The New Christianity.* Toronto: University of Toronto Press, 1973.

Blishen, Bernard R., and others, eds. *Canadian Society.* Toronto: Macmillan, 1971.

Caplan, Gerald. *The Dilemma of Canadian Socialism.* Toronto: McClelland and Stewart, 1973.

Christian, William and Campbell, Colin. *Political Parties and Ideologies in Canada.* Toronto: McGraw-Hill Ryerson, 1973.

Clark, Samuel; Grayson, Linda M. and Grayson, J. Paul. *Prophecy and Protest.* Toronto: Gage Educational Publishing, 1975.

Coady, Moses M. *Masters of Their Own Destiny.* New York: Harper and Brothers, 1939.

Coady, Moses M., and Laidlaw, Alexander F., ed. *The Man from Margaree: Writings and Speeches of M.M. Coady.* Toronto: McClelland and Stewart, 1971.

Cole, George D. H. *A Century of Cooperation.* London: Allen and Unwin, 1944.

Cole, Margaret. *The Story of Fabian Socialism.* London: Heinemann, 1961.

Crysdale, Stewart. *The Industrial Struggle and Protestant Ethics in Canada.* Toronto: Ryerson Press, 1961.

Grant, John Webster, ed. *The History of the Christian Church in Canada.* 3 vols. Toronto: McGraw-Hill Ryerson, 1972.

Gremillion, Joseph. *The Gospel of Peace and Justice.* Maryknoll, N.Y.:

Orbis Books, 1976.

Horn, Michiel, ed. *The Dirty Thirties*. Toronto: Copp Clark, 1971.

Horn, Michiel. *The League for Social Reconstruction: Intellectual Origins of the Democratic Left in Canada, 1930-42*. Toronto: University of Toronto Press, 1980.

Horowitz, Gad. *Canadian Labour in Politics*. Toronto: University of Toronto Press, 1968.

Hulliger, Jean. *L'enseignement social des évêques canadiens*. Montréal: Fides, 1957.

Lipset, Seymour Martin. *Agrarian Socialism*. Berkeley: University of California Press, 2d ed., 1971.

MacEwan, Paul. *Miners and Steelworkers*. Toronto: Samuel-Stevens, 1975.

Macpherson, C.B. *Democracy in Alberta*. Toronto: University of Toronto Press, 1953.

McNaught, Kenneth. *A Prophet in Politics*. Toronto: University of Toronto Press, 1959.

Mardiros, Anthony. *The Life of a Prairie Radical: William Irvine*. Toronto: James Lorimer & Company, 1979.

Morton, Desmond. *The Dream of Power*. Toronto: A.M. Hakkert, 1974.

O'Brien, David. *American Catholics and Social Reform*. New York: Oxford University Press, 1968.

Penner, Norman. *The Canadian Left*. Toronto: Prentice-Hall of Canada, 1977.

Robin, Martin. *Radical Politics and Canadian Labour*. Kingston: Industrial Relations Centre, Queens University, 1968.

Sharp, Paul Frederick. *Agrarian Revolt in Western Canada*. New York: Octagon Books, 1971.

Slater, Peter, ed. *Religion and Culture in Canada*. Waterloo: Wilfrid Laurier University Press, 1978.

Steeves, Dorothy G. *The Compassionate Rebel: Ernest E. Winch and His Times*. Vancouver: Booy Foundation, 1960.

Trudeau, Pierre E. *The Asbestos Strike*. Toronto: James Lorimer & Company, 1974.

Vidler, Alexander Roper. *A Century of Social Catholicism: 1820-1930*. London: S.P.C.K., 1964.

Young, Walter. *The Anatomy of a Party: The National CCF*. Toronto: University of Toronto Press, 1969.

Index